COUNTESS MARKIEVICZ, born Constance Gore-Booth in 1868 in County Sligo, Ireland, was a legendary figure in the Irish independence movement. The eldest daughter of a wealthy landowning family, she became a society beauty but was of too independent a spirit to settle fo

her. Despite parental oppositio

she met Count Casimir Markie

later their only child, Maeve, w

however, and the couple finally

During this time, Constanc

growing increasingly involved in politics. She became one of the leaders in the fight for Irish independence and campaigned for women's rights. She helped to found the future Republican Army, and was one of the organisers of the 1916 Easter Rising in Dublin. Arrested and sentenced to death for her part in the Rising, she was later reprieved because of her sex.

The last ten years of her life were spent either on the run or in prison. While there, she suffered enormous hardships - solitary confinement, rations that reduced her from 11 stone to 7½ stone and, at the age of sixty, hunger strike. She was also the first woman ever elected an MP to the British parliament, although she never took her seat there. In the Dail Eireann of 1919, an independent parliament set up by Sinn Fein MPs, she was the first Minister for Labour.

From early childhood, Constance had always been especially close to her sister Eva and the letters she exchanged with her while in prison were her link with the outside world. At this time, Eva - suffragist, trade unionist and pacifist - was deeply involved in protest against the First World War, and the correspondence between the sisters was something they greatly treasured coming, as it did, at a particularly dangerous time for both of them.

Proudly announcing 'I am a pauper,' Countess Markievicz was admitted to hospital in 1927, where she died of peritonitis. Despite attempts by the government to play down the impact of her death (her body was left to lie in state in a cinema, not a public place, and soldiers were posted to prevent volleys being fired over her grave), 300,000 people turned out to line the funeral route and lorryloads of flowers followed the coffin.

PRISON LETTERS OF COUNTESS MARKIEVICZ

WITH A NEW INTRODUCTION BY
AMANDA SEBESTYEN

Published by VIRAGO PRESS Limited 1987
41 William IV Street, London WC2N 4DB

First published by Longmans, Green & Co 1934

British Library Cataloguing in Publication Data
Markievicz, Constance Markievicz, Countess
Prison letters of Countess Markievicz.
1. Markievicz, Constance Markievicz, Countess
2. Revolutionists — Ireland — Biography
3. Politicians — Ireland — Biography
I. Title
941.5081'092'4 DA965.M35

ISBN 0-86068-781-3

Printed in Great Britain by
Anchor Brendon Ltd of Tiptree, Essex.

EDITOR'S NOTE

In bringing before the public the Prison Letters of Constance Markievicz, the Editor is sadly aware that only one-half of what would surely have been a lovely whole is being presented.

It had been hoped that in addition to Constance's letters, those written to her in reply by her sister, the poet, Eva Gore-Booth, would have been included, so that always the poet's words and the 'rebel's' might as 'strophe and antistrophe echoing go.'

Valuing these letters above everything, Constance carried them about her person in prison, wrapped in what is there by courtesy called a handkerchief but what we should call a duster. She was afraid that they might be taken away when she was out of her cell. She kept them carefully until she went into hospital for the operation in 1927. The day before she died she told me she wanted me to have Eva's letters at once, but alas! before I could get possession of what she valued so highly and what comprised some of Eva's most charming writing, the collection of letters was, by a tragic error, destroyed.

Eva, being a writer of exquisite prose, looked upon the allowed space of one sheet of paper as the limits within which to create a little work of art, supplying her sister's need of beauty and joy and laughter. These gems, which Constance loved so much, can never now be read by anyone.

So I reproduce Constance's letters, Eva's poems to her in prison, her account of a visit to Dublin after Easter Week to see Constance, her short account of the Rebellion and of Roger Casement's death, also a few other papers relating to this time. In no other way now can I make up for the lost letters.

In prison, letters and occasional visits are the only mitigation of the drabness of life. The authorities supply the prisoner with the one sheet of paper permitted, on the back of which are the grim regulations. The prisoner, we are informed, is allowed to write so that she may keep in touch with her 'respectable' friends, and, being respectable, they must never be exposed to 'slang or improper expressions,' or the letter will be suppressed.

In replying, the friend must not refer to public affairs, even if those who take part in them are the personal friends of both writers. The correspondents very likely do not wish the Governor's cold glance to fall on the recital of their intimate family affairs, so these are avoided too.

A dear friend of Constance's who has just read the letters says:

'I could never tell you how enthralling it was to me to read the letters. "Madame's" glorious self seemed to be with me again brilliantly alive. It has been like a wind blowing to flame again what was, in my discouragement, a dying spark, faith in life, in the Irish people, in the value of effort. I adore her sort of courage. It was one with happiness and with love. But what a magnificent thing she had in the love between herself and Eva. I find the cumulative effect of them [*i.e.* the letters] and the re-creation of the whole sequence of moods and phases so wonderful. The heightened sensitiveness of a prisoner is in so many of the letters. That excitement over every little pleasure and a kind of nakedness of the mind which feels acutely every fresh thought and idea. I miss Con to-day as though we had lost her yesterday.'

I have written a short introduction which does not profess to be a life of Constance Markievicz nor of her sister Eva Gore-Booth. Still less does it pretend to be a history of the Rising, for I am not qualified for such a task. It happens, though, that I saw some of the incidents of this Rising from an angle from which no other living person saw them. I also possess documents that will be of interest to those who knew and loved the sisters. These documents will also be of interest to those whose business it will be later on to write the history of the times.

I have therefore felt it best to tell my personal story simply and to publish the papers. It is not a complete picture, but it is, I trust, a true version of the happenings as I saw them.

CONTENTS

LETTERS

When I first read the Acts in [illegible] them in the old Prescott Library, in [illegible] Cass and [illegible] The [illegible] been [illegible] must was the [illegible] [illegible] experience.

[illegible] a [illegible]

[illegible]

for [illegible] and [illegible] the [illegible]
and [illegible] the [illegible]
[illegible] even though [illegible]
[illegible] the [illegible]

[illegible]

INTRODUCTION

When I first read these letters, in 1973, mice were running over them in the old Fawcett Library, in the backwater behind Caxton Hall where the big suffragette demonstrations had once been held. What struck me most was the very tender, delicate, painful way that political differences between families were expressed.

The Gore-Booths were a family torn apart by Ireland's wars of independence, as bitterly as families in that earlier Civil War whose sense of integrity led them on the one side to Parliament and on the other to the King. Constance, the eldest, and Eva, the third child, had always been the closest in their family. At the time these letters were written both were outcasts.

Constance was now Countess Markievicz, last surviving organiser of the tiny Dublin Rising of 1916. Her companions all executed, she faced indefinite imprisonment in English gaols that twenty years before had broken the Fenian conspirators with a combination of physical and mental torture. And braving the threat of Broadmoor, she smuggled out notes on prison conditions, which included rations that reduced her from eleven stone to seven-and-a-half.*

*It's impossible to talk about these prison letters without making some reference to the situation of Ireland today. But I had almost reached the end of my writing before I noticed that here, now, an Irish woman prisoner (on remand, unconvicted) can be strip-searched several times a day in an English prison for almost a year; strip-searching in front of male officers is routinely used to humiliate and break the spirit of Republican women in the gaols of Northern Ireland; an elected MP could be left to die on a hunger-strike over political status with hardly a person in Britain aware that the Terrorist Offence of which he was convicted (after a juryless trial) was to be arrested with six other people in a car where a gun was found.

The conditions in the gaols, the struggles over prison uniforms, the blanket strike and the dirty strike – they're all a continuation of the 1900s, 1910s and 20s which I describe. So too are the flowering of community self-organisation and then the pogroms and the economy's devastation. It seems that I, like most people born in England, (even though my mother's Irish) can hardly bear to look at Ireland until it's safely in the past. But the connections have become too strong to overlook.

Eva, a pacifist at the height of the War Fever, was exposing its horrors in the illegal paper *The Tribunal.* Conscientious objectors could face death in these same gaols, as, refusing to wear uniforms, they were stripped and soaked in water, some to die of pneumonia. Deserters at the front were being crucified in front of the guns, tied to a wooden cross in No Man's Land.

It was a terribly dangerous time for both sisters, and it drew them together until their minds literally met for minutes of each day. They became the dearest things in life to each other.

But all along there's a mixture of love and pain in these letters. Constance was a fighter and she knew that Eva didn't agree. And Eva was tough in another way, she'd chosen her political direction while Constance was still dashing from ballroom to studio. So there's a tension in those moments where they argue about revolutions in other countries – Russia, Italy – as if they didn't dare get closer to home.

THE WOMAN WARRIOR

There have been innumerable fictions written about the Countess Markievicz. She was such a picturesque and many-sided figure that perhaps it's inevitable. One way biographers have tried to reconcile the different visions of her is to suggest that she was principally an actress flinging herself into each new role. Her friend, the socialist and feminist Helena Moloney, wrote: "The work she did always had to be of a dramatic or even of a glamorous kind. She was made that way, she could only express herself in terms of action and gesture and drama." But even this is precisely contradicted by fellow rebel (later Professor) Liam O'Brian: "Gallant the Countess was, and elegant with natural grace. Natural above all, there was no posing, no theatrical gesture whatsoever."

The biographical note that follows this introduction of mine is a very clear example of a fiction constructed about Constance Markievicz. It's clearly a case for the defence; Esther Roper, Eva Gore-Booth's lifelong friend and political companion, entirely erases the figure of Constance Markievicz, the warrior, trying to reclaim her against attack: against Yeats' image – "her mind ... a bitter, an abstract thing"; Sean O'Casey's vicious in-fighter "oiling her automatic", a traitor to her sex; the bogey woman that the mother of Republican Grace Gifford could safely blame in the *Belfast Evening Telegraph* for her daughter's runaway marriage—"The Countess Markievicz has been responsible all along for dragging them into it..."

Roper's version stresses the Gore-Booths' record as a progressive land-owning family, the only ones to support all their tenants during the second great potato famine, giving out, as a contemporary described, "with their own hands from morning to night food to the needy ... an event unique of its kind in Ireland". Helping as a child in the soup kitchen of the great house, Lissadell, would have given Constance the background to manage a soup kitchen herself for the starving in the Dublin Lock-Out of 1913. But what Esther Roper doesn't mention is that Constance's own grandfather was held to have evicted all his tenants from a piece of land called The Seven Cartrons, giving them emigration money of £2 a head; they went on a 'coffin ship' and sank immediately out of harbour. Constance herself never forgot. In the debate which led to the Civil War, Constance opposed the new Treaty for giving a special space to the Anglo-Irish who "sent the people of Ireland to drift in the immigrant ships and sink at the bottom of the Atlantic".

Esther Roper mentions the progressive Home Rule tendencies of Constance's brother, Josslyn, and his co-operative dairies, (as Yeats said in his journal, "The eldest son is 'theoretically' a home ruler and practically some kind of humanitarian – much troubled by the responsibility of his wealth and almost painfully conscientious"). But Esther Roper doesn't say that Constance turned on her brother when his farm workers struck in 1920, and told him to remember that he came from a line of 'tyrants and usurpers'.

Esther Roper tells us that Constance went to Paris to study art, but not that this came only after prolonged struggles with her parents, and she doesn't quote the diaries where Constance raged like the young Florence Nightingale: "Success & art walled round with Family Pride, Stinginess & Conventionality. What is one to do? How am I to coerce them? How break away?"

Later in life, Constance was very angry and scornful of the kind of political education her family had given her: "Irish history was taboo, for 'what is the use of brooding on past grievances'." As a child visiting the peasants' mud-and-stone huts, a single room shared with the cow and the donkey (and the Gore-Booths were possibly the country's best landlords), Constance would notice a colour picture on the wall of Emmet or some other freedom fighter of the past. She never knew who they were until as an actress of nearly forty, taking part in the Gaelic Revival, she went to stay in a cottage belonging to the poet Padraig Colum. There she saw copies of the journals *The Peasant* and *Sinn Fein*, found out whose faces those really were, and the die was cast – she joined the movement for Irish freedom.

Esther Roper's choice of a portrait photograph of Constance with her daughter and the stepson who remembered her later as being "kind as she was beautiful", is an indirect statement on the most controversial aspect of her subject's life. Constance and her husband Count Casimir Markievicz, who was younger than she was, seem to have started to move apart early in the marriage. "Since the birth of their child she did not require him as a husband – this she told me herself," wrote a family friend to the biographer, Sean O'Faolain, going on, "he never at any time flaunted his infidelities in front of her . . . He was always a perfect gentleman, though he was, as Yeats said, a bit of a barbarian". Biographers describe the parting as painless, but the wardrobe mistress at the Abbey Theatre recalled the going-away party when Casimir departed indefinitely for Russia: "I remember how sad the Countess was on that night".

Constance was moving towards politics, he wanted to stay in the theatre – in their original Bohemian life, one foot in avant garde Nationalism but the other in Dublin Castle. Now he was likely to find, returning from a long journey, his house and his wife taken up with training the Fianna scouts who became the nucleus of the future Republican Army:

I have great trouble to find this house, but at last I find it and I send away the cabbie, I find the house at the end of the avenue all dark, all silent. I knock and knock but not a sound. I go around the back and I call out 'Constance!' No sound, I come round to the front and I knock and I call out 'Constance!' After a while a dirty little ragamuffin puts his head out and say 'Who da?' and I say "I want to see Countess Markievicz." He go away and I wait, no sound.

I knock again and I call 'Constance!' Another window go up and another dirty little ragamuffin say 'Who da?' I say 'I am Count Markievicz and I want to see the Countess Markievicz.' He go away and I wait. No sound. I hear much scuffling and running and last the door open. It is all dark but I see Constance. 'It's very dark, Constance,' I say. 'We have only one lamp', she says, 'and the gardener is reading with that.' We go into the drawing room, and there I find the gardener with his legs on the mantlepiece and he is smoking a dirty filthy shag tobacco. He does not stand up when I go in. I say, 'I am hungry, can not I have some food?' and they scuffle and they whisper again, while I talk to the gardener. At last they bring me cold meat and bread and butter. That is how I return to my home.

Her husband did come back when Constance was dying, and once or twice before. What was much harder to take - for her Irish contemporaries and maybe for us too - was the fact that her daughter Maeve was left to be brought up by her grandmother Georgina, a woman Constance only refers to in the letters as "G", and not very lovingly. There's a rather chilling little reference to "M's" engagement and "G" possibly opposing it.

In the 1870s the artist Sarah Purser was commissioned to paint a portrait of the two little girls, Constance and Eva. She recalled Constance as a difficult sitter but "the centre of her mother's hopes". Sure enough, Constance became an extremely popular society beauty, but broke away into art and later politics. "Oh dear, oh dear, this will be the death of me some day," Lady Gore-Booth would say as she drove around to her neighbours after hearing of yet another arrest or imprisonment. In fact, she died only a few months before her daughter, and towards the end, Constance did begin seeing her mother again for shopping trips. But for almost twenty years they hardly met.

When Maeve, now grown-up, met Constance, in a hotel foyer in 1923, she had to be told what her mother looked like. As she had been brought up at Lissadell by Lady Gore-Booth she didn't share Constance's politics; but from long before Constance joined any political movement, Maeve was being left behind as her mother went back to Paris and then to Poland. It was a common upper class practice, but taken to extremes.

Maud Gonne wrote later to Constance's stepson Stasko Markievicz: "I have heard people criticise Constance as a neglectful mother. But she was so unselfish she sacrificed everything for Ireland, and in this case did what she thought best for the child . . . Only people who knew her very closely and intimately knew how deeply she felt the sacrifice."

Maud Gonne was in a position to know, but there's not much suggestion of shared feeling in Constance's letter from Holloway: "My companions [Maud and Kathleen Clarke] I think of as 'Niobe' and 'Rachael', as they are the most complete and perfect – though now, alas, mournful! – mothers that I ever met! ... It's really very bad luck on the kids to lose *both* parents." This applied to her own daughter, too, but Constance's attention seems totally taken up with the fight.

The woman who is quite absent from Esther Roper's account is a woman who talked about "the joy of looking along a gun at the heart of an English soldier". Esther Roper doesn't say that when Constance died she was laid in state in a cinema because the Government couldn't allow her body any public place, while at the cemetery were Free State soldiers with machine guns to make sure that no volley was fired over her grave. One half of the city was mourning for her, and the other half for Kevin O'Higgins of the Free State Government, assassinated on his way to mass by the Republicans four days earlier.

The difficult fact is that *fighting was Constance's greatness* – a point missed equally by Esther Roper's protective biography and Yeats' famous and patronising poem, 'In Memory of Eva Gore-Booth and Con Markievicz':

> The light of evening, Lissadell,
> Great windows open to the south,
> Two girls in silk kimonos, both
> Beautiful, one a gazelle.
> But a raving autumn shears
> Blossom from the summer's wreath;
> The older is condemned to death,
> Pardoned, drags out lonely years
> Conspiring among the ignorant.
> I know not what the younger dreams –
>
> Some vague Utopia – and she seems,
> When withered old and skeleton-gaunt,
> An image of such politics.
> Many a time I think to seek
> One or the other out and speak
> Of that old Georgian mansion, mix
> Pictures of the mind, recall
> That table and the talk of youth,
> Two girls in silk kimonos, both
> Beautiful, one a gazelle.
>
> Dear shadows, now you know it all,
> All the folly of a fight
> With a common wrong or right.
> The innocent and the beautiful
> Have no enemy but time;
> Arise and bid me strike a match
> And strike another till time catch;
> Should the conflagration climb,
> Run till all the sages know.
> We the great gazebo built,
> They convicted us of guilt;
> Bid me strike a match and blow.

The assumption here is likely to be offensive to most readers of this book – that both sisters would have been better off keeping their looks and staying in their stately home, occasionally entertaining up-and-coming poets like W. B. Yeats (later to become a "public man" at the service of the Free State; and incidentally, burning down Free State Senators' houses was one of the favourite occupations of the Republican troops at the time of this poem).

But it is true that when we see a photograph of Constance and Eva in what was not particularly old age, only in their fifties, they do look like a couple of ghosts, tall and very, very thin with clouds of hair and lines deep on their faces as they smile at each other with tremendous love. We can stand back a little bit and admire the cheek with which Yeats – a person as Esther pointed out, "who never really knew" the Gore-Booths – insinuates himself in the role of a reminiscent old buffer of the landed gentry. The wonderful last stanza about the passing of time, and burning up of the revolutionary moment into a new age, is sparked off by what he sees as two wasted lives, although we might not agree. "Making the great gazebo" apparently was a bit of Irish slang for making a fool of yourself, and so the gazebo was a vantage point from which one viewed the world and it also meant that *all* sides in the Civil War had blown it.

In Yeats' other poem about Constance, 'On a Political Prisoner', he describes how much better off she would have been out hunting than in gaol, "her thought [become] some popular enmity". In the Civil War, writing in some of her republican magazines, I think she did use violence as a mask for disquiet and disillusion. But of course what Yeats prefers is hunting, the violence of the aristocrat, over popular organising, presumably the violence of the mob.

But in hunting is an analogy, a training ground for a very different view of Constance. That is of Constance as the ideal professional soldier with an ethic of absolute loyalty and a very quick mind, a superb organiser and trainer of other human beings with, of course, the physical skills and indefatigable energy that go with martial valour. (In all her terms in prison she chose hard labour, even in the last one, when none of the other Republican women prisoners did so, as they were all on hunger strike. Without siding with Yeats' view of aristocracy, we can agree that it was a terrible shame that a spirit of that kind should wear itself out behind bars.)

This is Constance the huntress, remembered by an old neighbour. She rode like a dancer, and "synchronised so naturally with the movements of her horse that it looked as if she could ride 'side-saddle' without a saddle at all." More importantly for her future life as a guerrilla,

> When riding to hounds, she had a remarkably quick eye for country and seemed instinctively to recognise the easiest line ... In Point-to-Point races she always took far more than the usual amount of care to familiarise herself thoroughly with the course beforehand, and I have never known her to deviate by a yard from the course as selected by her except in one case ...

The exceptional "one case" is important:

> Miss Gore-Booth ... had committed her horse to the jump when another representative of her own team rushed up almost alongside, and a collision seemed to be inevitable. Miss Gore-Booth pulled a little to one side, jumped the high hedge alongside the gap and got safely over both road fences leaving the easy line to the other competitor ... I afterwards measured the hedge. It was six feet three inches ... I afterwards expressed the opinion that the other rider was in the wrong and that she would have been fully justified in holding her course. She acknowledged that this was so, but added, 'But you must remember that it was a team race and we all thought that Mr – was riding the best of the Sligo horses. Besides I was the only woman riding and you can imagine what everyone would have said if I had knocked him out of the race.'

Constance Markievicz was described by her friend and sparring partner, Hannah Sheehy-Skeffington, (militant in the Irish Women's Franchise League and later Sinn Fein) as "never a feminist and barely even a suffragist". But in fact she had a very clear understanding from an early age of her situation as a woman and what that would allow her to do and not to do.

In her teens an older guest annoyed her by his attentions. One evening during a large formal dinner party, she suddenly felt his hand on her dress; she picked it from her knees like a dropped pear, held it up to attract everybody's attention and then said, 'Just look at what I have found in my lap.'

In 1896, the Gore-Booth sisters started a women's suffrage society in Sligo - only the third outside Dublin - and both young women truly showed themselves: Eva - "All of us, men and women alike, have duties to our neighbours and to our country and to society at large." Constance - "The sooner we begin to make a row the better."

As Constance said thirty years later, during the passionate and barely successful debate within Sinn Fein on giving women the vote, this meeting had been her "first bite of the apple of freedom". Like many Edwardian feminists, she omitted the word "obey" from her wedding ceremony. She helped her sister campaign for the barmaids of Manchester (though she, like many other feminists, was almost teetotal). And she was always ready to stand on platforms with the Dublin suffragettes in spite of their stated view that the Nationalists' Council of Women was "an animated collecting box" for a male organisation. She was also, of course, the first woman ever elected to the English Parliament - though she never sat there.

It seems clear, though Constance never complained, that she had a military talent of no mean order which she was never allowed to use for the obvious reasons of her sex. She began the future Republican Army and she trained its officers and its statesmen, and yet when its guns were first run into Ireland, the Fianna boys went off on a mysterious mission and the women and girls were excluded. Even earlier on, her own Fianna tried to put all women outside the door, saying that in a physical force organisation they were not welcome. Constance seems to have attempted to introduce girls into the scouts, but very few succeeded.

In the first Rising she was a lieutenant and was allowed initiatives on her own. True to her actress side, she'd already devised a uniform in discussion with her close friend and Rising companion, Dr Kathleen Lynn. A green tunic with silver buttons (the cause of a bitter quarrel with Sean O'Casey, who believed the Citizens' Army should fight in plain clothes), and breeches which she was always very fond of (in her old age she was likely to rip off her skirt and walk round in her bloomers to do her gardening or to repair her rattly old Ford. Much earlier there is a picture of her and Casimir, her husband, when young in Paris, coming back from a bicycling trip in knickerbockers).

Constance decided to wear skirts in Citizens' Army parades so as not to attract attention, but when she went to war she wore her breeches. On top, where she usually had a slouch hat with the red hand of Larkin's Transport and General Workers' Union, she had "her very best hat with the cock's feathers". She carried both a Mauser and an automatic.

In the Rising of 1916, as Esther Roper says, "There were a considerable number of Citizen Army women. They were on absolutely the same footing as the men". Constance believed that national independence and sex equality would come together–but she was wrong. Woman's suffrage was only carried by the barest majority within Sinn Fein, even at a time when women had been leading the movement through the Black-and-Tan years.

Eamon DeValera was the only commander who refused to have women at his post in the Rising.

DeValera's early years must account in part for his subsequent attitudes. His mother, Catherine, was widowed when he was three, and she was forced to place the child in the care of another woman while she went out to work. Shortly afterwards he was sent back from America to live with relatives in a small village in Ireland–a simple life he later romanticised. His mother remarried and, as Catherine Wheelright, became a prominent figure in Irish Nationalist circles within America ... DeValera's marriage to Sinead O'Flanagan exemplified his vision of women's true role; she bore him seven children and was rarely to be seen at any public occasion, even waiting at home for him when he was released from gaol after the Rising. (*Unmanageable Revolutionaries*, Margaret Ward)

By the time de Valera eventually took power as President, his national constitution of 1937 contained clauses "almost indistinguishable from Nazi decrees" ensuring that mothers stayed at home.

One of the signs that Constance would have made a great soldier was her life on the run as the underground Minister of Labour for Sinn Fein. Hers was the only office that was never raided by the police. She was

a martinet with regard to security ... not more than one person at a time was ever allowed to leave the premises ... every evening all important documents were taken away and hidden ... there were several pianos with rolls of music displayed so that in the event of a surprise raid the lady members of staff could masquerade as teachers.

Her life on the run, dodging in and out of disguises on her bicycle, all showed her sense of strategy. But in her years as a Minister and member of the Sinn Fein council she was often overridden by the men. She was the only woman there, and "verbatim reports of Dail meetings from 1921-2 will show that she received scant ceremony - once or twice not even common politeness".

During the Civil War, when the Republicans occupied the Four Courts, she wasn't even given any commission of her own. But she was a crack shot and she simply got in there and fought - outlasting all her male comrades who fell asleep - at nearly sixty she just went on for hours, shooting at a sniper no one could stop until she got him. That seems to me to be a sort of symbol of her life. Unquestioning loyalty - but increasingly a joy and flamboyance had gone. When she had first surrendered, in 1916, she'd kissed her gun before handing it to the British ...

I think the Republicans wasted her because they weren't prepared to have a woman as an army authority, as indeed no modern government ever has. (Harriet Tubman, "The Black General" of the American Civil War, mapped out a lot of the strategies that enabled the North to win from her knowledge of running the Underground Railroad for escaped slaves; but the Union government let her die with hardly even a pension . . .)

CON(VICT) 12

At no time in the five prison sentences that filled the last ten years of Constance Markievicz's life would you ever get any idea from her letters that she was really in danger. In the year 1920, 203 unarmed civilians were killed by the Black and Tans and British Auxiliaries. There were thirty-six assassinations in gaol – and Constance, serving her third term, would have been a prime target. But "Con(vict) 12" seems to have stayed always, and incredibly, "cheerful though captive". As she wrote to a friend: "One is just a little more careful to be ready to die, that is all."

It's only in her second jail term in Holloway that you see that stream of small complaints which is usually a sign of inner misery. This was the one time she was allowed no visitors at all. She *did* have political associates for once, but her references to Maude Gonne are tight-lipped. Perhaps the two women, both famous beauties, famous nationalists and fighters and also actresses, found it hard to co-exist in the same small space. Constance talks very sweetly about her other co-prisoner – Kathleen Clarke, the widow of Tom – but we know that one day Mrs Clarke got tired of being told, " 'I can't imagine why they arrested you, such a frail inoffensive little thing as you are'. [And] At last I rounded on her and said, 'Little and inoffensive I may be, but my charge-sheet is the same as yours', and after that she shut up."

It seems clear that even early in her political career, Constance didn't like rivals. Lady Gregory remembered her in her actress days as "rather a jealous meddler at the Abbey" Theatre. And when the talented labour organiser Delia Larkin left for America after the Dublin Lock-Out of 1913, it seems to have been because of personality clashes with Constance.

Until the last ten years of her life, there seems always to have been this shadow side to Constance's enormous energy, a damaging side even to her jokes. She might dress as a peasant girl to expose an admirer for arrogance to his tenants; but when she found a maid of hers stealing sweets, she put an emetic in them so the poor woman was vomiting for hours. She was a wonderful horse-woman, famous for her gentle touch; but her favourite and most famous horse died of a burst blood vessel racing for her. She loved dogs; but one of her dogs died early of over-exertion, after a life racing after her on bicycle trips. She had so much energy that she was almost dangerous to people around her, until she found a real way of channelling it.

But as the movement grew, she changed; she poured that energy into supporting and nurturing new leaders. You can see how full of optimism she is in the letters of the early '20s – the next generation of Republican women were very talented organisers and she was genuinely pleased to be out of the way and see the others coming forward.

By the time Constance was imprisoned for the third time, in Mountjoy prison, Ireland was in insurrection – not just an isolated rising – and the men's gaols were becoming colleges for new Republican leaders. Constance was reading history, learning about what the Bolsheviks were doing in Russia and giving herself a revolutionary education: "You can't understand the why of things unless you see all round."

There is a little one-line joke in her letters from this time, about barbed wire under her window. Nora Connolly's memoirs tell us what Constance never complained about:

> It was borne in on us very much how dreadfully lonely she must be with not a single associate, with no one to talk to, a very small courtyard to exercise in, barbed wire entanglements under her window, soldiers in trench helmets and war apparel, tanks, etc. We echoed the saying of the woman near the jail when she saw all the activity of the military: 'Yerra, God help ye, all that turnout for one lone woman'.

But Constance, alone with her books, was buoyed up by the sense of coming transformation. Her hopes seem sad now. "Maybe Lenin will win through after all! God speed him! and poor Russia. I wonder so on whose side C— is". "C" was her husband Casimir (the "Kathleen" or "Kitty" in these letters is Ireland - Cathleen ni Houlihan). And "C" was, in fact, on the other side. The pacifist Eva seems to have noticed the Bolsheviks' brutality towards their opponents. For Constance, it was the achievements of the popular uprising that inspired - and, for a time, hardened her heart towards her step-son Stasko, the son of Casimir's first marriage and a prisoner of 'the Bolshies'. (Towards the end of her life she wrote to him a very different letter. And in her last pamphlets and classes she distinguished "state socialism" from "co-operative socialism.")

In her letters from Mountjoy, Constance shows complete faith in her own side's humanity: "Some of the stories of sniping of [unarmed] police are so absurd: it's certainly not any of *our* crowd." An outsider herself, she was always intensely concerned with fairness. At the Rising's bitterest moment of surrender, she stopped one of her own side from revenge-killing a British soldier - "Don't, Joe, don't. It would be a great shame now." The same sense of justice comes up again, when as Sinn Fein's underground Minister for Labour in 1922, Constance, a Catholic convert in arms against the Protestant Ascendancy, wrote to a Catholic quarry manager in the North:

> Mr McCartan has received a notice from you ordering him to dismiss a Protestant workman . . . We wish to state that the Government of Dail Eireann cannot stand for intimidation and for the penalising of men because of their religion, and unless this intimidation is stopped we shall have to put the matter into the hands of the Republican Police.

Given that strong sense of honour, certain silences become notable in Constance's letters to Eva from the time of the Civil War onwards. We can read the sadness behind those gaps through the play she wrote so excitedly about in her last year of life. It is called *Broken Dreams*. It starts with a woman realising she has wasted her life on her brutal IRA husband; it closes with the man exposed, shot as a spy, and a right-on Republican rescuer named Eamon. But what remains is disillusion: "There was a traitor even among the apostles... you may expect to find them in a mere human movement."

THE FALLING OUT

Many historians – and certainly all the biographers of Constance Markievicz – treat the debate that led to the Civil War as a tragic mistake and are particularly unsympathetic to those "unmanageable revolutionaries", the women, who unanimously refused a Treaty with Britain and the compromise Irish Free State which would emerge. I think it's important for us to see that the issues raised there were not only those of honesty (Constance said taking the loyalty oath to a British king would be like planning a marriage when you were already thinking about getting divorced – very interesting that she used that particular symbol, when she and her husband had been parted for years); and of economic justice – would the whole people of Ireland get the benefits of the new Republic?

But there's one issue that historians don't often touch on that is particularly relevant to us now: the Treaty of the Free State left England in sole possession of all the naval ports and military strongholds. That situation is so like the present one, where American bases in England provide the greater imperial power with a foothold in a small island. A very crucial question of independence was at stake – military independence – and Constance was a soldier before she was anything else.

In the early days Constance wrote to Eva: "My conception of a free Ireland is economic as well as political: some agree with me, some don't, but, it's not a sore point. Easter Week Comrades don't fall out: they laugh and chaff and disagree. It annoys the enemy considerably."

But as she went through all the difficult years of the Civil War, on the run in Scotland and Northern England as well as Ireland, Roneo-ing and editing her own magazines, her writing gives the sensation that she was in deep trouble, digging up all the grievances that she and her old comrades from Easter week *had* had between each other and using them to beat the Free State with.

In 1916, Constance's close friend of Gaelic Revival days and an even closer friend of Eva's, the poet AE (George Russell), had stood by Constance when all the class she was born into were casting her off. He wrote this privately published but widely circulated poem:

Their dream had left me numb and cold
But yet my spirit rose in pride,
Refashioning in burnished gold
The images of those who died
Or were shut in the penal cell.
Here's to you Pearse, your dream not mine
But yet the thought for this you fell
Has turned life's waters into wine.

The hope lives on age after age
Earth in its beauty might be won
For labour as a heritage.
For this Ireland lost a son.
This hope into a flame to fan
Men have put life by with a smile.
Here's to you, Connolly my man,
Who cast the last torch on the pile.

Here's to the women of our blood
Stood by them in the fiery hour,
Rapt lest some weakness in their mood
Rob manhood of a single power.
You, brave on such a hope forlorn
Who smiled through crack of shot and shell,
Though the world cry on you with scorn,
Here's to you, Constance, in your cell.

Six years later at Christmas 1922, the poet wrote a very different, Open Letter to the Republicans in the *Irish Times*:

No ideal, however noble in itself, can remain for long loveable or desirable in the minds of men while it is associated with deeds such as have been done in recent years in Ireland . . . I do not like to think of you that the only service you can render Ireland is to shed blood on its behalf . . . Can you name those who, if you were all killed, would have left behind, as Pearse or Connolly, McDonagh or Childers did, evidence of thought or imagination?

To the survivor, Constance, those words must have been like a blow. At the very end of Constance's life, Mary Colum, wife of the poet whose magazines first turned Constance toward politics, describes her at AE's house again,

sitting in her usual place on the couch in the corner, a brown dog lying at her feet . . . But now, as she sat there, she whom I remembered as a beautiful woman, only second in beauty to Maude Gonne, was haggard and old, dressed in ancient demoded clothes. The outline of the face was the same, but the expression was different; the familiar eyes that blinked at me from behind glasses were bereft of the old fire and eagerness, she gave me a limp hand and barely spoke to me . . . I had known Constance Markievicz in her vibrant maturity, at the height of her youth and her courage, when she was engaged in masculine activities . . . Now I saw her, she was obviously a dying woman, sunk in dejection resulting either from imprisonment or from the loss of her hopes. What she had fought for had not really come into being; maybe nothing on earth could have brought it into being, so romantic and heroic was it.

In fact "what she had fought for" wasn't by any means an impossible dream, it was just a dream that had been lost, as first the British, then rival Free State and Republican armies devastated the co-operative dairies and farms of the new nation. There was no longer what Constance called "the material basis of freedom".

Most of her biographers have seriously underestimated her brains. She not only read in four languages (including Gaelic which she learned in prison), she was a political thinker. She learnt a lot from Connolly, the founder of the Irish Socialist

Party, and it was not just an emotional loyalty to him after his death that kept her on the road to what she called a "co-operative commonwealth". But times changed, and what before and just after the First World War had been the dream of millions of organised people – the liberation of the small nations, the federation of co-operatives – went down in blood all over Europe. What took its place were the mega-states of Italy and Russia, both welcomed at first by Constance, as by many others of "the world's wild rebels".

There is a terrible contrast between her words to Eva in 1920: "I don't agree about people being sheep . . . everyone wants to know and reads and thinks and talks", and these, written to an old friend just four years later:

> I never saw worse slums or met nicer people. 'Don't talk to me about politics, tell me how to get bread for the children,' was a very general cry. If one could only get the people to understand that politics ought to be nothing more or less than the organisation of food, clothes, housing and transport to every unit of the nation, one would get a lot further. Also if they would only learn to watch and heckle their leaders, aye, and distrust them, fear them even more than their opponents . . . If the people would only read, study and make up their mind as to where they wanted to go and as to how to get there, we would easily win out, but alas, it's always their impulse to get behind some idol, let him do all the thinking for them and then be surprised when he leads them all wrong.

By the time Constance came to her last prison in the North Dublin Union in 1923, the Civil War was almost over. The boys that she had trained in her Fianna, armed scouts, had grown up, become fighters for the Republic (and statesmen too, like Liam Mellows, who was the only person apart from herself who spoke in the Dail for "a government which looks after the rights of people before the rights of property"), and had already been killed by members of what used to be their own side.

You can tell from her last few letters that Constance was absolutely exhausted, but she went on hunger strike for the first time at nearly sixty, in this gaol. Typically, she comments that her rheumatism got a lot better, which of course is a very common experience, as the fast is one of the oldest forms of healing known to humanity; she also mentions that "one of the girls was very bad". What she doesn't mention is that as she was recovering herself from the hunger strike, Constance nursed this girl, Baby Bohun, back to health, put her own mittens on her shrunken hands and helped her backache by supporting her with her own body.

So many people had died that by the end she obviously found it very difficult to find workers with the same degree of intelligence and commitment. Before she went into the North Dublin Union, she had been going round on a dray raising popular support, and as soon as visitors came to her when she was recovering from hunger strike, she asked whether the dray had still gone on, and was very disappointed to find out that it hadn't. The Republicans by this time had become a minority sect, and she was still trying to work for a huge popular movement.

At the end of her life she would have become lonelier still, as she followed de Valera into his new party, Fianna Fall. It meant leaving the Republican Council of Women, who hoped so much for her return that they left their presidency open for her in case she changed her mind. She was faced with the prospect that she might actually have to take the Oath of Allegiance. Before she died she said to Baby Bohun, "How could I ever meet Paddy Pearse or Jim Connolly in the hereafter, if I took an oath to a British King?" But one of her longest associates and fellow prisoners, Eithne Coyle, said in a 1975 interview that "Madam was no fool ... she had more than average intelligence to realise all the implications of staying with de Valera ... poor Madam". It was lucky that she died when she did.

She said herself that she "often longed for the peace of the Republican [Burial] Plot", and increasingly more and more of her life centred on contact with the dead. Not only had she introduced W. B. Yeats to his first séance – and the Gore-Booth family had always been interested in Irish folklore and spirit lore – but there were waves of spiritualism in response to the massive deaths of the First World War. In Ireland's case there was also a tradition which went back much further through horrendous famine, emigration and executions. Political allegiance came almost always to be phrased in terms of loyalty to the dead. Constance herself wrote some rather doggerelly revolutionary hymns which expressed this feeling even before the Rising and the deaths of her own friends:

We have sworn by prison, torture and death
By the fate of Emmet and Tone;
By the martyr men of our noble race
By the peaceful days that have gone,

That to Ireland's days we'll devote our lives,
That we'll stand where our forebearers stood,
That as Ireland's soldiers will live and die
In ranks with men of our blood . . .

A LOST LEADER?

It must have been harder and harder for Eva and Constance to talk as Constance threw herself into more and more bellicose activity. It's an irony that Eva seems further away from us, although she was interested in so many of the things that Women's Liberation is interested in today; in her later years she was talking on Animal Liberation, for instance, to the Tunbridge Wells Theosophical Society.

From her political campaigning through the 1900s Eva Gore-Booth was making very cogent criticisms about the male chauvinism of the Trades Union Movement:

We have seen the gradual widening of the social chasm between the men who have emerged into political power and position and their women comrades who are still washing dishes and cooking dinners . . . The low rate of wages among women is, of course, not due to original sin or to some strange sex aberration which makes them unable to understand the usefulness of money. Neither is it due to want of organisation ... There are many causes given to the low rates earned by women ... but I venture to assert that there is not one of them that you can impartially examine and not find that it is but a new form behind which masquerades the ancient and ubiquitous fact of the political subjection of women.

It's a pity Eva has come down to us with such an aura of saintliness because she was not only a considerable scholar (teaching herself Greek and Latin as well as three European languages which she shared with Constance), but a very sharp analyst, and she was able to inspire a lot of people. In fact she could be called the personal inspiration of the militant suffragette campaign, because its architect, the young Christabel Pankhurst, had no interest in politics whatever before taking the courses on Shakespeare that Eva was giving to the mill girls of Manchester. From then on Christabel's conversion to 'the Cause' was sudden and total. Helena Moloney wrote that the women's movement in Ireland, "which aroused such a deep feeling of social consciousness and revolt among women of a more favoured class, passed over the head of the Irish working woman and left her untouched". But Constance had come to know another very different movement – the radical suffragists of Lancashire, with whom Eva spent ten years of her life until her health broke down, gaining her whole political education and becoming their main propagandist and writer. Here were the biggest exceptions to Helena Moloney's rule: very highly organised women workers with leaders from their own ranks, demanding the vote specifically for themselves.

It was these masses of working women who gave the Pankhursts a springboard to launch into London. But long before they had done so, local suffragists had become critical of the militant campaign. A letter from Eva Gore-Booth describes her objections:

Our members ... for the first time are shrinking from public demonstrations. It is not the fact of demonstrations or even violence that is offensive to ... the average working woman whose human dignity is very real to her. It is being mixed up and held accountable as a class for educated and upper class women who kick, shriek, bite and spit . . . It is not the rioting but the *kind* of rioting.

While the Pankhursts moved to war, Eva became a pacifist. These words are from *The Tribunal*, edited by Basil Boothroyd, which she wrote for regularly:

It is not capitalism nor secret diplomacy that makes wars possible. It is the idealism, the poetic imagination of the people, who see in the heroic bloodstained khaki-clad figure a national Messiah, and infinitely prefer him to the pale Galilean whose advocacy of meekness and passivity they neither endorse or understand. Pacifism will conquer war when pacifists can show the same courage and the same devotion as soldiers, the same healthy pugnacity towards opposing forces, and the same readiness to give their all for the realisation of a good cause.

But by the 1920s all Eva's interests were reflected through an intense Christian-Theosophical mysticism – it must have been almost impossible for her to find common ground with Constance. Eva's poetry was always in that Shelleyan style which combines transcendental symbolism and flowery traditional language with visionary politics. Constance herself writes rather neatly about the two styles that are coming into being, one much bolder, curt and jagged. Although she appreciates her sister's beautiful writing, she herself is more in the post-War style and that is why her letters are easier for us to understand today than Eva's poems. Before the First World War it was quite possible for poets like Swinburne and William Morris (and Oscar Wilde) to combine a radical vision with a very traditional and highly wrought style – afterwards, it really wasn't. It's very hard for us to appreciate Eva's poetry, although some of her political writing is excellent.

It's not often understood how much the younger sister was really the political inspiration of the elder. Eva found her way first: she met her lifelong friend Esther Roper in Italy in 1896, and went back to Manchester with her to spend her life with the radical suffragists and mill workers; it wasn't until quite a few years afterwards that Constance found the movement for Irish freedom. It is fitting that Esther Roper edited this book, not only because she was one of the group of women praying around Constance when she died, but because it was in fact the passionate friendship of Eva and Esther which was the beginning of a revolutionary road for both of the Gore-Booth sisters.

We don't have Eva's letters. We can deduce that it was a strain for her to be supporting her sister, much as she loved her, from the verse drama that they made together. Eva wrote *The Death of Fionavar and the Triumph of Maeve* in the first year that Constance was in gaol, and Constance illustrated it herself with quills from rooks' feathers (she also made embroideries that year with threads pulled from dish rags). Constance gives us highly realistic windswept thoroughbred horses with rather incongruous wings, and borders of butterflies and caterpillars to remind us that her very first ventures in political journalism were Nationalist Gardening Notes: "It is very unpleasant work killing slugs and snails. But let us not be daunted. A good Nationalist should look upon slugs in the garden in much the same way as she looks on the English in Ireland." When she was in Mountjoy prison the governor came round and asked what they all wanted. Constance said that she wanted dung, and when the sacks of dung arrived she typically refused to let anyone heave them up except herself, saying she could carry more than any man. And at the end of her life gardening was still a great solace. She didn't have a house of her own then, but she'd set to work on any old dusty backyard and start planting. Sometimes she would come back from a stormy meeting as a Rathmines and Rathgar District Councillor – fighting against the jobs blacklist on those who refused the oath of allegiance, fighting to retain public spaces for her own Fianna, or just fighting for the old and unemployed as it became more and more clear that the new Irish Government was not in any way the Workers' Republic she had dreamed of – and she would spend another two hours hard at the garden.

The story of the play I think shows in a mythic form the struggles that Eva was going through to support and love a woman who was living as a sort of warrior queen, a "Maeve of the Battles". Eva shows Maeve piling up the victories, but then discovering that her own daughter has died of pity on the battlefield; turning inwards, she examines herself, gives away all her land and her possessions, divides it between her commanders and the common soldiers (making the commanders as angry as Con's old Dublin Castle friends). The central figure moves from "savage heroism" to pacifism:

She begins to lose her interest in fighting and her ambitions. It is not exactly that sorrow possesses her, but her ideas of the value of things slowly change and she begins to feel it impossible to rule and lead armies, and not worthwhile to fight for narrow, ambitious ideals.

Constance seems not to have remarked on this. I think that Eva could have unconsciously been thinking of the Maeve who was Constance's own daughter as a kind of sacrifice; but in fact it seems to have been Eva herself who performed the sacrifice for change, because after her death the last ten months of Constance's life were indeed lived quietly and almost entirely among the poor.

THE STYLE

In *Constance Markievicz and the cause of Ireland* by Jacqueline van Voris, there is a description of a little room in Lissadell, midway between the two great rooms of the house, which Constance and Eva used for their painting and their reading. In different ways Constance seems to have recreated it throughout her life. There is a picture of her in her studio, at a bare table surrounded by art objects, blowing smoke through her fringe. Later on she had the very beautiful Surrey House ("Scurry House") with Casimir in Dublin, and she extended it with total generosity to all her new friends:

crowds used to gather into it at night – we had tea in the kitchen, a long table with Madam cutting up slices of bread about an inch thick and handing them around ... she had lovely furniture and splendid pictures. Then we used to go into the sitting room and someone would sit at the piano and there would be great singing and cheering and rough amusements. She had lifted her lovely drawing room carpet but had left her pictures on the walls, and on the bare boards there was stamping of feet.

From the time she got out of gaol she never had a house of her own, but she always loved beautiful things and kept a few that had been stored, it was a dwindling number because she'd always be giving them away if anyone liked them (together with the dwindling daughter's portion she continued to draw from the family lands). Here's a description of the last places she lived in in her life; "Con's room was bright, colourful and lovely but at times it was so untidy that it would take a mountain goat to get through it. This was due to political distractions and not laziness. The rest of the house was painfully ugly."

Her clothing seems to have alternated between the magnificent and literally rags. When she visited America in 1922, she asked prostitutes for tips on make-up, as well as finding out about chewing gum. She also had a great penchant for drag. Not only was there her Citizens' Army uniform, but she made herself with great care some fifteenth-century armour as Joan of Arc in a suffrage pageant in the year before the First World War.

Among the suffragettes the figure of Joan the Maid consoling a woman prisoner was often a coded message for love between women. In spite of this, and in spite of the passionate friendship of Eva and Esther Roper, there's never been in any of Constance's biographies a suggestion of a love relationship either with Dr Kathleen Lynn, who was with her at the Rising and by her bedside at the end, or with any of the other close women friends that she had. I haven't had access to her letters to any of these friends; I do know that she once said, "I'm not interested in men, for I've had the pick of too many men."

Her bloomers, and her hair which she cropped at nearly sixty because "I see no reason why old women shouldn't be as comfortable as the young" were all part of her radical chic. She kept open a space in the grimmest battles and the barest tenements for a kind of Bohemian free-handedness and glamour. Percy French's song about the 90s' Dublin Art Club suits her well.

If you're highly democratic
And your mode of life is essentially erratic.
From no fixed address,
But you sleep in someone's attic

Join the Arts Club, Join the Arts Club.

Amanda Sebestyen, London, 1986

The most thanks possible to my editors, Gail Chester of Ultra Violet and Ruthie Petrie of Virago; and to the Fawcett Library in their new home at the City of London Polytechnic.

Further reading on Constance: *Daughters of Erin,* Elizabeth Coxhead (New English Library, 1968); *The Rebel Countess,* Anne Marreco (Weidenfield, 1967), *Constance Markievicz,* Sean O'Faolain (Cape, 1934), *Smashing Times: A History of the Irish Women's Suffrage Movement,* Rosemary Cullen Owens (Attic Press Dublin, 1984), *Ireland's Abbey Theatre,* Lennox Robinson (Sidgwick, 1951), *Constance de Markievicz: In the cause of Ireland,* Jacqueline van Voris (University of Massachusetts, 1967), *Constance de Markievicz,* Jacqueline van Voris (The Feminist Press, NY, 1972), *Unmanageable Revolutionaries: Women and Irish Nationalism,* Margaret Ward (Pluto, 1983). **Attack:** *Autobiographies, vol 3: Drums Under the Window,* Sean O'Casey 1945 (MacMillan 1981).

On Eva: *One Hand Tied Behind Us,* Jill Liddington and Jill Norris (Virago, 1978), *Poems of Eva Gore-Booth* with letters, autobiographical note and biographical introduction by the editor, Esther Roper (Longmans 1929). Eva's many poems, pamphlets and plays, including *The Death of Fionavar* with Constance's illustrations, have never been republished and are in the British Museum. **Attack:** *The Suffragette Movement,* Sylvia Pankhurst 1931 (Virago, 1977).

On both: *With Wooden Sword: A Portrait of Francis Sheehy-Skeffington, Militant Pacifist,* Leah Levenson (Gill & MacMillan, 1983). Copies of Constance's Republican paper *Forward* and Eva's pacifist *The Tribunal* are at the British Newspaper Library, Colindale.

The world's true will
Has brought, in this dark hour of pain and strife,
A violet to life.

EVA GORE-BOOTH.

Remember no one has it in his power to make me unhappy.

CONSTANCE MARKIEVICZ.

BIOGRAPHICAL SKETCH

CONSTANCE GEORGINA GORE-BOOTH, born on 4th February 1868, was the eldest child of Sir Henry Gore-Booth, Bt., of Lissadell, Co. Sligo. Eva Selena was the third child, and was born in 1870. Their father was one of the largest landowners in the west of Ireland. It must not be assumed that he was out of sympathy with the peasants who were his tenants. On the contrary, he maintained throughout his life a friendly relationship with them. During the famine of 1879-80 stores of food were kept at Lissadell and freely given to the sufferers. He told me with pride that he had always refused police or military protection when in the troublous times of land agitation they were offered to him. He did not need them, for he was a good landlord, never exacting high rents, and ready to deal justly with his tenants. Lady Gore-Booth started home industries to help the women, and I saw beautiful needlework and lace made in her school, and afterwards sold in England by her efforts for the benefit of the makers. Later on the eldest son took an important part in the Irish Co-operative Agricultural Movement, devoting his time and energies to the building of creameries, the cultivation of bulbs, and other activities.

It was in congenial soil that these children grew up, on terms of intimacy and friendliness with the country people, from whose lips they learned much of the stories and legends of Ireland. But the extremes of poverty which they saw around them seem to have bitten deeply into the minds of both sisters. Even then it was absolutely natural to them to believe in equality and to fight for the downtrodden and suffering, and to wish to share all they had with others.

From an early age both of them were fearless riders, and Constance especially was famous for her daring on land and sea. I remember hearing from her father that on one occasion when he returned from one of his arctic exploration voyages and his little yacht lay in Sligo Bay, Constance came out in a canoe half full of water to greet him. The sailors implored him to break up the canoe in which she was risking her life. But it would have been useless; she did not know what fear meant, and could not be dragooned into 'safety first.' Constance's younger brother tells this story also: 'I saw the following Rob Roy canoe episode myself. The steamer *Justin*, bound for Sligo from Philadelphia, ran ashore on the Wheaten Rock, outside the Bay. I walked over to see the work of lightening to refloat the ship, and I hadn't been there long before Constance came *sailing* round Raughley Point in the canoe, much to the amazement of all the men, who stopped work to stare. This was full Atlantic.' I have often been taken by Constance and Eva on wild expeditions in a pony-cart with ramshackle harness, tearing over rough and stony ground at a speed that would cause the hair of an ordinary quiet person to rise, but neither of them were ever the least perturbed, and the ponies seemed to enjoy the joke. Both she and Eva had some mysterious sympathy with horses. No wonder both could draw and paint them so well. Constance built up in this healthy outdoor life a magnificent constitution which enabled her to stand the strain and stress of later life. Eva, on the other hand, was always very delicate, but she too developed the capacity of standing hardships from which stronger people would shrink. This was useful later when she organized and spoke at campaigns of outdoor meetings in Northern England in the midst of winter snow and fog.

I was struck by the understanding between both sisters and the peasants. Often when we were out picnicking they would take me into some cottage to tea. I there once heard the story of the Miss Gore-Booths riding at the head of a procession escorting Parnell through the streets of Sligo to some meeting; at which, of course, the conventionally-minded were shocked. Through their efforts, what they called a 'tin tab' was built for entertainments, meetings and plays, and a good deal of local talent came out in this way. The freedom and friendships of those days resulted in natural friendliness with workers everywhere and a complete unconsciousness of class distinctions.

Constance early showed a talent for painting and wood-carving. Eva had a real poetic gift, and not a day passed on which she did not practise her art with concentrated energy. They were wide readers. When I first knew them at Lissadell they habitually spent hours each day, Constance sketching and Eva reading aloud every book—poetry or prose—that came within their reach. They were beautiful girls, tall, slender, and full of life—as was their younger sister also.

Both of them were, so to speak, saturated with the beauties of nature, for Lissadell, where their youth was spent, is one of the loveliest spots on earth. They travelled too, and appreciated keenly all that other countries had to give—in music, architecture, painting, sculpture.

Both Constance and Eva were presented at Court in the usual way, and for years spent the 'season' in London—Constance enjoying everything to the full, Eva, on the other hand, not caring for the social side of it, though taking great pleasure in the opportunities it brought of meeting and talking to writers and thinkers and artists of all kinds. Concerts and theatres were an absorbing delight to them. I have memories of Constance in early days. She was radiantly beautiful, living the normal life of girls of her class. It was, I think, her extraordinary vitality that swept everything before it and made her so much admired and sought after: as popular in ball-rooms and other society functions, in every sport and occupation of country life, as she was later to be among working people in both islands. These people were attracted by the radiant energy and keen spirit which she brought to every happening in life as it came. I can see that lovely figure full of gaiety and mischief as it positively rushed along to dance a night away. Even more clearly can I see the same figure years after, seated high up on a coach driving four restless horses into the middle of a crowded square in an English factory town, where a political campaign was at its height, and the delight of the bystanders in her skill and enjoyment of the fun.

In later life circumstances separated the sisters, but though they never lived together again, but followed very different paths, the strong bond between them was not broken. Indeed, as this story will show, it did but grow deeper. Eva's life I have sketched elsewhere.[1] It is enough to say here that she chose to leave this spot whose beauty shines in every line of poetry she wrote, to live for many of the best years of life in the north of England, working with ability and happiness among the industrial women workers there. I give just one poem showing how she loved 'the great waves of the Atlantic' and 'the little waves of Breffny.'

[1] Biographical Introduction to *Collected Poems of Eva Gore-Booth.* [Longmans, Green & Co.]

THE PERILOUS LIGHT

The Eternal Beauty smiled at me
  From the long lily's curvèd form,
She laughed in a wave of the sea,
  She flashed on white wings through the storm.

In the bulb of a daffodil
  She made a little joyful stir,
And the white cabin on the hill
  Was my heart's home because of her.

Her laughter fled the eyes of pride,
  Barefoot she went o'er stony land,
And ragged children hungry-eyed
  Clung to her skirts and held her hand.

When storm winds shook the cabin door
  And red the Atlantic sunset blazed,
The fisherfolk of Mullaghmore
  Into her eyes indifferent gazed.

By lonely waves she dwells apart,
  And seagulls circling on white wings
Crowd round the windows of her heart,
  Most dear to her of starving things.

The ploughman down by Knocknarea
  Was free of her twilight abode ;
In shining sea winds salt with spray,
  She haunted every grey cross-road.

Some peasants with a creel of turf
  Along the windswept boreen came,
Her feet went flashing through the surf,
  Her wings were in the sunset's flame.

Beyond the rocks of Classiebawn
The mackerel fishers sailing far
Out in the vast Atlantic dawn
Found, tangled in their nets, a star.

In every spent and broken wave
The Eternal Beauty takes her rest,
She is the Lover of the Brave,
The comrade of the perilous quest.

The Eternal Beauty wrung my heart,
Faithful is she, and true to shed
The austere glory of Art
On the scarceness of daily bread.

Men follow her with toil and thought
Over the heavens' starry pride,
The Eternal Beauty comes unsought
To the child by the roadside.

The Gore-Booths had owned land in Salford and Manchester for generations, but Eva did not know the place. We met first in Italy. I was already working for the Enfranchisement of Women in the Lancashire industrial district. Two years later she joined me in Manchester, and we lived there twenty-seven years. Constance often stayed with us and was deeply interested in industrial conditions. Eva did most able work for Women's Trade Unionism and political emancipation, becoming Secretary to a Women's Trade Council and worker at the University Settlement. Some of her early poems give a charming picture of the life.

THE STREET ORATOR[1]

At Clitheroe from the Market Square
  I saw rose-lit the mountain's gleam,
I stood before the people there
  And spake as in a dream.

At Oldham of the many mills
  The weavers are of gentle mind;
At Haslingden one flouted me,
  At Burnley all the folk were kind,

At Ashton town the rain came down,
  The east wind pierced us through and through,
But over little Clitheroe
  The sky was bright and blue.

At Clitheroe through the sunset hour
  My soul was very far away:
I saw Ben Bulben's rose and fire
  Shining afar o'er Sligo Bay.

At Clitheroe round the Market Square
  The hills go up, the hills go down,
Just as they used to go about
  A mountain-guarded Irish town.

Oh, I have friends in Haslingden,
  And many a friend in Hyde,
But 'tis at little Clitheroe
  That I would fain abide.

THE GOOD SAMARITAN[1]

. . . .

At evening in the sunset flame
Out of the mill the workers came;
She who with four great looms weaves
Found Justice fallen among thieves.

The Egyptian Pillar, by Eva Gore-Booth.

Stone-breakers resting from their toil
Have poured out wine and oil.
The miner hurrying from the mine
Has seen a flash of light divine,
And every tired labourer
Has given a helping hand to her.
The workman leaning on his spade,
Or the tramp resting in the shade,
The navvy who the roadway mends,
These are our comrades, these our friends.

. . . . . .

During all these years she spent her holidays in Ireland, and kept in touch with her friends there. Many of her most characteristically Irish poems and plays were written in Manchester.

Constance was still living her usual life—interested chiefly in painting, for which she had a marked talent. After a session at the Slade she went to Paris to study. There, later, she met and in 1900 married Count Casimir Markievicz, a fellow-artist, a man of great gifts and charm. He was a Pole by race, but a Russian subject. The marriage, to our great amusement, took place at St. Marylebone's, London, the Russian Legation, and a registrar's office. Such were the difficulties of marrying a Russian subject then. The first six months Constance and Casimir spent on his family's estate near Kiev. They, like many of the landowners in that district, were Poles, and lived in a patriarchal manner. She told us how the eldest son's wife built an extension of the house for servants' bedrooms, but had the greatest difficulty in persuading the maids to sleep there. They preferred to stretch their blankets across their mistresses' bedroom doorways. The experience of Russian life interested Constance greatly, but she was glad to get back to Paris. They brought back with them Casimir's little son by his first marriage. Soon after, they returned and settled in Dublin. Their only child was born at Lissadell, in 1901.

Dublin was, at the beginning of the century, a place teeming with activity, political, artistic, literary, and Casimir and Constance took part with zest in every side of it. They painted, acted, wrote and produced plays. Their house became a centre of this Renaissance in Irish life. Gradually she became more and more interested in its patriotic side. Later on, during the War, the English authorities in Dublin demanded that Constance should register as an alien, since she had married a Russian subject. It seemed to her an intolerable insult, that an alien Government should call her an alien in her own country. I presume she must have said so forcibly. At any rate, she did not register, nor, as far as I know, was she again asked to do so.

In 1909 Constance organized the Irish Scout Movement. It had been proposed by the English Boy Scout leaders to extend their movement to Ireland, and this roused the Nationalists to start their own organization. Constance undertook this work and founded Fianna Na h-Eireann (the name of the old heroic Irish brotherhood).

It was a significant rule of this association that they pledged themselves never to join any English armed force. The boys received an ordinary scout training, and were, moreover, taught by Constance to shoot. She lived for a time at 'Belcamp,' a large house with grounds on the outskirts of Dublin, and it was here that she organized their training. However, the clan did not like country life, and she gave up the place and settled at Surrey House in Dublin. This became a gathering-place for writers, painters, politicians, trade unionists, and Fianna boys. It was here we first met one of the most impressive figures of the Rebellion, James Connolly.

During the Lockout of 1913, Constance was drawn into the industrial movement, of which at the time Jim Larkin was the picturesque Dublin leader and James Connolly the Belfast representative. Twenty thousand men and women had been locked out by the big employers of labour under peculiarly harsh circumstances. Æ.'s [George Russell] fine letter to the press, entitled 'Open Letter to the Employers of Dublin,' exposed the terrible conditions of starvation in which Dublin's population were living.

Constance plunged into the struggle. For six months she worked day and night, and organized a food kitchen and milk depôt. She collected the funds, cooked the food, visited workers in their homes, and organized a band of helpers from all classes. One of her helpers was Joseph Plunkett, another Francis Sheehy Skeffington. It was largely owing to her efforts that the children of the 20,000 strikers were saved from sheer starvation.

Many tales were told of her work. I will only give one here, told me by Mrs. Skeffington. 'The children, ever the hungriest and the most eager, used to file past with mugs, tin cans, porringers, old jam crocks, which she filled, and with a jolly word for all, for Madame had a personal contact and real sympathy with the poor that removed all taint of the Lady Bountiful and made her a comrade among comrades. One day a youngster came along, a boy of about ten, with his little soup-can, only to be recognised and pushed aside scornfully by the others with a taunt, "Go away, your father is a scab." Madame, seeing the hurt look in the child's face and the quick withdrawal, called him back. "No child is going to be called a scab. He can't help his father. When he grows up he'll be all right himself, won't you, sonny? And now have some soup."' In Dublin, Constance was called either 'The Countess' or 'Madame.'

I agree entirely with her friend, Mrs. Sheehy Skeffington, when she says, 'This was her biggest, finest achievement, greater than her manning the barricades in 1916 and facing sentence of death. She espoused an unpopular cause, and braved conventions in her championship of the poor and lowly.'

'I first saw Constance Markievicz,' Mrs. Skeffington says, 'on the boards of the Gaiety Theatre, Dublin, where she was acting as Eleanor in George Birmingham's comedy, *Eleanor's Enterprise.* The play was produced by Count Markievicz, himself a dramatist and producer of no mean parts. Constance also played in his drama, *The Memory of the Dead*, a play of '98, in which the rôle of rebel heroine was written and cast for her. As an actress, her high-pitched voice and English accent, and her short sight, which in later years entailed the wearing of glasses, were disabilities. But her temperament suited rebel and heroic parts, and in these she shone. Later, too, her acting gifts helped her with various disguises, necessary when she was "on the run," a much-wanted Cabinet Minister. She often chose the rôle of an elderly and rather feeble old lady, with Victorian bonnet and cape. It was all right so long as she did not speak. But her voice instantly gave her away.[1] During all the time when she was "on the run," staying a night here and there with a friend (we all had lists of friendly houses where, if pressed, we might pass the night), though Constance

[1] I must add to this that one day when 'on the run' the spirit of mischief entered into her and she determined to make the policeman on point duty take the dignified old lady across. For once her voice was feeble and shaky and her footsteps too, and she nearly danced with amusement when he very kindly put her safely on the opposite footpath.

was well known to tram-conductors, newsboys, basket-women and all over Dublin, none of them ever gave her away or even pretended to recognise her as she passed. "The Coun*tess*," as Dublin called her (accent on the second syllable), had the freedom of the city, literally.

She herself wrote plays, all of a rebel and propagandist character—*Blood Money*, *The Invincible Mother*, *Broken Dreams*. The Fianna and Cuman na-mBan or The Republican Players staged these, and she herself helped to produce them. Owing to the haste with which these were thrown together, feverishly dashed off like her sketches and poems, they did not rank as literature, but there is fire and quality in them for all that, and, of course, propaganda.'

Mrs. Skeffington, who at the time was working hard for the enfranchisement of Irish women, says: 'Madame, though only a mild suffragist (she held that suffrage would come with a lot else when Ireland was free), was always interested in direct action of any sort against authority. She was also keenly interested in people, and her home was a meeting-place for rebels of all sorts. She would rush in and say, "Come along to-night. I want you to meet So-and-so. The gas is cut off and the carpets are up, but you won't mind. Tell Frank to come along." Then we would meet the particular "lion" and talk round the big fire, sitting on her large divan in the big bow-window, by the light of innumerable candles stuck around.

'It was to this house that Connolly was brought after his hunger strike, when Lord Aberdeen hastily released him.

'It was from here that Jim Larkin went forth disguised, to address the multitude in August 1913 from the windows of the Imperial Hotel, O'Connell Street, owned by William Martin Murphy who had locked out the tram workers of Dublin.'

From this time onwards her interest in industrial matters grew rapidly.

She helped in the Trade Union Movement at Liberty Hall and became a friend of James Connolly, who succeeded Larkin as leader of the Transport Workers Union, which included every kind of worker in its ranks. He was a man of wide experience, a skilled organizer, an able writer, as his *Labour in Irish History* proves, and with all this, a man of the greatest personal kindness and sympathy. I remember one night sitting at supper at Surrey House with Constance, Eva and James Connolly. We were discussing industrial questions and Socialism, when suddenly a woman rushed in in a state of agitation, saying that a young girl member of the Union had left her home and disappeared into the slums. Without a moment's hesitation he got up and left the house to find her. Having found her and taken her back to her home, he returned about midnight to continue the conversation and drink tea, instead of the supper he had left. I remember going to Liberty Hall one day when lunch was being served to the workers, and being shocked by their look of utter poverty.

Thus there was at this time in her mind a deep sense of the urgent importance of this industrial movement as the only hope for the workers; and at the same moment her leadership of the Fianna Na h-Eireann made more and more claims on her organizing power and activity. She did not speak much to us of the revolutionary side of her life, though, of course, I saw numbers of Fianna boys at her house.

I confess I utterly miscalculated the likelihood of a rising. One day about twelve months before 'Easter Week,' Eva and I sat in a window of a Dublin house watching the march past of men and women of the Citizen Army and Volunteers, Fianna boys, women of Cuman na-mBan, and a crowd of sympathizers on their way to visit the grave of some Irish hero of the past. There were few uniforms, though Padraic Pearse, their leader, was in full uniform. When it was over, thinking with admiration of all the gifted people in those ranks, I said with relief to Eva, 'Well, thank goodness, they simply can't be planning a rising now, not with such a tiny force.' I had become sadly accustomed to the tramp of endless troops through London on the way to the Front. But I did not adequately realize, as Connolly and the others did, the power that an intrepid failure has to rouse Ireland. I forgot the reality behind the words, 'We have our dead.' Constance, knowing how opposed her sister was to violence, said nothing, wanting to spare her anxiety as long as possible. So it was that the news of Easter Week came as a terrible shock.

To go back a little in the history of the modern movement, I should record the founding of the 'Inghean A na h-Eireann' [Daughters of Ireland], a patriotic body of women, by Maud Gonne and Helana Molony, in 1900. A paper 'Bean na h-Eireann' was written and printed on a hand-press by a group of women about the same date. In 1908 the Irish Women's Franchise League was started by Hanna Sheehy Skeffington and others. Then in 1909, as I have said, came Fianna Na h-Eireann.

The Ulster Volunteers were formed in 1913 to oppose by force the Home Rule measure then before the House of Commons. Support and immunity were promised to them by certain English Cabinet Ministers. In consequence of this, Professor Eoin MacNeill published articles in the Gaelic League weekly journal, urging the formation of Nationalist Volunteers. If force was to be used in Ulster against Home Rule, why not by Nationalists in support of it? So in November 1913 the

'Irish Volunteers' were formed. But just before them, as a result of the catastrophic failure of the great Lockout in Dublin, the Irish Citizen Army had been formed from members—including some women members on full equality with men—of the Irish Transport and General Workers' Union, by James Connolly and James Larkin. As auxiliary to the Irish Volunteers there was Cuman na-mBan [Women's Council]; also Padraic Pearse started an Officers Corps at his school, St. Enda's. Meanwhile Constance Markievicz, as Chief Scout, was drilling Fianna Na h-Eireann.

Early in 1914 there was what was called the 'Curragh Camp Mutiny,' when officers of the Irish garrison declared that, if ordered to Ulster to act against the Ulster Volunteers, they would disobey orders. These officers at once resigned their commissions. John Redmond at this time demanded that on the Executive of the Nationalist Volunteers there should be an equal number representing the Irish Parliamentary Party and the Volunteers themselves. This was agreed to, whereupon Pearse withdrew from the Executive.

In March 1914 the Ulster Volunteers landed a cargo of arms at Larne, without any attempt being made by Government officials to hinder them. Baron von Kuhlman, as German agent, watched these events from Belfast and reported them to Berlin. Inevitably they were known also to every man and woman in Ireland.[1]

In July, the Nationalist Volunteers of Dublin landed a cargo of rifles from a yacht at Howth; Volunteers and Fianna members placed them in cars and wagons and started for Dublin. On the way they were met by the regular forces, who demanded the rifles, but the Volunteers got away with them. The Crown forces

[1] See *Ourselves Alone*, by Alice Stopford Green; *Ireland for Ever*, by Brigadier-General Crozier, C.B., C.M.G., D.S.O.

marched back to Dublin, where they were hooted by an idle crowd, some of whom threw stones. The officer in command gave orders to fire; the men loaded, knelt down and fired, killing and wounding men and women in what became known as the Bachelors Walk affair.

In August the World War broke out.

In September the Home Rule Act was placed on the Statute Book, but it was agreed that the measure should not be put into effect until an amending Bill had been passed. When a Coalition Government came into power in England containing several strong anti-Home Rule members, including Sir Edward Carson, the Chief of the General Staff of the anti-Home Rule Volunteers in Ulster, everyone in Ireland knew that while he was in office the Act would never be put into operation, and the Nationalists felt they had been betrayed.

The Nationalist Volunteer Force divided. (1) Those who agreed with Mr. Redmond when he offered them to the Government as a defence force, on the condition that they were equipped and kept in the country, called themselves National Volunteers. This was the major part. (2) Those who remained with Prof. MacNeill—about 10,000 in number—called themselves the Irish Volunteers. As was natural, the latter body and the Citizen Army, which had its own leaders, drew closer together. When, in 1916, conscription was imposed on England, the National Volunteers began to drift back into the Irish Volunteer ranks.

It cannot be too often repeated that James Connolly was not a militarist. Armed risings he regarded as out of date. His whole energies were given to the Labour Movement. But, alas, England's treatment of the Home Rule Act and the recruiting in Ireland filled him with indignation, and he came to think that the moment had come for armed rebellion, perhaps

Ireland's only chance. Not that he imagined that the small force of which he was one of the leaders could beat the English Army and Navy. He knew such a thing was impossible, but he believed this to be now the only way to prove Ireland's determination to be free. She should not be the 'only small nation left in thrall.' It was said in Dublin at the time that when a friend told him there was a report that Roger Casement had been arrested, which meant that there was no possible chance of help of any kind from outside, he replied to the friend's appeal that he should abandon the struggle, 'No, now less than ever.' He would not give up the rising however desperate the situation might be. Ireland would rise and make one heroic effort.

And so it came about that just after noon on Easter Monday, 24th April 1916, the Irish Republic was proclaimed at the base of Nelson's Pillar, Dublin. This historic document was written by Padraic Pearse. I give it in full:—

POBLACHT NA H-EIREANN

The Provisional Government of the Irish Republic

To the People of Ireland

Irishmen and Irishwomen, in the name of God and the dead generations from which she receives her old traditions of nationhood, Ireland, through us, summons her children to her flag and strikes for her freedom. Having organized and trained her manhood through her secret revolutionary organization, the Irish Republican brotherhood, and through her open military organization, the Irish Volunteers, and the Irish Citizen Army, having patiently perfected her discipline, having resolutely waited for the right moment to reveal itself, she now seizes that moment, and, supported by her exiled children in America and by gallant allies in Europe, but relying in the first on her own strength, she strikes in full confidence of victory.

WE declare the right of the people of Ireland to the ownership of Ireland and the unfettered control of Irish destinies to be sovereign and indefeasible. The long usurpation of that right by a foreign people and Government has not extinguished the right, nor can it ever be extinguished except by the destruction of the Irish people. In every generation the Irish people have asserted their right to national freedom and sovereignty; six times during the past three hundred years have they asserted it in arms. Standing on that fundamental right, and again asserting it in arms in the face of the world, we hereby proclaim the Irish Republic as a sovereign independent State, and we pledge our lives and the lives of our comrades in arms to the cause of its army, of its welfare and of its exaltation among the nations.

THE Irish Republic is entitled to, and hereby claims, the allegiance of every Irishman and Irishwoman. The Republic guarantees religious and civil property, equal rights and equal opportunities to all its citizens, and declares its resolve to pursue the happiness and prosperity of the whole nation and of all its parts, cherishing all the children of the nation equally and oblivious of the differences carefully fostered by an alien Government which have divided a minority from the majority in the past.

UNTIL our arms have brought the opportune moment for the establishment of a permanent national Government representative of the whole people of Ireland and elected by the suffrages of all her men and women the provisional Government here constituted will administer the civil and military affairs of the Republic in trust for the people. We place the Irish Republic under the protection of the Most High God, Whose Blessing we invoke on our arms, and we pray that no one who serves that cause will dishonour it. In this supreme hour the Irish nation must by its valour and discipline, and by the readiness of its children to sacrifice themselves for the common good, prove itself worthy of the august destiny to which it is called.

SIGNED on behalf of the Provisional Government:—

THOMAS J. CLARKE
SEAN MACDIARMADA
P. H. PEARSE
JAMES CONNOLLY
THOMAS MACDONAGH
EAMON CEANNT
JOSEPH PLUNKETT

Padraic Pearse was chosen as Commandant-General of the Republic's forces, and James Connolly was chosen to command in Dublin. He was already Commandant of the Citizen Army.

Now the Irish Citizen Army and the Irish Volunteers combined to become the 'Irish Republican Army.' The day before, Professor MacNeill, believing the moment hopeless, had countermanded the parade of the Irish Volunteers called for the Sunday. He thus prevented a general rising; only Dublin and a few counties rebelled. The General Post Office and the South Dublin Union were seized and the rebels occupied Jacobs' Factory, the College of Surgeons, the Four Courts, Boland's Mills and St. Stephen's Green. It was in the Green that Constance was stationed as officer under Mallin, who commanded that section of the Citizen Army. By night, Government troops began to arrive from all over the country, and by Tuesday there were 20,000 soldiers in Dublin. Most authorities consider 800 was about the number of the rebel forces in the city, and of these I believe 250 were in the Citizen Army. Martial law was proclaimed and fierce fighting went on the whole of Easter Week. Very little news came through to England. The rebels were in possession of the G.P.O. and prevented communications with the outside world. In London we knew nothing except the brief notices issued by the Government. Stephen's Green was raked by machine-gun and rifle fire from the surrounding buildings. The trenches dug by the rebels were of no use against such an attack; they therefore retreated in an orderly fashion to the College of Surgeons on the Tuesday. Powerful shells were thrown into the Post Office, Liberty Hall and other buildings occupied by them. The roar of big guns went on till Friday. Fire broke out in the city (over 200 buildings were involved). At last the Post Office took fire and became untenable. Street fighting raged, till finally the rebels' ammunition became exhausted. Padraic Pearse decided to surrender at 3.45 P.M. on Saturday, 29th April 1916. He issued a general order:—

'In order to prevent further slaughter of unarmed people and in the hope of saving the lives of our followers now surrounded and hopelessly outnumbered, members of the Provisional Government at present at Headquarters [1] have agreed to unconditional surrender and the commanders of all units of the Republican forces will order their followers to lay down their arms.'

Pearse signed this first. It was then signed by James Connolly and also by MacDonagh.

General firing ceased on Saturday afternoon, but

[1] The General Post Office.

individual sharp-shooters did not get word of the surrender at once and the city was not quiet for a couple of days.

Through all this week Constance had been first in St. Stephen's Green and later at the College of Surgeons till the surrender. Later we heard stories at first hand from those who had been with her on the Green. She was jovial to her comrades, friendly to the prisoners, quite unafraid all through. Many years afterwards she described to me the last night at the College of Surgeons. There were wounded to be nursed, as well as military duties to be done. In all this she took part. Through the night those assembled there prayed for the dead and the living. A great peace was over them, waiting for the end. Constance wanted to join in the prayers, but at first they could not understand why a non-Catholic should wish to take part in Catholic prayers.

In her earlier life religious observances had not meant much to her. I think she hated to belong to a church that represented the richer rather than the poorer people—all the peasants being Roman Catholics. Later, in Dublin, it was the same thing. She told me she had come to believe very little in religion. But now face to face with death she was deeply impressed by the reality of spiritual things to these men and women among whom she had lived. As she shared their prayers there came to her a vision of the Unseen, which wrought such a change in her that from that moment to her, too, the things that are seen became temporal and the things that are unseen, eternal.

As she told me the story after her sister's death, I felt that some change had actually taken place in her life, and that from that time she had developed slowly and painfully until in the hospital ward in 1927 she was as one already in an unseen world. I knew the future was more real to her then than the life in which we spoke and suffered at the moment.

After the surrender, at the end of Easter Week, she was taken to Kilmainham Gaol with the other rebels. On 6th May she was court-martialled and condemned to death. She rejoiced to think she would be with her friends, but suffered terribly each morning when she heard the sound of rifle shots, which she knew meant the execution of some of them. These executions were as a matter of fact hideously drawn out.

At the time we were not even allowed to know the charge against Constance, but later she managed to give her sister the official document. I therefore insert it here.

FORM FOR ASSEMBLY AND PROCEEDINGS OF FIELD COURT-MARTIAL ON ACTIVE SERVICE

Proceedings

A. Order convening the Court

State the place and country

At Dublin, this 4th day of May 1916.

Whereas it appears to me the undersigned, an Officer in Command of the Forces in Ireland on active Service, and a competent Military Authority under the Defence of the Realm Regulations, that the persons named in the annexed Schedule and being subject to Military Law, have committed the offences in the said Schedule mentioned.

AND I am of opinion that it is not practicable that such offences should be tried by an ordinary General Court-Martial; nor is the offence one of a minor character. I HEREBY convene a Field General Court-Martial to try the said persons, and to consist of the Officers hereunder named.

(I am unable to appoint:—

(1. Three Officers to form the Court.)

(2. A Field Officer a President.)

(3. Three Officers having more than one year's service.)

for the following reasons, namely:—)

President.

Rank.—Brig.-Genl.
Name.—C. J. Blackader, D.S.O., A.D.C.

Members.

Rank.—Lt.-Col.
Name.—G. German,
Regiment.—5th Leicester Regt.

Rank.—Lt.-Col.
Name.—W. J. Kent,
Regiment.—R.F.A.(T.).

(Signed) J. G. MAXWELL,
General Commanding the Forces in Ireland. Convening Officer.

SCHEDULE

Date, 4th May 1916. No.

Name of Alleged Offender (a)	Offence Charged.	Plea.	Finding, and if convicted, Sentence. (b)	How dealt with by Confirming Officer.
Constance Georgina Markievicz	1. Did an act to wit did take part in an armed rebellion and in the waging of war against His Majesty the King, such act being of such a nature as to be calculated to be prejudicial to the Defence of the Realm and being done with the intention and for the purpose of assisting the enemy.	Not Guilty.	Guilty. Death by being shot. The Court recommend the prisoner to mercy solely and only on account of her sex.	Confirmed. But I commute the sentence to one of Penal Servitude for life.
Alternative	2. Did attempt to cause disaffection among the civilian population of His Majesty.	Guilty.		

(*a*) If the name of the person charged is unknown, he may be described as unknown with such addition as will identify him.

(*b*) Recommendation to mercy to be inserted in this column.

J. G. MAXWELL, *Convening Officer.*

C. J. BLACKADER, Brig.-General, *President.*

Promulgated this 6th day of May 1916.
Kilmainham Gaol, Dublin.

H. ANDERSON, Captain.

TRIAL OF CONSTANCE GEORGINA MARKIEVICZ

Prosecution

1st *Witness.* Walter McKay duly sworn states:—

My name is Walter McKay, and I live in University Club, Stephens Green, and am employed as a page boy. I was 17 years old last Sept. I remember last Easter Monday, April 24th and between 1 and 2 o'c. that day I was standing at the Club door. From there I could see Stephens Green, and I saw a few rebels dressed in green uniform they were pulling the civilians out of the Green and as they were doing this the accused drove up in a Motor car, blew her whistle and leaned out of the car. She gave orders to a Sinn Feiner after he had shut the gate of Stephens Park. She then drove up towards the Shelbourne Hotel—I saw her again about 1.15 P.M. she was then behind one of the monuments in the Green, she had a pistol in her hand which she pointed towards the club and fired.

I ran upstairs and saw where the bullet struck. After firing she walked up towards the Shelbourne Hotel dressed in knickers and puttees. I was in the Club the remainder of the week and on Tuesday night there was firing from the Green.

Cross-examined by the Accused

I was at the Meath Industrial School, Blackrock.

I never saw the accused on the Green before the occasion referred to.

I saw the accused blow a whistle just one blast. I did not hear the order but I saw her say something to the man who then went away.

The witness withdraws.

2nd Witness. Captain Henry de Courcy Wheeler, Reserve Officer attached to General Low's Staff, duly sworn states :—

I remember Sunday last, April 30. I was in the Castle yard that day. From there I proceeded to the College of Surgeons.

I met the accused at the side door of the College of Surgeons in York Street. Commandant Michael Mallin of the rebels was with her. The meeting took place under a flag of truce. Subsequently the rebels who were in the College of Surgeons marched out and surrendered. The accused was one of the number. She was armed with a pistol and ammunition in a Sam Browne belt. She handed her arms to me. I offered to drive her in a motor car to the castle. She refused, and said she preferred to march with the men as she was second in command. About 120 rebels surrendered at the same time as the accused.

The accused declines to cross-examine the witness.

The witness withdraws.

Prosecution closed.

The accused declines to call witnesses.

The accused in her defence states :—

I went out to fight for Ireland's freedom, and it doesn't matter what happens to me.

I did what I thought was right and I stand by it.

Statement ends. C. J. BLACKADER, Brig.-General.

Signed this 4th day of May 1916.

C. J. BLACKADER, Brig.-General,
President of the Court-Martial.

Subject to what I have stated in the last column of the Schedule, I hereby confirm the (finding and) sentence of penal servitude in the case of Constance Georgina Markievicz.

Signed this 6th day of May 1916.

J. G. MAXWELL,
General (Field) Officer, in Chief
Command of the Forces.

Constance stated in her interview with her lawyer, at Aylesbury Prison, later on, that 'there were in fact three distinct charges at both trials [*i.e.* preliminary trial and Court-Martial both within a few hours] which are not stated separately in the official report, but were as follows :—

1. Participating in the Rising, to which I pleaded "Guilty."

2. Assisting the Enemy, to which I pleaded "Not Guilty."

3. Causing disaffection, to which I pleaded "Guilty."'

The page-boy's evidence was worthless. Constance showed that he could not possibly have seen what he said he did from the place in which he stood.

The fact that she took part in the Rising as an officer in the Citizen Army, was in itself considered sufficient to call for the death sentence. Perhaps the knowledge that she was the Founder and Leader of Fianna Na h-Eireann, and thus 'caused disaffection,' had something to do with it.

The swiftness and lack of deliberation shown in these trials was ghastly.

Constance told me that during the first week in Kilmainham, when she was lonely and sad one night, an English soldier on guard outside her cell waited till all was quiet and then unlocked the door and came in. He offered her a cigarette and sat down himself to smoke with her. He was most kindly and sympathetic, telling her the news and answering questions. She never forgot this human action, coming as it did at a time when she was worn out after a week's violent activity followed by the strain of solitary confinement. She always wanted to thank him, but did not know how to find him and could not make inquiries lest she should get him into trouble.

Constance was not allowed legal aid at her trial. Mr. Gavan Duffy, in the face of the greatest difficulties, went over to Dublin, and he and Mr. T. M. Healy, K.C., interviewed the officials, but they could not get permission to appear for her and they came away feeling that the military authorities meant to take her life. What Constance, in common with all the Irish prisoners, owed to George and Margaret Gavan Duffy it is impossible to put into words. They literally gave up everything for the prisoners and earned the love and gratitude of all of us. Mr. Healy's *Letters and Leaders of my Day* show how deeply he too felt the sufferings of those who had taken part in the Rebellion. I know from personal experience how constantly he helped the sufferers of Easter Week.

Indeed, I think in England too, all men of goodwill came to sympathize even where they most deeply disagreed. The executions at Kilmainham and Pentonville were the worst days' work ever done by England to Ireland. Irish people who had taken no part in the revolt became permanently embittered and utterly alienated ; before long the whole country was against English rule. The loss to Ireland of these rare spirits was tragic in the extreme. What might not these Republican leaders have done in the rebuilding of Irish life—for education, for the industrial movement, for foreign relations, for peace between the nations. Instead of this, all the wisdom and experience of the leaders were thrown wantonly away. It was a tragedy, but it was also a crime on the part of the English authorities for which both nations have had to pay in blood and tears. As Mr. Nevinson says, it was inevitable that the Court-Martial should condemn Constance to death ; she had been second in command, under Mallin, of the Citizen Army force in Stephen's Green, and was also leader of Fianna Na h-Eireann. I believe he is correct in saying that it was owing to Mr. Asquith, the Prime Minister, that she was reprieved, though whether he went over to Dublin for that purpose I do not know. Certainly, the day before the reprieve was announced, one of his secretaries who knew Eva, was allowed to tell her that she might have certain hope that the extreme penalty would not be exacted.

From the moment the Rebellion had been crushed, Eva had worked night and day to prevent the taking of vengeance. It was not only for her sister that she worked, but for the others, especially for James Connolly, against whom there was an intensely bitter feeling in London.

The facts of the murder of Francis Sheehy Skeffington, an extreme pacifist, by an officer [afterwards pronounced insane], when they became known, added to the horror. At first the Prime Minister denied the truth of the accusation made by Mrs. Skeffington, but inquiry, alas, proved it only too true. Mr. Healy, who represented Mrs. Skeffington at the Government Inquiry, said Captain Colthurst was court-martialled, convicted, and declared insane and sent to Broadmoor Criminal Asylum, but was soon discharged, and it was believed given half-pay.

He gives details of these days following Easter Week. 'After their surrender no arrangements for decent custody were at first possible. This led to conditions which left a memory as bitter as that enkindled by the executions. In the Rotunda Gardens there were herded together in the open, hundreds of men and women from Saturday to Monday, without any sanitation or other provision. Men gnashed their teeth at the shame to which both sexes were exposed. . . . The horror may have been inevitable before decent arrangements could be improvised, but it made a seed-bed of hatred.'

I can myself bear witness to the misery of the crowds, who still on 12th May were waiting outside Richmond Barracks, unable to find out whether their friends had been taken there as prisoners, and if so, whether they were alive or dead. I shall never forget the descriptions of the conditions inside, given us by the priest (once a doctor) who had been called in to administer the last rites to the dying. Mr. Healy goes on to say: 'I never knew such a transformation of opinion as that caused by the executions. Besides the looting by the soldiers and ruffianism against innocent people, the ill-treatment of prisoners, the insolence of the military in the streets, the foul language used to women and the incompetence shown by officers, have aroused a contempt and dislike for which there is no parallel in our day. . . .' He makes some statements, though, which I am thankful to see. At the time of Connolly's death it was freely said that Mr. William Murphy had urged the authorities not to grant a reprieve. 'William Murphy was owner of *The Independent*. A leader was printed there without his knowledge or approval which haunted him till his death.' 'He was greatly affected by the thought that he had been accused of advising the shooting of Connolly and said that so far from its being true, he used to pray for Connolly, owing to the antagonism he showed him.' [They were leaders of the opposing sides in the Strike of 1913.] The story is told of Con Colbert (Fianna Na h-Eireann member and friend of Constance). 'He had insisted on taking the place of his Commandant when surrender was resolved on, saying, "You're a married man; I'm single. You'll be shot. Resign." "Never," said the Commandant. "Then," said Colbert, "we'll depose you." So it was done. Colbert gave the surrender and was tried and shot.'

Ceannt left a letter which was not made public till 1926. I feel I must insert it here. 'I bear no ill-will towards those whom I fought. I found the common soldiers and the higher officers human and companionable, even the English who were actually in the fight against us. Thank God, soldiering for Ireland has opened my heart and made me see poor humanity where I expected to see only scorn and reproach. I have met the man who escaped from me by a ruse, under the Red Cross. But I do not regret having withheld my fire. He gave me cakes!' It was of Ceannt that Constance spoke at her trial at Mallow.[1] It is reported that members of the Courts-Martial in 1916 who tried the insurgents, were affected by their bearing. General Blackader, who presided, soon resigned his commission. . . . The officers of the Courts-Martial hated their task.

Amongst those who ministered to the prisoners were the Franciscan Capuchin Friars from Church Street, Father Albert, Father Augustine and Father Aloysius. Only those whose friends suffered know all the loving service given by them. Perhaps this is best shown by quoting a few letters written to Eva by Father Albert.

FRANCISCAN CAPUCHIN FRIARY,
CHURCH STREET,
DUBLIN,
December 23, 1916.

DEAR MISS GORE-BOOTH,—Many thanks for your most welcome letter. I was delighted to have even a

[1] Page 90.

word about that dear friend of ours. Thank God she is so well and in such splendid spirits. The ordeal she had to go through was terrible. I shall never forget those awful days in Kilmainham.

I was there in the early morning when the executions took place, and I was with eight of the men who were shot. But it was not all gloom. Never could I have imagined that men could die so bravely, so nobly and so prayerfully. They went out to meet their fate like saints and martyrs, to offer up their lives to the Saviour of men for Ireland : to that sweet Saviour who also died for a noble Cause. It was a time of awful strain on our friend, but she bore up wonderfully.

I was sure, from statements in the Press, that she had already benefited by the relaxations recently introduced for the men. I cannot understand how men, even Englishmen, can be so unfeeling and callous to one whose position ought to appeal to everything that is manly . . .

[*Rest of letter missing.*]

FRANCISCAN CAPUCHIN FRIARY,
CHURCH STREET,
DUBLIN,
March 30, 1917.

MY DEAR MISS EVA GORE-BOOTH,—Many, many thanks for your delightfully interesting letter about our very dear and beloved friend. I was overjoyed to hear such good news and to know her health is better and that she is in such splendid spirits. Isn't she wonderful, thank God.

I read your letter for some great admirers of hers here, who take a personal interest in her. They were almost as delighted as I was myself when they read it.

I gave it a few days ago to a Nun who was a great friend of Commandant Daly and his staff during Easter Week. She was most grateful to read your most interesting account. I don't know when I shall get it back, as a great number of Madame's friends want to read it. Priests from Maynooth, nuns, nurses in hospital (tell your sister that the nuns and staff in Jervis Street and Richmond Hospital are particularly good), patients in North Dublin Union, etc., etc.

I am so glad she got the little card I sent for S. Patrick's Day. I shall write again for Easter. I intend asking the Governor if I can send a little book I would like her to read, and I'm sure he won't object. It is called *Mysteries of the Mass in reasoned prayer*. If she is not allowed to receive it I shall ask if it can be given to you and you can keep it for her. I have told a number of her friends that she will be allowed to receive cards at Easter, so she may be expecting a fine lot. She will probably have one from Sr. Brigid (to whom I referred above), one of our best and most devoted friends. Tell your sister that when she comes home she will have to spend the first few days in Church Street district, because there is no place in Dublin where she has such friends. She knows it well, as she often came here to assist personally the poor and the destitute. I did not know her then, though my sympathies were identical with hers. But since Easter Week, I have become acquainted with nearly all that were in the fight as soldiers or Irish Aid workers. There is a grand spirit amongst us, thank God, and though we are in the minority, we look to the future with the greatest confidence.

Madame may be glad to know that Misses M——, C—— and P—— often come over here, and I meet often from time to time Dr. K. Lynn, Miss F—— M——, Miss M—— (who was with her at the College of Surgeons), Mrs. James Connolly, Mrs. Mallin, Mrs. E. Kent and Mrs. De Valera (Mrs. De Valera's husband is doing penal servitude for life at Lewes). They are all wonderfully well and are looking forward anxiously and lovingly for her return and the return of all the other dear exiles of Erin.

I enclose newspaper cuttings, one *re* the Resolution of the Cork County Council, one *re* Resolution that is to be brought forward on Monday next at the Dublin Corporation.

I have been in communication with our friend Alderman Kelly about the latter. There was a feeling that resolutions should not be multiplied, as it would weaken their value. However, I told the Alderman (Madame knows him well) that her case was quite distinct from all the other Irish prisoners, and if her name could not be introduced in the resolution, or if a special one on her behalf could not . . .

[*Page missing.*]

—— has come to Dublin to take up a course of gardening. She suffered a good deal from nerve trouble and she needed more open-air exercise. I told her a few days ago that when the Countess came home, she would probably be starting garden work and that she would have an opportunity to be one of her gardeners. A large number of ladies here in Dublin are taking up gardening. It is splendid for them, and later on it will give much needed employment.

Should the Countess have some post-cards for Easter from A. and K. B——, she'll know that they are from my two sisters.

I would be grateful if you would let me know if I can do anything further for her, or if I could send her anything—say a nice Religious Picture for her cell, a Prayer Book, Rosary Beads or anything.

FRANCISCAN CAPUCHIN FRIARY,
CHURCH STREET,
DUBLIN,
April 25, 1917.

DEAR MISS GORE-BOOTH,—For the past few weeks I have been wondering how is our dear friend the Countess. I hope she is very well and in good spirits. She is wonderful to have borne so bravely all she has had to endure and so cheerfully. I often think the Lord must have some great future in store for her. The sufferings and privations of the past twelve months have brought out all the grandeur and nobility of her character and has certainly endeared her a thousandfold to us here in Ireland. I only wish you could meet some of her friends to whom I have been speaking recently. You would be proud to hear them speak so beautifully about her, praising her love and devotion to the poor, her intense patriotism, her bravery, fearlessness and her unselfish devotion to the highest ideals. Her influence over the men and boys was most remarkable: they had the deepest and most beautiful reverence for her. There was not one of those—and I have met hundreds of them—that would not die for her. It is not surprising that she was so devoted to such men. I don't think they could be found outside Ireland.

We had a grand High Mass at Mount Argus yesterday for all the men who died for Ireland last year. It was the anniversary of the Declaration of the Irish Republic. All Public demonstrations and processions have been forbidden by the British Military Authorities here since Easter Sunday, and these restrictions are to continue until May 13th. But in nearly every part of the country there have been religious celebrations (though some of the clergy have been very nervous), and the hoisting of the Republican Flag. The tri-coloured flag is flying from a high building at the top of Church Street for the past few days. I don't know how it has escaped the Police, who are ever ready to pounce upon every manifestation of Irish Independence.

At Mount Argus yesterday, I met a great number of Madame's friends, including Mrs. Mallin, Mrs. Connolly, Dr. K. Lynn, Miss French Mullen, Mrs. Grace Plunkett, Mrs. Kent, Miss Carney, Miss Maloney, etc. They are all wonderfully well. Mrs. Heuston, mother of Sean Heuston,[1] who was executed the same morning as Commander Mallin, wished very specially to be remembered to Madame.

She told me Sean was a great friend of hers and was always speaking about her.

I suppose you have heard that poor Partridge has been released on account of delicate health. We are hoping he may soon be able to return to Ireland. When he does, he will be able to help us do more for Madame and the men at Lewes.

I wonder has she got any further little concessions?

Great numbers of public Boards have passed resolutions on her behalf and they have sent them to the Home Secretary.

But these British Ministers seem to be very hard and unsympathetic, especially where Ireland is concerned.

Small nations and their rights evidently don't appeal to them.

I enclose some newspaper cuttings *re* our resolutions. Father B—— of Carlow worked these for us. The chairman of the council, Mr. S——, who is a great Redmondite, came out pretty strongly.

You need not return any of the cuttings. If there is anything we can do for her, won't you let us know. It would give me the greatest pleasure to do anything in

[1] A member of the Fianna.

my power to help such a dear friend, to whom we owe so much.

I am looking forward to seeing her in the summer, if not in Ireland, then at Aylesbury.

Tell her we never forget her. I am sorry I have not succeeded before in praying her home, but at the right moment the Lord will open to her the prison gates and send her back once more to us. Everything is in His hands.

Here is Constance's own account of Easter Week, given to members of the Cuman na-mBan some time later :—

SOME WOMEN IN EASTER WEEK

You ask me to write you an account of my experiences and of the activities of the women of Easter Week. I am afraid that I can only give you a little account of those who were enrolled like me in the Irish Citizen Army, and those who were with me or whom I met during the Week. Some were members of Cuman na-mBan, and others, just women who were ready to die for Ireland.

My activities were confined to a very limited area. I was mobilised for Liberty Hall and was sent from there via the City Hall to St. Stephen's Green, where I remained.

On Easter Monday morning there was a great hosting of disciplined and armed men at Liberty Hall.

Padraic Pearse and James Connolly addressed us and told us that from now the Volunteers and the I.C.A. were not two forces, but the wings of the Irish Republican Army.

There were a considerable number of I.C.A. women. These were absolutely on the same footing as the men.

They took part in all marches, and even in the manœuvres that lasted all night. Moreover, Connolly made it quite clear to us that unless we took our share in the drudgery of training and preparing, we should not be allowed to take any share at all in the fight. You may judge how fit we were when I tell you that sixteen miles was the length of our last route march.

Connolly had appointed two staff officers—Commandant Mallin and myself. I held a commission, giving me the rank of Staff Lieutenant. I was accepted by Tom Clarke and the members of the provisional Government as the second of Connolly's 'ghosts.' 'Ghosts' was the name we gave to those who stood secretly behind the leaders and were entrusted with enough of the plans of the Rising to enable them to carry on that Leader's work should anything happen to himself. Commandant Mallin was over me and next in command to Connolly. Dr. Kathleen Lynn was our medical officer, holding the rank of Captain.

We watched the little bodies of men and women march off, Pearse and Connolly to the G.P.O., Sean Connolly to the City Hall. I went off then with the Doctor in her car. We carried a large store of First Aid necessities and drove off through quiet dusty streets and across the river, reaching the City Hall just at the very moment that Commandant Sean Connolly and his little troop of men and women swung round the corner and he raised his gun and shot the policeman who barred the way. A wild excitement ensued, people running from every side to see what was up. Thc Doctor got out, and I remember Mrs. Barrett—sister of Sean Connolly—and others helping to carry in the Doctor's bundles. I did not meet Dr. Lynn again until my release, when her car met me and she welcomed me to her house, where she cared for me and fed me up and looked after me till I had recovered from the evil effects of the English prison system.

When I reported with the car to Commandant Mallin in Stephen's Green, he told me that he must keep me. He said that owing to MacNeill's calling off the Volunteers a lot of the men who should have been under him had had to be distributed round other posts, and that few of those left him were trained to shoot, so I must stay and be ready to take up the work of a sniper. He took me round the Green and showed me how the barricading of the gates and digging trenches had begun, and he left me in charge of this work while he went to superintend the erection of barricades in the streets and arrange other work. About two hours later he definitely promoted me to be his second in command. This work was very exciting when the fighting began. I continued round and round the Green, reporting back if anything was wanted, or tackling any sniper who was particularly objectionable.

Madeleine ffrench Mullen was in charge of the Red Cross and the commissariat in the Green. Some of the girls had revolvers, and with these they sallied forth and held up bread vans.

This was necessary because the first prisoner we took was a British officer, and Commandant Mallin treated him as such. He took his parole 'as an officer and a gentleman' not to escape, and he left him at large in the Green before the gates were shut. This English gentleman walked around and found out all he could and then 'bunked.'

We had a couple of sick men and prisoners in the Band-stand, the Red Cross flag flying to protect them. The English in the Shelbourne turned a machine-gun on to them. A big group of our girls were attending to the sick, making tea for the prisoners or resting themselves. I never saw anything like their courage. Madeleine ffrench Mullen brought them, with the sick and the prisoners, out and into a safer place.

It was all done slowly and in perfect order. More than one young girl said to me, 'What is there to be afraid of? Won't I go straight to heaven if I die for Ireland?' However it was, they came out unscathed from a shower of shrapnel. On Tuesday we began to be short of food. There were no bread carts on the streets. We retired into the College of Surgeons that evening and were joined by some of our men who had been in other places and by quite a large squad of Volunteers, and with this increase in our numbers the problem of food became very serious.

Nellie Gifford was put in charge of one large classroom with a big grate, but alas, there was nothing to cook. When we were all starving she produced a quantity of oatmeal from somewhere and made pot after pot of the most delicious porridge, which kept us going. But all the same, on Tuesday and Wednesday we absolutely starved. There seemed to be no bread in the town.

Later on Mary Hyland was given charge of a little kitchen, somewhere down through the houses, near where the Eithne workroom now is.

We had only one woman casualty—Margaret Skinnader. She, like myself, was in uniform and carried an army rifle. She had enlisted as a private in the I.C.A. She was one of the party who went out to set fire to a house just behind Russell's Hotel. The English opened fire on them from the ground floor of a house just opposite. Poor Freddy Ryan was killed and Margaret was very badly wounded. She owes her life to William Partridge. He carried her away under fire and back to the College. God rest his noble soul. Brilliant orator and Labour leader, comrade and friend of Connolly's, he was content to serve as a private in the I.C.A. He was never strong and the privations he suffered in an English jail left him a dying man.

Margaret's only regret was her bad luck in being disabled so early in the day (Wednesday of Easter Week) though she must have suffered terribly, but the end was nearer than we thought, for it was only a few days later that we carried her over to Vincent's Hospital, so that she would not fall wounded into the hands of the English.

The memory of Easter Week with its heroic dead is sacred to us who survived. Many of us could almost wish that we had died in the moment of ecstasy when, with the tri-colour over our heads we went out and proclaimed the Irish Republic, and with guns in our hands tried to establish it.

We failed, but not until we had seen regiment after regiment run from our few guns. Our effort will inspire the people who come after us, and will give them hope and courage. If we failed to win, so did the English. They slaughtered and imprisoned, only to arouse the nation to a passion of love and loyalty, loyalty to Ireland and hatred of foreign rule. Once they see clearly that the English rule us still, only with a new personnel of traitors and new uniforms, they will finish the work begun by the men and women of Easter Week. CONSTANCE DE MARKIEVICZ.

Here, also, is a letter from a Colonel in the English Army—an old friend—in command of troops in Ireland in 1916:—

MAIN BARRACKS.

DEAR MISS EVA,—Your letter is painfully interesting. I do hope my letter gave your sister a ray of pleasure. It is dreadful to think of the charming high-spirited girl I used to know being a prisoner. It is wonderful her keeping up her spirits.

Perhaps they will find her some kind of work that might suit her clever artistic fingers.

An enormous Army doctor was in here yesterday who described being captured by the Countess in person, who deprived him of his belt and allowed him to look after wounded Sinn Feiners.

Her pistol was enormous and he was terrified of its going off. I don't know what the dear child would say if she knew I was commanding the garrison here, defending bridges and controlling the district.

Shall we ever have peace and quiet ? Anyway, we cannot manage without belonging to an Empire.

Small states seem to be demolished.

J—— L——

Immediately on hearing of Constance's reprieve, Eva applied for permission to visit her, and on the night of 11th May we crossed to Dublin. Here is an account of this—and of our visit to Mrs. Skeffington—written by Eva herself, for a speech she made a few days later to a small Society in London :—

'As the *Leinster* steamed into Dublin Bay on that May morning of 1916 the world seemed transfigured with beauty and delight. There was nothing to remind one of that blind will of domination, violence and greed that has for centuries made of these blue waters a highway of destruction. White sea-gulls flashed against a blue sky and the mountains had about them the radiance and peace of the early morning hours. The sea shifted and glittered and dreamed. It was hardly possible to believe that any man could look upon the vessel's shining track merely as the road to Empire and domination. Yet, as the syren suddenly shrieked out its harsh warning, the sight of a great mass of khaki-clad soldiers crowding round the gangway shook the glamour of the scene and brought queer memories of past generations.

Soldiers of all times, of the same nationality and on the same quest. Soldiers in the queer bulky armour of the early Middle Ages, soldiers in the gay colours of the Elizabethans, soldiers in Cromwell's drabs, soldiers in the stiff reds of the last century, and now soldiers in khaki. Soldiers with bows and arrows, soldiers with spears, soldiers with swords and muskets and all manner of old-fashioned weapons, soldiers with quaint and unwieldy cannon, and soldiers with rifles and revolvers and machine-guns. Soon there would be soldiers with tanks and aeroplanes. An endless procession of soldiers, with every kind of weapon, always on the same errand, always going, as they are going now, to conquer and hold down Ireland.

And Ireland the Unconquerable suffering them helplessly, watching them land in their thousands, with that same old self-conscious gesture of hers, half-passionate, half-cynical, partly tragic and wholly contemptuous. Like the human soul smiling through an agony of weakness at the secret of her enigmatic strength.

It was easy to pass unnoticed through the rather sheepish crowd on the pier, who were doing their best to look Prussian and efficient. The soldiers were not at all aggressive. It was hard to believe they were engaged in crushing a Rebellion and holding down an oppressed nation. By the most vivid stretch of the imagination, you could not credit them with any sinister designs.

Dull and lethargic they seemed for the most part, sometimes they were quite amiably frivolous. One wondered if Cromwell's soldiers were like that.

"Stay where you are, for God's sake!" I heard a laughing soldier say in mock-tragic accents to a group of civilians who were in too great a hurry to land. "If I let you go over there, I shall be court-martialled and shot at dawn!"

Ten minutes after that the world turned black, as I read the words that shrieked in huge letters from every hoarding in the town: "Execution of James Connolly." "James Connolly shot this morning."

In days past I had known James Connolly, most kindly and humane of men. A man who had that quality, rare indeed among politicians, that however absorbed he might be in fighting for a cause, he did not forget to answer the appeal of individual suffering.

Afterwards, the story went round that one of those told off to shoot him was a miner, one who had personal cause of gratitude to him. But he did not know who it was he was going to shoot. Anyway, he stood there with the rest, submissively waiting for the word of command. So would any other soldier, the very man who joked about executions would have done it. Without anger or hate or any conscious cruelty, but simply because he was told to. So insidious a thing is that vile creeping obedience that deprives man of his sense of right and wrong, his very soul and will and mind.

Realisation of the happenings of the past weeks rushed upon us in a flood as we drove through the smoking ruins of O'Connell Street.

The driver seemed rather nervy, surly and suspicious, most unlike the usual talkative Dublin driver. He confined himself to a long grumble about being starved with his family during the Rebellion, not being allowed out of the house for three days. It had been impossible for him to get food for himself and his children.

Driving past Stephen's Green, he began to tell us some rather fictitious details about dead bodies of men and women being carried away at night and buried secretly.

And my thoughts rushed back to that dreadful Sunday in London when I had read in *Lloyd's Weekly News* a circumstantial account of the finding of my sister's dead body in Stephen's Green, and of the terrible days that followed, when I had almost wished the discredited story had been true, so much worse does it seem to the human mind to be executed coldly and deliberately at a certain hour by the clock than to be killed in the hurry and excitement of battle. Perhaps this is because such a death is so wholly unnatural.

In every form of natural life, destruction comes silently and unexpectedly or, at the worst, wrapped in a haze of uncertain hours and vague moments. The foreknowledge of the exact minute of death is a form of mental torture entirely invented by human beings, in the fiendish ingenuity of vengeance sanctified by pious traditions. The world, as God made it, may be cruel in many things, but it is not cruel enough for that supreme and unnatural outrage.

This slow and excruciating and delicately applied brain torment has been brought to a terrible pitch of perfection by a generation that prides itself on the abolition of the rack, and the rougher methods of their ancestors, too blunted themselves to realise the more refined and exquisite possibilities of brain and nerve torture.

But the worst had not happened. My sister, condemned to death for her part in the Rebellion, had been reprieved.

And now I was on my way to visit her in prison.

After visiting the kind friend who had by some means procured the permit, the three of us started for Mountjoy.

The Dublin streets were terrible. They had a sort of muddled desperate look, rather like but infinitely more tragic than the look one used to see in London on an air-raid night, just after the warning was given. As if everybody, even the very houses, were crouching down, hiding from something.

Oddly enough, we chanced on the same car that had driven us from the station earlier in the day. But the car driver was transfigured when he heard the address to which we were going.

All his surliness and suspicion vanished in a moment, and as we got down at the gate of Mountjoy, he turned on us with a beaming smile. " It's little I thought this morning when I drove you from the boat, it was to the prison I'd be taking you ! "

From his manner you would have thought (as doubtless he did) that the dingy prison gate was the entrance to some very select Paradise, sacred to the greater Saints and the more exalted Archangels.

Prisons are all the same, built after the same dreary pattern. Very imposing and grand on the outside, they gradually get squalider and squalider the farther you get into them. We were let in through a little postern door in the main gate by a long-suffering porter who spends the livelong day opening and locking the gate. He does not guard the prisoners, but he is like a sentinel in a besieged city, opening the door for a moment to let in a cart of supplies and shutting it again hastily in the face of the enemy. For to all that live in that gloomy place, our free and kindly human life is the enemy to be shut out at all costs—except the prisoners, and sometimes one thinks that the only people in a prison whose point of view has not become wholly perverted and insane are the prisoners. For they have no " duty " to prevent their being kind and loving to their neighbours.

The Mountjoy porter looked at our permits, and presently the big iron gate was unlocked and we crossed the yard into that inner building which is the prison itself. As I walked through the long corridor, my mind was obsessed by one horrible thought: " They have shot all her friends; James Connolly and Eamon Ceannt only that day: did she know? should I have to tell her? " Afterwards I knew that this was a quite unnecessary anxiety. She knew everything. The shots that killed Padraic Pearse and the others she had listened to morning after morning in her cell at Kilmainham.

Suddenly there was her face behind a sort of cage: it was cut into sections by the cross-bars. But one could half see, half guess how calm and smiling she was.

She talked very fast, and was full of all sorts of commissions she wanted carried out, asked a great many questions and seemed only really puzzled by one thing: " Why on earth did they shoot Skeffy? " she said. " After all, he wasn't in it. He didn't even believe in fighting. What did it mean? "

At the time I could not answer her: afterwards I found out. Nobody who has not gone through the ordinary prison visit can realise how unsatisfactory it is, nor what a strain it is, to fling one's intimate conversation across a passage with a wardress in it, to a head appearing at a window opposite. And then to know that these few minutes must last one for months, and that one has probably forgotten something important.

There was much to hear: her adventures in the Rebellion, details of her court-martial, her anxiety for the wife of a dead colleague who was ill, in hiding and without money. Many and very insufficient directions as to how to find her. About her own treatment the prisoner had not much to say. She was a " convict " and a " lifer " and that was all about it. And anyway, it was splendidly worth while.

For one glorious week, Ireland had been free . . . and then back she went to stories of that wonderful time, of the night-scouting and the trench in Stephen's Green and the machine-gun on the Shelbourne and how they were forced to retreat into the College of Surgeons. And how they could have held out for days, and the shock and grief of the order to surrender on that Sunday morning when I had run up and down London trying to find out if she was really dead. And she told of the executed colleague who had marched with her down Thomas Street where Emmet had been hung a hundred years ago, for the same cause, by the same power. They had discussed together what seemed to them the only doubtful point in the immediate future : whether they would be shot or hung.

This rebel had a very strange story. He had been in the past for many years a private in the British Army. In India long ago he had met another Irish soldier, who told him when next they met he would not be fighting for England.

In South Africa, years after, he came on him again, a prisoner condemned to death for fighting with the Boers against England.

This man made such an impression on the other Irish soldier, awakening in him such a sense of shame to be found on the side of Empire and the conquistadores and oppressors of Ireland, that he got away from the Army as quickly as possible and joined the growing rebel army in Ireland. Now he, too, had been shot.

At the end of twenty hurried minutes of rapid talk we said good-bye for the next four months, and the oddly becapped head disappeared from the window, vanishing into what unimaginable scenes of dullness, dinginess and squalor.

The next morning we set out early to try and find my sister's friend and spent many weary hours walking through endless poverty-stricken streets, questioning naturally suspicious and incredulous people, and causing many a fit of nerves no doubt, to those who were afraid of being suspected of rebel tendencies, and who now obviously thought we were Government spies. In the course of our wanderings we passed one of the great fortress-like barracks that seem to over-awe Dublin. Round the gates a miserable crowd collected, of patient white-faced men and women, standing under the great gray wall in a sort of hopeless gray dejection. We were told they had been there for days. They were the relatives and friends of prisoners, waiting to try and get some news of them. And the story goes that four of the soldiers having been killed in the fighting, the young officers in the barracks had sworn to have forty rebel lives in exchange.

No one will ever know what went on in those barracks behind those towering walls.

An old woman came towards us in the road, crying and begging for news of her son who had been deported to England. She was sure they would try to force him into the Army. "He won't don the khaki. He won't don the khaki," she reiterated drearily. Perhaps it was some vague tradition of what had happened after the last rebellion that made her so certain of what would happen to him. "A year ago," she wailed, "his work was taken from him because he would not don the khaki, and he'll not don the khaki if they shoot him for it."

Poor soul, I hope her son came back safe and sound and without any khaki. At the time it seemed impossible to persuade her that there was the slightest hope that he would not be shot.

In the end we found a little chapel full of people,

where a priest was saying Mass. After the service was over, we went to the vestry and appealed to him for help. Though not a Sinn Feiner, he was a very sympathetic man, and he had been outraged and horrified at the treatment of the Irish prisoners behind that terrible wall, starved, deprived of water and every necessity of life, left to lie for days crowded together, 500 lying on the floor in unspeakably insanitary conditions, some of them wounded, one of these with only his boots for his pillow. So that many of the men were hardly conscious when they were court-martialled. The priest told us of the people waiting there outside day after day, begging for news and of the utter callousness of the authorities. His voice was choking with grief and indignation. He had been a doctor in his youth. It was the horrible inhumanity of the whole thing that he minded. One poor girl was in prison for waving to my sister as she passed marching among the other prisoners on her way to the barracks. Yes, he could find the woman we wanted : he knew some of her relations. It would be quite easy.

At lunch at our hotel we listened with some interest to a conversation between a soldier and a local Unionist. They were shouting to one another from different tables. "I must say," said the Unionist, "your people were pretty free with your bullets. A friend of mine, a strong Orangeman, had stayed in his house for three days as directed, and at the end of the third day he opened the front door to get a little air and the soldier in the street shot him dead."

"Stupid sort of thing to do, to put your head out at a time like that," said the soldier, shrugging his shoulders.

Truly, life is cheap in these days and death needs little formal apology or introduction. Fresh from that Flanders shambles the soldiers forget that many civilians have kept a pre-war standard of value, for their own lives at all events.

At the same time, talking to Mrs. Sheehy Skeffington that afternoon, one realised there was much more in the story of her husband's murder than mere military carelessness and indifference. Both she and her husband were strong pacifists and they possessed no weapons, but the windows of the room in which she sat were still broken by the volley fired into it by the soldiers when there was no one in the house but herself and her little boy of seven. Since then the story of her husband's murder has been often told, but at that time the horror of it was still fresh. She showed us the poor little parcel returned from the barracks, containing a watch, a tie and a collar, worthless things that bore pathetic witness to the almost insane truth,—that those who did not scruple to steal human lives were yet most honourable and honest in their dealings with property—to them a much more important matter.

Hearing Mrs. Skeffington talk, one realised that though her husband never had a weapon in his hand, militarism was wise in its generation, and in Sheehy Skeffington militarism had struck down its worst enemy—unarmed yet insurgent Idealism. It was not for nothing that the half-mad officer who carried out the murder was promoted a week afterwards.

The authorities knew their business well.

All his life Skeffington had never "ceased from mental fight" against all forms of tyranny, oppression and cruelty. He was a born rebel, a questioner of ancient traditions, a shaker of ancient tyranny. He refused to go out against tyranny with a gun, not because he acquiesced in authority, but because he did not acquiesce in any violence between human beings.

In a social state founded entirely on blind obedience to certain traditions and ideas, mental freedom means disaster, and the man who knows no obedience is the enemy.

If the unthinkable had happened and Skeffington had been in the British Army, he would not have shot James Connolly or Padraic Pearse. Not only would he have died protesting against these terrible crimes, but he would have tried to rouse the conscience of every soldier he came near. Individual conscience in the Army means mutiny. It is the deadly and most fatal enemy of militarism.

Skeffington, on fire with hatred of violence and cruelty, attending forty recruiting meetings, speaking in the street against war, defending the cause of Labour, denouncing all oppression in the name of Liberty, Mercy and Kindness, was a greater danger to the authorities than many a more violent revolutionist. For revolutions and counter-revolutions are familiar in this weary world, but his voice was the voice of a new era, a terrible possibility, that nightmare of individual evolution and militant goodwill that shakes the dreams of militarism with a strange threat.

Truly, it was easy enough to understand "why they shot Skeffy," though the only crime they could accuse him of was an effort to persuade a hooligan crowd not to loot the shops.

Militarism has a true instinct and a short way with its enemies. But perhaps the future is with Skeffington.

Dublin was thrilling with horror that afternoon at the revelation of the murders in King Street. A deputation had gone to the Prime Minister to place the facts before him, and to insist on an investigation into how many inoffensive citizens had been dragged down into the cellars and brained with the butt-ends of the rifles of perhaps drunken soldiers. People smiled. They might indeed pretend to insist, but everyone really knew that such investigations are never made.

Meanwhile Dublin was a city of mourning and death.

Roger Casement had been taken from Arbor Hill Barracks to the Tower. There was a feeling of strain and embarrassment everywhere. People broke down and wept for very little, even in the streets. Dazed and miserable, with the sound of the bombs still in their ears, they were beginning to collect in groups and tell one another stories of individual sufferings, injustices and atrocities.

It was not till later that they began to hold up their heads in pride, thinking of the strange heroisms of the dead, and rejoicing in the fact that once again in her long struggle for liberty Ireland had shown the world that she did not acquiesce in her age-long slavery, any more than she had done in the days of Elizabeth, Oliver Cromwell, William Pitt, George III., or any of her old conquerors and tyrants. That was the Irish point of view. The English one was different.

On the way back to London about a week later, travelling up from Holyhead, was a woman in the carriage with us who talked about the Rebellion. "Dreadful people the Irish," she was saying, "so cowardly too, and ungrateful, to stab us in the back like that, after all we've done for them!"

Between these points of view no reconciliation seems possible. Except perhaps in the future: that universal reconciliation of humanity in goodwill, which was the creed of that troublesome idealist, Francis Sheehy Skeffington.'

I can only add a few details to Eva's account of our visit to Dublin.

Mountjoy Prison must be very old, judging by the building in which our interview took place. The three visitors were shown into a bare white-washed room at the end of which was a small barred window opening. Crossing outside this was a narrow passage on the opposite side of which was another barred opening, and it was behind this grille that Con's face at last appeared, looking ghost-like.

A wardress walked up and down the passage between the two grilles. After greeting us, Con asked almost at once whether Connolly had been shot. We had been warned that on no account must we answer this question. Though no word was spoken she must have seen the answer in our faces, for with the tears running slowly down her cheeks she said, 'You needn't tell me, I know. Why didn't they let me die with my friends?' It was a terrible moment. Under all other circumstances in prison she kept gay and brave. This was absolutely the only time I ever saw her show emotion there. But she had worked for years with Connolly at Liberty Hall, and he was her friend. Also she must have known that he had been dangerously wounded, and that they had had to wait till he was well enough to be strapped on to a chair before they could take him out to shoot him, as they had done a few hours before this interview took place. It was a ghastly story, and for a moment she was overwhelmed. Soon she drew herself up and said, 'Well, Ireland was free for a week.'

After that most of the time was spent in telling us how to find the wife of her Commandant, whom she feared would be in great trouble. Her husband was executed, and the birth of a child expected daily. She asked Eva to do everything for her that could be done. She did not think of herself.

On me the notice of James Connolly's execution, the hideous surroundings of the prison, the utter devastation of the streets with their ruined, smoking houses, the terror of the people in the slums, who by now saw a spy in everyone, the squalor and starvation only too plain there—these things made an impression never to be wiped out. Rebellion and revolution are the natural outcome of conditions of life as terrible as those I saw in the slums of Dublin. 'Loyalty' is not, could not be bred in such places. I felt no difficulty that day in understanding why Ireland had risen against England's rule, not only because I am half-Irish myself, but because on the spot it appeared clearly inevitable. Nor could I doubt that more hatred and rebellion would inevitably be bred by such a vengeance as had been taken.

We went to Surrey House, which had been seized by the military authorities. The place was in chaos—furniture broken, papers, ornaments, books, pictures, lying smashed on the floor. I noticed a box of lantern-slides which had been overturned and every single slide crushed to bits by someone's boot; a beautiful leather dressing-case ripped across by a bayonet, and so on. The garden had been dug up in search of arms, but nothing had been found. As we came out we were surrounded by a crowd of people who started in amazement, mistaking Eva for Constance. Many people told us Eva went in danger of her life because of her striking likeness to Constance. Some soldier would fire at her, they feared. For hours on end we tramped the streets until our search for the Commandant's wife was successful, and we were able to carry out Constance's earnest wishes. But I knew after this visit some of the horrors of war, even though only on a small scale.

Eva wrote an account of the Rising for the *Socialist*

Review at the time, which I insert here. An Irish newspaper which reprinted it said of it :—

The writer of the following sketch of the recent insurrection belongs to a well-known and widely respected Co. Sligo family. The article appeared in the August-September number of the *Socialist Review*. Whether viewed from a literary standpoint, or as an effort to get at the real genesis and facts of the rebellion, nothing has, in our opinion, so far been printed which can compare with it.

THE IRISH REBELLION

When the news of the Irish Rising trod hard on the heels of the startling story of Casement's dramatic landing in a collapsible boat on the Irish coast, people in this country took for granted that the two events were connected. It was easily assumed that Casement's sudden appearance was part of a mysterious concerted plan, and that he had come to take part in the Rising. It now, however, appears that the real meaning of that strange adventure was a frantic effort on Casement's part to reach Ireland in time to stop the Rising.[1] It is claimed for him that in a spirit of reckless self-sacrifice he left a position of safety to face almost certain death in a heroic attempt to save his country from the disaster he foresaw.

No light was thrown on Casement's real object at his trial, and when the story came out of his interview with Father Ryan, most people were baffled and perplexed by the whole business. It seemed so impossible

[1] [It must be clearly stated that Roger Casement was not against the Rising, only, knowing what he did, he feared that at the moment failure was inevitable. He was not able to get reliable information as to Irish events and hopes of success, and so came, at risk of his life, to warn his country people of the situation.]

to believe in an attitude of mind that would enable a man to go through that terrible ordeal without mentioning a fact which, whatever the 'blame' of his conduct in Germany may have been, was bound to tell in his favour and save him, maybe, from a dreadful fate. Such, at least, is the plea urged in his behalf by his friends, and backed by substantial evidence.[1] But it found little acceptance in England. People on this side of the Channel could not believe that an Irishman would rather be hung than state publicly that he had tried to stop the Sinn Fein rising, and so seem to blame his fellow-countrymen in their failure and defeat. And inability to understand this fact is significant of one of those mental barriers which make it so difficult for English rulers and officials to adjust their strict notions of the divinity of law and order to what is to them the old idiosyncrasies of the Irish temperament.

[1] It is stated that on 6th April Casement was in a Nursing Home in Germany, when he heard through a spy's report that there was going to be a rising in Ireland. He went straight to Berlin, where with great difficulty he got a submarine to take him to Ireland. The submarine broke down off Heligoland and he had to wait for some days to get another. His object in going was to stop the rising. The captain of the second submarine did not know Ireland, and landed him on a part of the coast where he was subsequently arrested, as recorded at his trial. Casement begged to be allowed to communicate with the leaders to try to stop the rising, but was not allowed. He succeeded, however, in confiding a message through Father F. M. Ryan, O.P., who testified as follows in a letter to Mr. Gavan Duffy, the solicitor for the defence :—

ROSCREA, CO. TIPPERARY,
July 12, 1916.

DEAR MR. GAVAN DUFFY,—Sir Roger Casement saw me in Tralee on April 21, and told me he had come to Ireland to stop the rebellion then impending.

He asked me to conceal his identity, as well as his object in coming, until he should have left Tralee, lest any attempt should be made to rescue him. On the other hand, he was very anxious that I should spread the news broadcast after he had left. Sincerely yours, (Signed) F. M. RYAN, O.P.

In England the State has gradually taken to itself a sort of sanctity in the eyes of the majority. Loyalty is the highest virtue, rebellion is the 'sin of witchcraft' (whatever that somewhat anachronistic sounding crime may be). Authority is enthroned in the souls and minds of men. Indeed the divine pretensions of the Roman Emperors could have brought them no fairer harvest of submission. In Ireland the position is reversed. The Republican Proclamation points out how 'six times in 300 years the Irish nation have asserted their right to national freedom and sovereignty in armed rebellions.' The element of foreign ascendancy has prevented the State from assuming a semi-sacred character. Tradition has grown up slowly from generation to generation in the Irish mind and the idea of rebellion has gradually assumed the sanctity that among English people is associated with the organized authority of the State. So that in Ireland the great rebels are all national heroes and martyrs, and their names are household words, revered and honoured as in England the names of kings and queens are revered and honoured—with this difference, that in Ireland the halo of tragedy is round the heads of all the heroes, and nobody speaks lightly of those who have won great honour through extremes of suffering and self-sacrifice. Loyalty as conceived by masses of Irish people is not, as it is in England, a faithful adherence to the successful and governing classes, but a passionate clinging to an often lost cause, and to the memory of dead and defeated heroes. In a past number of the *St. Enda's Magazine* Pearse has given expression to this strange, troubled patriotism so common in Ireland :

'It has been sung of the Gael that his fighting is always merry and his feasting is always sad. Here at St. Enda's we have tried to keep before us the image of Fionn during his battles—careless and laughing, with that gesture of the head, that gallant, smiling gesture, which has been an eternal gesture in Irish history; it was most memorably made by Emmet when he mounted the scaffold in Thomas Street, smiling, he who had left so much; and more recently by those three who died at Manchester. When people say that Ireland will be happy when her mills throb and her harbours swarm with shipping, they are talking as foolishly as if one were to say of a lost saint or of an unhappy lover, "That man will be happy again when he has a comfortable income." I know that Ireland will not be happy again until she recollects that old, proud gesture of hers, that laughing gesture of a young man that is going into battle or climbing a gibbet.'

To understand this paragraph is to understand one side, at all events, of the Sinn Fein rising. The stories of irrepressible gaiety that have filtered through from Dublin, the pleasant tea-party in the midst of the machine-guns in Stephen's Green, 'the Countess in male attire, smiling and garrulous, discussing the situation with her English prisoner, and ordering the bill to be sent to the Irish Republic'; the man in the Post Office who played 'The Wearing of the Green' and 'Who Fears to Speak of '98?' on the bagpipes all through that terrific bombardment that reduced O'Connell Street to a heap of smoking ruins; the man who put up a recruiting notice (on what had once been a wall at the corner) bearing this inscription: 'Men of Ireland, join the British Army and save your towns and fields from the fate of the towns and fields of Belgium'; and last, but not least, that sardonic Jacobin who cut out the heads of two high personages from the picture in the College of Surgeons and wrote underneath in large letters, 'Deleted by the Censor.' Pearse's gesture of a young man mounting the scaffold seems to find its echo in the story of the mock execution of the girl scout of fifteen whom all the torture of that ghastly scene could not move to betray her comrades. 'You're a brave girl and you deserve the Victoria Cross,' said one of the soldiers at last, struck by the courage with which a child could face unflinchingly the prospect of immediate death. 'You can keep your Victoria Cross,' she said, surely with that very gesture of Pearse's, the gay gesture of defiance in the face of defeat and tragedy which to his mind was the eternal heritage and ideal of the Gael.

Pearse's own death was in the great tradition. Those unfaltering eyes of his that he begged might be unbandaged that he might have his last look at Ireland seem to have unnerved the soldiers. Twice the order was given to fire, with no result.

Connolly, dying in frightful agony, carried out on a stretcher and propped up to be shot, could yet pray for the soldiers who formed the firing party. 'Never let what you are doing to-day disturb you,' said MacBride to the officer, who, it was said, showed some emotion. 'I have been looking down rifle barrels all my life, and I'm not afraid now.' Macdonagh thanked the court-martial who had just condemned him to death. He said: 'It would not be seemly to go to my doom without trying to express, however inadequately, my sense of the high honour I enjoy in being one of those predestined to die in this generation for the cause of Irish freedom.' From the English point of view, these men were doubtless rebels and deserved their fate. But surely many thoughtful Englishmen must feel dubious of the wisdom of shooting a man who dies thanking you for the high honour you have done him in allowing him so glorious a death.

It seems a tragedy indeed that a rising which on its intellectual side was a mixture of Dumas, Mazzini, and that eternal saga of gentle fighting and courteous dying that haunt some of the finest minds in Ireland, should end in those incendiary bombs and executions that are the usual vindications of military power, and which translate their victims into the realm of romance and glory for ever.

And yet there is another side to the whole question which, though perhaps more prosaic, is even more tragic still. Behind the dreams of the Sinn Feiners and the generous idealism of Casement, and the world-wide Republican dream of Connolly, there was a substratum of that kind of solid facts that are always the groundwork of revolution. Writing in the *Daily News*, 12th June, Clara Moser (Hon. Sec. of the Housing Sub-Committee of the Dublin Watch Committee) discusses the rebuilding of the Sackville Street area. She points out that one important aspect of the case has been overlooked. 'It is usual,' she says, 'to find the most filthy areas behind and often surrounded by the best class of property. According to the report of the Departmental Committee appointed by the Local Government Board to inquire into housing conditions in Dublin, there were in 1914, 37,552 persons occupying houses which were fast approaching the state of being unfit for human habitation, and 22,701 persons occupying houses unfit for human habitation and incapable of being made so. So long as these conditions are allowed to exist . . . there will be bred in the minds of the inhabitants that form of discontent which ends in desperation, and which must always be expected to break out in ruinous violence.' Can anyone who followed the course of the Transport Workers' strike and the ruthless way it was crushed by the starvation of three-quarters of the population, wonder that such desperation should have found an outlet in rebellion? It is impossible here to do more than touch on the economic state of Ireland, but if it was more realised in England people would arrive at a better understanding of Irish discontent with the present organization of government. We hear with enthusiasm of the noble work of the English doctors and nurses who have gone out to Serbia to fight the epidemic of typhus. Typhus is endemic in South Connemara. In one recent outbreak the local doctor, who had applied to Dublin in vain for help, had to do every bit of nursing and doctoring himself, even down to putting the dead into their coffins. We do not hear of units, fitted up at great cost by English philanthropic societies, going over to Ireland to combat this pestilence, nor to wage war on the terrible condition of dirt and poverty, of which it is the result. Though England may often seem to be the Good Samaritan of Europe, by some malign fate and in spite of the good intentions of many individuals, her rule in Ireland seems to be followed too often by the old round of misery, poverty, destitution, dirt, disease, starvation, strikes, despair, rebellion, execution, and everlasting bitterness.

As far as Nationalist aspirations are concerned, they may once have found expression in the national representation at Westminster, but when Mr. Redmond started the recruiting campaign for the British Army (that campaign that was to prove that all Ireland was united in loyalty) great numbers of hitherto mild malcontents went over to the extremists who, of course, regarded such an action as treachery to Irish ideals and traditions. It is difficult for English people to realise the anger roused by this campaign amongst masses of the Irish people, brought up in that fierce tradition of secret hostility that has, alas ! been handed down through the centuries. It is perhaps necessary to live in Ireland to understand the root fact known to every person there, Unionist or Nationalist, Sinn Feiner or Orangeman, that Ireland is not a county of

England, but an island surrounded by sea, with a separate and, indeed, a terrible history of its own, often unaffected by events of national importance to English people, and torn and rent by internal happenings that are wholly unknown or quite irrelevant to the mass of English people, rumours of which indeed often barely penetrate into the minds of those who sit in high places and rule both countries. A sort of perverted malice seems to have taken charge of the relations between the two.

The Sinn Fein rebellion was a blow to all who hoped for a gradual lessening of hostility. But the severity with which the rebellion was crushed was, many of us believe, a far worse blow. England had her opportunity, an opportunity of treating the Irish Rising as De Wet's Rising[1] was treated in South Africa. The rising was crushed, her enemies were at her feet. What a glorious opportunity for killing with clemency the old tradition of hatred and the memory of the atrocities of '98 that have festered so long in the imagination of the Irish people. By some malign fate, as ever, England showed her hardest side in her dealings with Ireland. Those irresponsible and extraneous shootings and horrors which seem to be inseparable from the advance of a conquering army in a hostile country were not enough. Fourteen deliberate executions of men widely known and admired were carried out under heart-rending circumstances. And thus Ireland's old tradition of defiance and hatred gets new lease of life, and her ideal gesture remains through the ages 'the laughing gesture of a young man going into battle or climbing a gibbet.' The cry of Kathleen ni Hoolihan is ever in her people's ears :

> 'He died for love of me; many a man has died for love of me.'

[1] In 1914.

And,

> I will go cry with the women,
> For yellow-haired Donough is dead,
> With a hempen rope for a neck-cloth,
> And a white cloth on his head.

And again,

> They shall be remembered for ever,
> They shall be alive for ever,
> They shall be speaking for ever,
> The people shall hear them for ever.[1]

Indeed, it is only in the sense of physical frustration and failure that the way of severity has been able to crush the Sinn Fein rebellion. For there is no solution of the Irish question possible that is not founded on goodwill between the two nations.

EVA GORE-BOOTH.

We returned to London, where we had now been living for over a year. We had been obliged, with deep regret, to leave Lancashire on account of the bad effects on health of the cold climate.

We tried to find out where Constance would be imprisoned for the main portion of her sentence, but could get no information.

On a hot Sunday afternoon in June, we were sitting in the flat thinking and talking of Constance. We knew that at the end of a month in a local prison, long-term prisoners are sent to a convict prison. We also knew that Irish men prisoners had been sent to Lewes Gaol, but we had no news whatever as to her movements. Suddenly, for no reason whatever, I felt I must go to Euston Station to meet the Irish Mail. I was reluctant to say so, for Eva was tired out. However, I did so.

[1] 'Kathleen ni Hoolihan,' by W. B. Yeats.

She asked 'Why?' I was obliged to reply, 'I have no reason whatever, only I feel I must.' She looked very much astonished, but said, 'Very well, then, I will come with you.' 'No, don't,' I begged, 'it will all be for nothing, I expect.' 'Oh no, if you go, I will go with you,' she said. Mercifully she kept to that. In the late afternoon we went wearily enough. The station was hot and quiet when we got to the arrival platform, and I felt exceedingly silly. 'You go to one end of the platform and I to another,' suggested Eva, and she chose the furthest end. I waited alone, watching idly while various policemen and detectives came along and someone I took to be a staff-officer from the War Office. Then the train came in, a number of passengers emerged, none of whom I knew. I got more and more depressed, when suddenly looking up, I beheld coming towards me the strangest little procession ever seen by my astonished eyes. First a brown cocker spaniel, well known in Dublin as 'The Poppet,' then a couple of soldiers with rifles, then Eva and Constance together, smiling and talking hard. Lastly an officer with drawn sword, looking very agitated.

What had happened I heard later from Eva. She had walked to the end of the platform. When the train came in, she glanced up at the carriage that stopped opposite to her, and there looking out of the window was her sister. When Constance got out, surrounded by the soldiers, and saw Eva, she forgot everything in her joy, and before anyone could prevent her she rushed to her sister, flung her arms round her neck and kissed her. The officer implored them to stop and to walk quietly down the platform. This they did at once, but much conversation must have been got in on the way. I, of course, shouted a greeting as I tried to get near. A detective opened the door of a taxi and Constance got in accompanied by an escort. All information as to her destination was refused. The dog jumped in too, no one apparently venturing to touch him. As the car drove off Eva called out, 'Send Poppet back to the flat if they won't let him in.' Then as she turned away, she added quietly, 'I heard a detective tell the chauffeur to go to Holloway Prison.' When we were well out of the station she showed me a legal document which Constance had thrust into her hand. It gave the names of the Court-Martial Judges, the charge against her, and the verdict, in fact all the information which had been denied to Eva or her legal representative.

Owing to untrue and malicious charges brought against Constance by certain low newspapers in London, it was important to know the exact nature of the charges. About an hour later our door-bell rang and the spaniel was brought in. He, by the way, had rushed on to the boat at Kingstown at the last minute. I tell the tale just as it happened. I am not in the least psychic, nor have I ever had a similar experience. I can only suggest by way of explanation, the fact that, as Constance told us later, when she had suddenly been taken from Mountjoy and put on the steamer and realized she was going to England, she was filled with an intense longing to see Eva, and a deep regret that she had not been able to tell her beforehand of her journey.

I could tell many stories of her life in prison which amused or interested me at the time. For instance, of a Prison Visitor, whom I will call the Duchess of A——. She was a family friend who had known Constance in her youth, was full of human kindness, but not, I think, gifted with a sense of humour. Finding it difficult, I presume, to know what to say to a 'rebel,' she asked impressively, 'Do you say your prayers?' 'Well, you know,' said Constance, in telling me the tale, 'I really felt a bit insulted, but I thought I would get my own back, without showing my feelings, so I opened my eyes wide and replied, "Of course; why, don't you?"'

A most amusing, though most annoying, thing happened at Christmas-time, 1916. Eva wrote a poem, illustrated it herself, and sent it to her sister as a Christmas-card. To her great disappointment Constance never got it till a week after the 25th. She afterwards declared that a Home Office Committee sat to consider whether it might not be the signal for a rescue party. Apparently the angel singing outside a barred window was considered suspicious, or so we concluded. I reproduce the inner pages of the card to show how suspicions are aroused in prison circles. At the time it seemed to us merely mad, but afterwards when wonderful escapes were made by Irishmen (who, of course, were in prisons where many other Irish inmates could help), we could only suppose that the authorities imagined Constance endowed with miraculous powers enabling her to fly or make herself invisible, or some equally exciting thing. As a matter of fact, she did not wish to escape, and no such effort was ever made to rescue her.

On another occasion Constance suddenly met in the passage Mrs. Wheeldon, in my opinion quite unjustly convicted of an attempt to assassinate Mr. Lloyd George. The 'rebel' managed, as they passed, to greet her warmly and said, 'Oh, I know you, you're in for trying to kill Lloyd George.' 'But I didn't,' protested the innocent and peaceful lady, as she was hurried away. When she told me the story, with some lurid remarks on the politician concerned, I said to her, 'You know very well you wouldn't hurt a hair of his head yourself. Now what would you do to him if he was wounded and on your own doorstep?'

'Take him in and look after him, of course,' she said promptly, but not too pleased to have been made to admit the undramatic truth. Her hatred never went beyond words: they, I admit, were emphatic and bitter enough at times. But if I had had the misfortune to be her enemy, I would have trusted myself, personally, to her without hesitation.

There was in prison with her a woman who had been sentenced to seven years' imprisonment for shooting her lover. He was, I believe, practically unharmed. She was almost crazy with anger and fear when she did it, because she had just told him she was going to have a child and his reply was to inform her of his forthcoming marriage to another woman. Constance was deeply concerned about this prisoner. She had already served some years and was cut off entirely from her child, who had been taken from her when he was a year old. No child was allowed in prison between the age of one and fifteen years. Constance begged Eva to try and get her out. Mrs. Cobden-Sanderson, a wonderful friend to all in trouble, undertook the difficult task, and so successful was she that presently the woman was released and put under Mrs. Cobden-Sanderson's supervision. They (the mother and a small boy of about four years of age) came to see us. He was a charming, shy person. He walked into the room and said in a breathless whisper, 'I've got a champagne coloured jersey on. Shall I show it you?' This he did with great pride and then sat by himself while everyone else talked, absorbed in the pictures of a volume of *Colour*. The mother, in spite of a nervous weakness, spent the next two years working doggedly in a small hotel, where a housemaid's place was got for her. When last I heard—before Mrs. Cobden-Sanderson's death—she was preparing to go to one of the colonies where she and the boy would begin a new life together. Is he an artist, I wonder, or has he forgotten colour ?

Each person in the prison became an individual to Constance, not a 'number,' as in the regulations. Nothing that anyone had done made a barrier between them. But her great consolation was the visits of the Roman Catholic chaplain, who was a saintly man, full of human understanding. Now that Father Scott is dead, perhaps I may tell a little story that appealed to me greatly. Knowing that the smells of prison were to her peculiarly hard to bear, once when she was ill and he came to give her instruction, his first act was to produce from his pocket a large bottle of eau-de-Cologne, and sprinkle it about. What made the deepest impression on her was his gracious courtesy to what the world would call the most degraded of women. He, too, knew no difference of class ; the more hopeless the case, the more gentle and kindly was he. Constance always remembered him with gratitude and appreciation. We knew him well, for we used to visit him often at the Presbytery and shared her feeling for him.

Constance's prison task at first was sewing, but she soon got ill with so much sitting still. Then she was transferred to the kitchen, where her work was washing and cutting up vegetables and scrubbing stone floors, and hard work it was. The food was very poor [it was war-time]. Once she lost weight alarmingly. She could not eat the red, coarse meat provided and the brown bread made her ill. Eva begged that she should have one glass of milk a day instead of meat, but I don't think she would ever have succeeded in her efforts but that Mr. Healy came to the rescue, and in some way got the Home Office to agree to it.

One day Constance said to me, 'The only thing

prison does for people, as far as I can see, is to teach them to use bad language and to steal. I was so hungry yesterday that I stole a raw turnip and ate it.' The impassive wardress made no comment. Constance never grumbled at conditions, and she received great kindness from some of the officials in prison. No prisoner is allowed to talk in the passages, but the first sounds we heard while we waited in the dreary 15th-class waiting-room, was always her gay ringing laugh as she came along the corridor from the cells, talking to the wardress in charge of her.

After months of effort she was allowed 'paper and pencil' for drawing, but, alas, when it came the paper was lined and the pencil as hard as nails. In time the Home Office relented and Eva was permitted to pay for suitable materials, so that Constance might have an occupation for the weary hours after 5.30 P.M. when she was shut into her cell. Hers was a much worse fate than any other Irish 'rebel's.' A resolution of the House of Commons allowed to the men, who were all placed in one prison, a certain amount of 'association' each day, but nothing that anyone could do could persuade the authorities to extend this privilege to Constance. Eva tried to get them to make a women's side to Lewes Gaol; obviously her sister needed this alleviation as much as any one of the men. Her closest friends had been executed and she had been condemned to death, and then plunged into what was almost solitary confinement, as there was no one of her own mental level in the prison most of the time she was there. Association with the other Irish prisoners could easily have been supervised,—there were no ordinary prisoners in Lewes. But no. Mrs. Grundy, or rather, Mr. Grundy dictated that no woman prisoner shall under any circumstances see the face of a man prisoner, not even when that man was a political prisoner, and a personal friend. The sense of proportion seems for some inscrutable reason to have been denied to most human beings. The sense of propriety in this case swallowed up everything else. We did not ask privilege for her, only that ordered by the House of Commons for 'the Irish prisoners.'

If anyone thinks we asked too much, I would advise a course of visits to that most dreary spot on earth—a prison. To me, it is a misery to enter one, though I have visited many in my time. It rouses every rebellious instinct I have. I ask myself how in Heaven's name shutting out the sun, the wind and the sight of the trees could make a rebel loyal or a thief honest—or indeed do anything but fill the heart with bitterness and hatred of all mankind. I once went into a hospital cell. The place was clean, there was an iron bedstead and a window, but—the glass was frosted three-quarters of the way up and it opened upwards only, at the top. So even the sick were deprived of the joy of trees and flowers, for there were both outside. As I went along the passage to go out, I passed a party of women who were engaged on some work—I don't know what. A whistle blew, and the women turned their faces to the wall while we passed. And this was in the year 1916. Some upright citizen will say this is all sentimentalism on my part, but it is not, it is merely common sense. I marvel at the patience and courage with which a fiery soul like Constance's went through the ordeal and learned from life before the end, as she did, the lesson of love and of pity. But how many of us could say, as she said to her sister, 'Don't worry about me. Remember no one has it in his power to make me unhappy,' and this when she was being banished from all that makes life lovely.

At last, on 16th June 1917, came the news of the amnesty. Next day all the men went home, and a courteous Home Office official arrived to say Eva would be allowed to go next day to Aylesbury and bring her sister away. Accordingly, armed with all the gay clothes that we could beg or borrow, we went, and were admitted to help her to dress. Soon Constance, herself again, thin but beautiful, in a blue dress instead of that twice too large, hideously ugly cotton garment supplied by a paternal Government, left that prison for ever.

One day she had in London seeing her friends and —like a scene from her former life—spending a little time drinking tea and talking to friendly M.P.s on the terrace of the House of Commons. Then home to Ireland.

It was a strange journey. We left Euston by the early morning boat-train. Irish men and women sang patriotic songs on the platform, and friendly porters looked on smiling. When we arrived at Holyhead the platform was packed with people waving flags and singing and cheering wildly. I remember standing by Constance's side trying to get on the gangway of the boat. Her clear voice called out, 'Which is the right side for us to get on?' A coal-black face was thrust out of an engine-room, and with a broad grin replied, 'It's always the right side if you're on it,' and disappeared again amid the laughing cheers of the crowd. Once on the boat there was nothing but kindness. In the cabin the stewardesses had provided for Constance and her friends a breakfast including lovely grapes and peaches. They pressed round her full of delight and smiling welcome. Alas! these friendly people were all drowned later on when the boat was torpedoed.

We zigzagged across the water, and at last arrived

at Kingstown Harbour, where the people were delirious with excitement and pleasure. It was difficult to reach the train for Dublin. Arriving there, we gave up any effort to hurry. Stepping down from the train was like plunging into the waves of the Atlantic—we were swallowed up. The deputation of welcome did their work somehow, and in time 'the Countess' and her friends were placed in cars which were to drive to Liberty Hall for the official welcome. Constance and Eva were in Dr. Kathleen Lynn's car, and I, some way behind, tried to see it all. We simply could not move at first. Constance had to stand nearly all the time so that she could be seen by the vast crowds. It seemed as if all Dublin must be there. It felt hours long before my car arrived at Liberty Hall and I was admitted. Traffic all along the line was controlled by the 'rebel' band, the police most sensibly remaining in the background. When I did get into that shattered building, roofless and windowless, which in the old days had been so full of life, I could feel as real only those sombre figures in mourning—the widows of the men executed in Easter Week—who had come to welcome back their friend.

All the time Constance was in Aylesbury Prison she was receiving instruction, but she did not join the Roman Catholic Church until she returned to Dublin in 1917. Mrs. Skeffington writes on this subject:

'Impressed by the great devotion of the boys of Fianna Na h-Eireann, and by the heroic ease by which simple unlettered men of the Irish Citizen Army went to meet their deaths, Constance Markievicz declared her desire to become a Catholic, to be with the boys in death by a baptism of desire, if need be. She asked the Rev. T. Ryan, then Chaplain of Kilmainham (who told me the story), to promise to be with her at the end.

When her death sentence was commuted she was removed with some other women to Mountjoy Prison. (One of these is sister to the present Minister of Agriculture, Dr. James Ryan.) The chaplain there, the Rev. Fr. McMahon, started to give her instruction, with a view of having her formally received into the Church. When I went to see the women prisoners in May 1916, the chaplain was coming out of Mountjoy gate—"the Joy" as it is quaintly called in Dublin by the poor. He said to me "I can't understand Countess Markievicz at all. She wants to be received into the Church, but she won't attend to me when I try to explain Transubstantiation and other doctrines. She just says 'Please don't trouble to explain. I tell you I believe all the Church teaches. Now, Father, please tell me about the boys!'" From another source I heard that she shocked the padre by defending Lucifer as a 'good rebel,' but that, I think, was part of her habit of leg-pulling of authority. I did not see her then: she was not permitted to see anyone, being a "lifer," and shortly afterwards she was removed to Aylesbury.

She delayed joining the Church formally until she was released from prison and allowed back to Ireland in March 1917.

She said she did not want a religious ceremony while she was in jail. She was received in Dublin, taking the baptismal name of Anastasia.

Later, Father Ryan attended her funeral in Glasnevin in 1927, as he told me, to fulfil her request to be with her at the end. There were very few clergy present at her obsequies, just a few rebel priests like Father O'Flanagan and those belonging to Westland Row, the parish where Sir Patrick Dun's Hospital is situated. The clergy generally never quite approved of such an independent rebel as Madame.

As to her religion generally, I would say that she

belonged to the church of St. Francis of Assisi, rather than that of St. Paul.

The ritual and the ceremonies, the music and the beauty of the Catholic Church, its art and cultural background attracted the mystic in her. She defended the socialist Connolly against an attack by a Jesuit, Father McKenna. She held Socialism to be possible within the Church. Individual clerics she often sharply disagreed with. Over her bed was a picture of Da Vinci's Christ.'

Constance had not been allowed to know anything about the trial and execution of Roger Casement, except the mere fact, while in prison. But to us outside, the months that followed had been the continuation of the Easter Week tragedy. He had, of course, been taken prisoner on Good Friday, 21st April, before the outbreak, had been brought over to England, kept in the Tower for some weeks where he was badly treated—Mr. Nevinson says ' with gross indignity '—and then transferred to Brixton Prison. On 26th June he was tried at the Law Courts by the Lord Chief Justice (Lord Reading), Mr. Justice Avory and Mr. Justice Horridge, and after four days, he was condemned to death. Then came the Appeal, which was heard in the Court of Criminal Appeal on 17th July before five judges, with Mr. Justice Darling presiding. Eva and I were present at one sitting, but not at the end. Mr. Gavan Duffy got permission for us to sit in the Gallery, which was, as far as I remember, not much above the level of the raised dock. The judges, coming into Court, were received by the assembly standing, as is the custom. When they had taken their seats, Roger Casement was brought by two warders up the steps into the dock. He courteously bowed to the Judges who, following the inhuman practice of such places, took no notice. Then he turned and caught sight of Eva, who had risen to her feet when he appeared. His face lighted up with a rare and beautiful smile. Even his enemies must have been impressed by his dignity and calmness. As Mr. Nevinson says, he looked 'by far the noblest man in Court.' I shall see the picture of that worn but gallant figure, alone but undefeated, to my dying day. Everything else that morning was to me utterly shocking and agonizing. To hear responsible men blandly discussing the placing of a comma in an ancient document as a point on which the life of a human being, in their very presence, might depend; to hear jokes made; to feel that gorgeous raiment was valued as contributing to 'the dignity of the law'—all this was to an ordinary mortal terrible. It swept away the feeling of respect one was supposed to have for such institutions. The only person who appeared to be above the conflict, in apparent detachment from all personal matters, living as it were on a spiritual plane apart, was Roger Casement himself. Not too far apart, though, to be able to sympathize with the agony we were suffering for his sake. 'Give my love to Eva,' he wrote that night. 'I thought her looking so tired in Court to-day.' Such selflessness stabbed us to the heart when we watched the cruelty surrounding him.

Surely most of those taking part in the trial must have been touched to sympathy and sorrow. Long after it was all over, it happened that I met one of the Jury at the first trial. He openly lamented that he could do nothing to prevent the verdict of guilty. 'What could you do when the prisoner said definitely that he *had* used certain words on a certain day and in a certain place, and those were the only questions you had to decide. I would have given anything,' he added, 'to go across the Court, put my arm round his neck, and tell him what I felt for him.' We were not in Court when the Appeal was dismissed, and I never saw Roger Casement again. For the remaining weeks we, among many others, worked night and day to get a powerful Petition for reprieve. It is true that some most remarkable signatures were obtained. The educated public who knew his former services to humanity, utterly refused to believe in the possibility of his execution. Had we not received him with honour when he returned from Putumayo so short a time ago and were we not at that very moment entertaining with respect a patriot who had organized his countrymen against the Austrian rule in like circumstances? But there was never any hope, in my opinion. He himself had no illusions on this point. Relentless foes sat in seats of power and they poisoned the public mind by circulating lying stories (that had nothing to do with the case) against the personal character of Roger Casement. Only those who did not know him believed them, and it was a vile way of hunting a man to death. It is often called un-English but it was done in London in 1916. On the evening of 2nd August, Eva accompanied Gertrude Bannister [Roger Casement's cousin], Mrs. J. R. Green, Mr. Nevinson and Mr. Philip Morrell, to Buckingham Palace to beg the King to use his prerogative of mercy, only to find that it was no longer the King's Right. It was vested in his Ministers; the King could only inform his Ministers that he had been appealed to, which I believe he did.

The Cabinet with whom the decision lay contained some of Roger Casement's bitterest political enemies. They made their decision, and on the morning of 3rd August one of the rarest spirits of our day escaped at last from the cruelty of men into freedom and peace.

English men and women watched with him from afar that night and at least one Englishman knelt with Roger Casement's dearest friends in the dust of the pavement outside the prison gates as he passed away. Thousands mourned in pity and shame that such a deed was done.

A couple of years later Eva told the story in *The Catholic Bulletin*, a Dublin monthly paper, and I give it here.

FOR GOD AND KATHLEEN NI HOULIHAN.

The two years now closing have been to many years of death and exaction. Tragedy after tragedy has overwhelmed our world with pity and terror. But to Irish people especially that pity and terror has come mixed with a strange exultation. And to the little band of lovers and friends who watched in breathless suspense and agonised hope that supreme and long drawn out agony, that dragged slowly on through three terrible months to its inevitable end, there were sudden flashes of intense realisation, moments when the heart's tragic defeat was merged in the mysterious victory of the soul. In some silent compelling way, sorrow itself seemed to be drawn up at times into that calm atmosphere of beauty and peace that wrapped round in a strange smiling security the untroubled spirit of Roger Casement, as he moved serenely through tempests of reviling and torture and the scorn of men, without fear and without hatred. 'He sent grateful messages to all who prayed for him and loved him—that I was to tell all that he died for Ireland, and that he wished them to know that he had no bitterness in his heart for anyone. . . . He was wonderful, the peace, the tranquillity, the courage with which he faced death and talked of it. . . . My heart is divided between joy and sorrow.' Such was the witness of one who was with him a day or two before the end. But the simple and spiritual beauty of his nature expresses itself most clearly, perhaps, in the letter to a friend, an old Irish peasant woman, dated 14th July; a letter so poignant in its pathos, so selfless in its detachment, that the darkness of certain death that hangs over its simple and gay friendliness seems only like one of those cloud shadows, that at twilight so often deepen the beauty of the sunlit hills of Ireland, with the sudden wistfulness of an unseen and secret presence.

My dear Brigid,—I am writing to you through a friend, asking her to send this letter on to you, as she will be able to find out where you are. Your letter came to me yesterday, here in this prison cell, and it was like a glimpse of the garden, with the wallflowers and the Japanese cherry, to get your message.

First, I want to tell you that your Crucifix, the medals and the scapular came to me three weeks ago, but the letter only yesterday. They are always with me, and please God will be as long as I am here.

Remember me to so many, and thank those friends who pray for me—and don't pay any attention to the lies. They are compliments really, and we need not mind compliments, you and I, Biddy dear.

Do you remember the *Cradle Song* I liked so much? Get Cathal to sing it for me, and give him my love and thanks from my heart, also to Colm, if he is near you, and Dinny and Seaghan Dhu, whenever they come back to you and the old room again. I dreamt last night I was lying before the fire in it, and the boys were there telling stories, and you standing at the door with the pipes. . . . I have thought of you often, and of the garden, and of the last time I saw you, and the message I gave you. Do you remember? I know you carried it out, dear Brigid, because I heard you did. And so farewell—and may God's blessing rest on you and yours and be with you in your work—and may the heartfelt thanks of one in much sorrow and affliction of soul be part of your reward for your affection.—Always your friend,

Roger Casement.

The *Manchester Guardian*, describing the passing of the death sentence on Roger Casement, comments thus on the prisoner's attitude: 'Sir Roger Casement heard these words and smiled wanly, looking down, one thought, as if to reassure his friends who were near the dock. Then erect and quite self-possessed he turned and disappeared behind the green curtain. He had kept his dignity, his almost incredible detachment, to the last.'

That 'incredible detachment' was a constant source of wonder and inspiration to his friends. History holds up for our admiration the figure of Sir Thomas More apologising to his executioners for having to ask them to help him to climb the scaffold, and adding with smiling politeness, that 'for his coming down he would shift for himself.' That story might have been written of Roger Casement at any moment during those long months through which he faced a certain and horrible death, with something more than courage, a supreme gentle courtesy so selfless that it had forgotten the very meaning of fear. 'I was going to read it out in Court,' he said in one of his last letters of a certain document, but he explained that the print was very small, 'and besides I felt sorry for the jury. They had had enough, and their kindly faces deserved a change of scene from that dreadful Court.' It is not often that a prisoner just about to be condemned to death concerns himself about the discomfort and boredom of the jury, and one cannot help wondering what rare secret of character was hidden behind those simple words. There are many degrees of selfishness in human beings and there are many unselfish people. But the certainty of a lonely and horrible death would find out the weak point in most of us, and it would seem natural and pardonable in most people, if, at the supreme and tragic moment of their destiny, their minds were concentrated on their own agony, to the exclusion of other people's petty discomforts. But Roger Casement was not like most people. There was something in him that made it impossible for him to be self-absorbed, however strange and desperate his circumstances might be. Perhaps the keynote of his nature might be found in that sentence with which he explained his loyalty to Ireland, and the reason he felt no loyalty to the Empire that governs her by force. 'Loyalty,' he said, 'is a sentiment, not a law. It rests on love, not on restraint.' The same might be said of the shining qualities in his own character. They were not founded on mere laws or external restraints, but on a great universal love of human beings, and goodwill to all men. It was his nature to consider and feel for other people's difficulties, sufferings and hopes with no careful and forced unselfishness, but with an enthusiastic and eager affection, that no private suffering of his own could dull, and that made him lose entirely the limited personal point of view common to most people. It would be easy in defence of this view to quote the known facts of his noble and self-sacrificing cause,—to say that he threw away health and ordinary human happiness through years of hard and terrible work, in unhealthy climates, trying to bring to light atrocities and cruelties in Putumayo and the Congo, and saving thousands of innocent victims from outrage, mutilation and death. Indeed, it might be said of him that the desolate and oppressed never appealed to him in vain. The loyalty that is founded on love had a very different effect on his life to that of the more common form of loyalty founded on mutual hate, self-interest and fear. Instead of making him bitter against others, it deepened his sympathies with all oppressed nations, and made him, besides being the champion of Ireland, a fighter in the cause of enslaved nationalities and individuals all over the world. And let no one imagine that his international activities and sympathies did not react for good on the cause of his own country, by accentuating her position in the eyes of the world (as all his work tended to do) as one of the oppressed small nationalities of Europe, a comrade of Poland, Finland and the rest, in her struggle for freedom, and not merely as a rather rebellious and troublesome province in a corner of the British Empire.

Roger Casement was one of the world's great champions of the weak against the strong, of good-will and freedom against militarism and empire, of life against death, and thus he takes his place with the seers and prophets of all ages. But if Roger Casement was in a sense international and had room in his heart for all the oppressed and defeated, yet to him had come more specially the call of Kathleen ni Houlihan in her great need. And it was for the sake of her he loved with all the passion of his idealistic and romantic nature that he left his safe asylum and, in full knowledge of what must be the result of his action, made his way to Ireland to be ready with help and advice in the hour of danger and difficulty. 'We salute you as we would salute Wolfe Tone,' wrote 'three obscure citizens of Ireland' to the condemned prisoner of Pentonville, in one of those many touching tributes of love, admiration and gratitude from his own people, that were indeed his due, who had given up for their sake everything that most men hold precious. For truly never was there a man who more deliberately threw away his life and liberty in a cause that was dearer to him than life or liberty. 'I am going with a halter round my neck,' he told a friend before he left Germany. And from that day onward, I do not think he ever faltered in the certainty that he was one of those who are (as Thomas MacDonagh put it in his speech before the court-martial) 'predestined to die in this generation for the cause of Irish freedom.' He was never of those whose courage has to be bolstered up with illusions.

To-morrow [he wrote] I go to the Appeal Court to hear my counsel against the Indictment. And I shall return here. That is the one thing I am sure of. However interesting from the point of view of treason law in this country, I anticipate no other interest than that of listening to the arguments for and against and coming to the place I started from in the morning. If I had Solon for an advocate the result, I fancy, would be the same.

Up to the last his sympathy for suffering in all countries never failed. On 16th July he wrote :

I am glad, indeed, to hear the news from Putumayo and the Fathers there. The Franciscans were loved in Peru from of old. It is a good thing to think of them there now in that dreary region, and I am glad for their sake. Once I grieved at it, and thought I was sending them, or asking for them to be sent out to bitter trial and disappointment, but it is not so, and they will see the fruit of their privations and of their self-sacrifice in the lives they save, and in the increase of life and happiness around them, to replace the old dreadful and mortal misery.

But in those last weeks of cruel loneliness it was to Ireland that his heart turned :

To-day [he wrote] my mind is far away down by O'Sullivan Beare Land and over there where I shall never be again, not even in dreams, by Clare and Aran and Garumna. I wonder how it will all be a hundred years hence, and whether any of the old speech and thought that sprang from it and prayers that grew from it will survive. Goodbye, my dear friend, and I hope all your young ones will grow up in that Gospel and no other and that it may be well with them hereafter. . . . I shall not forget you wherever memory goes with me.

The growth of Roger Casement's religious convictions in the isolation of prison life could be surprising to no one who understood the character and ideals that had been his through years of active work. If it be a fact, as he said, that true religion rests on love, it is easy to see how the long years of selfless devotion and affectionate friendships had brought him into harmony with the unseen purposes of the universe, and very near to the Divine meaning of human life. 'I can only accept in my soul from love,' he said, and indeed, to one who had such a great heart and such a universal love for the brother whom he had seen, it could have been no great step to that other mysterious love. In religious matters, as in all things, he was very honest with himself, would not let himself be hurried by emotion into taking any step without the consent of his mind as well as his heart.

And then [he wrote] I don't want to jump or rush—or do anything hastily—just because time is short. It must be my deliberate act, unwavering and confirmed by all my intelligence. And alas! to-day it is not so. It is still, I find, only my heart that prompts, from love, from affection for others, from association of ideas and ideals, and not yet my full intellect. For if it were thus the doubts could not beset me as vigorously as they do. I am not on a rock but on a bed of thorns. . . . You must continue to help me as you have done in the way you wot of, and in the way you say so many more are doing.

His was no facile deathbed conversion, prompted by fear or sentiment, but a gradual adjustment of the whole mind and soul into relation with the unseen, an adjustment that began with pain and struggle and uncertainty, and ended in the peace of a personality in harmony with itself and with God, exalted above fear, trouble or bitterness.

We cannot know much of the working of his inner

mind during the long and lonely hours of his imprisonment, nor of those mental processes that led up with growing and gathering conviction to the unfaltering certainty of that confession of faith which was perhaps the last voluntary action of his life. But we can find traces in his last message to his friends of that religious exultation and other-world peace that was a marvel to those who were privileged to see him. 'Give my love to all my friends, and to all who have worked for me. My last message to every one is "Sursum Corda," and for the rest, my goodwill to those who have taken my life, equally to all those who tried to save it. All are my brethren now.'

Roger Casement was ready and willing to die, as he said, for the cause of Irish freedom. And indeed it might be said of him, that while many have died for their countries and for great causes in all ages, no man has ever in the annals of history done more than he did, by the manner of his dying, to exalt and glorify the country of his love. 'He died,' said one who was with him at the last, 'with all the faith of an Irish peasant woman. . . . He marched to the scaffold with the dignity of a prince and towered straight as an arrow over all of us on the scaffold. He feared not death and prayed with me to the last. I have no doubt that he has gone to Heaven.'

EVA GORE-BOOTH.

No progress was made in the direction of peace between England and Ireland in 1916, as was inevitable. Nor did the findings of the Inquiry into the murder of Mr. Skeffington and two other journalists make things better. The Prime Minister soon announced the appointment of Mr. Lloyd George to act as mediator. Ireland merely said this was because without a settlement it was very difficult to get the United States into the War on the Allied side. The Irish there had been so furious at the executions that they had become Pro-German.

Partition was coming nearer. In 1917, the Government constituted a Convention of Nationalists and Orangemen to try and sink their differences. Protestant and Roman Catholic Bishops were on this body, but of course Sinn Fein was left out. The chairman was Sir Horace Plunkett, and the secretary, Mr. Erskine Childers. Lord Dunraven (a cousin of Constance) was a member and on the side of Home Rule throughout. But the Orangemen were immovable and the Convention came to nothing, though Home Rule had been on the Statute Book and inoperative for nearly four years. Then in 1918 the last awful mistake was made, when it was decided to force Conscription on Ireland—all men from eighteen to fifty were to be called up at once.

It seemed incredible to everyone connected with Ireland that England could really for a moment contemplate forcing men to fight for her who not two years before had risen against her, had seen their leaders executed and hundreds of their men and women imprisoned. Even in 1909, when Fianna Na h-Eireann was founded, feeling was so strong that one of its regulations forbade Fianna members ever to serve in an English force. It was common knowledge that the population was far more anti-English in 1918 than it had been in 1916. It became clear that they would resist Conscription to the death. Indeed the authorities must have feared a rising, for machine guns were placed on the top of the Bank of Ireland overlooking the place where the Convention had been held. At Mr. de Valera's instigation the Lord Mayor of Dublin called a Conference in May to make plans for resistance.

Its members were Mr. Dillon, Mr. Devlin, Mr. Healy, Mr. de Valera, Mr. Griffith, Mr. William O'Brien, and three Labour Representatives. Mr. de Valera advised that a deputation be sent to Maynooth, where the Irish Bishops were sitting. The result was that the latter passed a unanimous resolution against Conscription. There was a universal stoppage of work for a day to show the feeling of the people. The Irish leaders kept to their resolution that passive resistance should be tried, though they quite expected the authorities would use force. We were present at a private meeting in London when Irish Labour Representatives put the Irish case to English Labour, and deeply impressive I thought it.

My brother went to Dublin to see Constance and to get first-hand information as to the state of affairs. He reported the feeling against Conscription as intense. He saw people of all sorts, from 'Æ.' and James Stephens to Sinn Fein women, preparing lint and other materials which would be needed for Red Cross work if force was used. Constance, of course, was in the thick of the fight. Men were being arrested in hundreds for refusing to serve. Mr. Kevin O'Higgins (afterwards Minister of Justice) was handcuffed by police before the eyes of his father and mother, when being taken to Dublin by train. All Tullamore turned out to see him off, including the priests. His mother kissed the handcuffs when he went.

Then the Chief Secretary, Mr. Shortt, discovered an imaginary 'German Plot,' and the arrest of leaders began. Mr. de Valera and Mr. Griffith were taken (two other Sinn Feiners were at once nominated in their places as alternative members of the anti-Conscription Conference). Next, Constance, Maud Gonne McBride and Mrs. Tom Clarke were arrested, and they and Mr. de Valera and Mr. Griffith were deported to

England. Constance was for six months in Holloway Gaol without trial.

At last the military authorities seem to have been convinced that Conscription would not succeed, and it was withdrawn.

In November of this year the Armistice was signed and the World War ended, but there was no peace for Ireland, nor were the prisoners released.

My brother had taken with him when he went to Dublin the MS. of a small book of poems written by Eva after Easter Week. It was accepted by the publishers, and when it was issued in Dublin some months later with the title *Broken Glory* it was marked ' Passed by the Censor, 1918.' Really there is no limit to the odd things that Governments will do!

The General Election of December 1918 was carried out in Ireland as in England under the New Register, with women enfranchised. The old Irish Party was wiped out and Sinn Fein triumphed at the polls. Constance was returned as Member for St. Patrick's Division of Dublin and thus became the first woman M.P. She received a letter in Holloway, from Mr. Lloyd George, the Prime Minister, exhorting her to be present in the House of Commons on the opening day of the coming important Session. It evidently was sent to all M.P.s indiscriminately, for if there was one person in England more determined than herself that she should not be present, it was Mr. Lloyd George. I believe she much enjoyed answering this letter. But what an entirely ludicrous thing to send it. I suppose institutions cannot be expected to have a sense of humour. The only sign of Constance there ever was in the House of Commons was a peg for coats with her name inscribed below, which, I was told, appeared that Session.

We did not see her in Holloway, unfortunately. She

and the other Irish were internees, not prisoners, they were never brought to trial on any charge whatever, yet they were required to sign an undertaking not to discuss politics, before permission was given to see visitors. There was a general agreement to refuse this undertaking, so Constance saw no one. The prisoners demanded either to be tried for their alleged crime or else to be released. Neither demand was granted, and soon it was practically solitary confinement for Constance, as the other women prisoners were released owing to illness.

In August, Mrs. Skeffington had been in the prison a few days. I will give her own account of it later. She was able to give Constance all the American news, otherwise the latter was kept in ignorance of her country's affairs. Some alleviation was allowed her. She could wear her own clothes and have food sent in. This was a great relief, for she found prison during an English winter a great strain. Above all, she prized the permission to have paints and paper. I have the two gifts she sent to Eva from Holloway. One is a gay book-cover for *Broken Glory* which she designed and painted there: it is inscribed

To Eva, Christmas 1918
from C. de M.
Holloway Jail.

The other is a water-colour sketch of an Irish landscape, with a rainbow appearing through the mists: it showed that her hand had not lost its cunning, nor her imagination its power.

In March 1919 she was released, but in June she was once more arrested in Dublin, conveyed under heavy escort to Mallow, and on the 20th tried in private and condemned to four months' imprisonment.

This trial was interesting for one thing. She was

accused of saying in her speech at Newmarket, Co. Cork, that 'Sinn Feiners should treat the children of the police as spies, ostracise them, treat them as lepers, and refuse to sit near them in church or school. She denied the authority of the Court to try her and did not defend herself on the general charge. But the one thing she did say was that she would never advocate the persecution of policemen's children. She begged her friends never to hurt or make unhappy a little child. She did not think any of her friends at Newmarket took her as advocating the annoying or persecution of children, even policemen's children, and she asked them in the name of Eamon Ceannt, executed in Easter Week, who was himself a policeman's son and who died for Ireland, to respect children. What she did say at the meeting was, "Be careful of what you say to your own children for fear they would say anything to a policeman's child," but she would never raise a finger to hurt a child.' She was sent to Cork Prison. Extraordinary precautions were taken to avoid publicity. The train was heavily guarded, and on arrival a large force of constabulary escorted her motor car through the city to the gaol. There, equally strange precautions were taken, soldiers and police guards being placed in and around the prison. Still she very much preferred an Irish to an English prison. Even there things felt more like home, and she was allowed for reasons of health to work in the garden. She was quite proud of the rock garden she made for the Governor of Cork Gaol, and I am sure she put her whole heart into the work. She was the most generous-hearted and ungrudging of prisoners.

In 1919 the Irish M.P.s, who were pledged not to sit in the House of Commons, summoned a Parliament to meet in Dublin. They of course summoned every person elected in Ireland, but non-Republicans did not attend. The Republicans numbered 73 per cent. of the Representatives elected. Dail Eireann assembled, and on 21st January the Declaration of Independence was formally made. This was the constitutional birth of the Republic.

For the first six months both sides marked time. Ireland hoped her position would be referred to the Peace Conference. A large number of Irish officers, including the General who had commanded the 16th Division in the War, appealed to the British Government to take this way. General Gough, who had headed the resignations at the Curragh in 1914, was now on the side of those Irish Nationalists who had served under him in France, and who asked to have applied to their country those principles for which they had been fighting overseas. There was really little crime in Ireland. Passive resistance was the order of the day, and people were trying to secure the release of those in prison on suspicion of complicity in 'the German Plot' of whose existence there has never been any satisfactory proof.[1]

Mr. de Valera made a dramatic escape from Lincoln Prison, and at last there was a general release of prisoners. Then Dail Eireann met again, Mr. de Valera was elected President, and a responsible Cabinet formed.

Constance had kept in touch with industrial matters since her release from prison in 1917, and was much trusted by Liberty Hall, consequently it was natural that she should be chosen Minister for Labour in this Government. She did excellent work during the year she was in office. I remember her showing me, with real pride, a list of disputes she had been instrumental in settling. All the time she was in prison she had been reading general economic literature and thinking deeply on these subjects, I know, and when she

[1] Constance was in Holloway on this charge.

stayed with us in London, at her request we asked various experts to meet her at our flat to discuss economic problems. The remarkable fact about this Government was that though it was proclaimed illegal, and the English Government was in nominal possession, yet the former's decisions were respected and carried out. People appealed to it who did not belong to the Republican party. They found its judgments fair. Unionist writers say the Republican Court's land decisions were welcomed by both sides. This Republican Government also appealed to Ireland for a quarter of a million for the carrying out of their work, and the money came in. The farming class, freed from conscription, were grateful and subscribed well, it is said.

The Irish-American delegates came over to inquire into the condition of the country at the time when things were beginning to be worse again. The English authorities were making arrests, and Mr. de Valera's civil army began to operate as rescue parties. Police who were regarded as spies were on several occasions assassinated, I regret to say. The Dail appointed a Commission to undertake an industrial inquiry into the possibility of developing Ireland's resources. This body was declared illegal. Meetings of the County Councils summoned to confer with them on the utilisation of water power were prohibited. In August 1919 a party of soldiers were attacked at Fermoy and their arms stolen. Retaliation by the other side followed.

In September 1919 the English Government proclaimed Sinn Fein an illegal association in certain counties, and the Dail was proclaimed an illegal assembly. It must be remembered that its members were elected in 1918, under the new British Franchise Act, as the country's representatives, and the Home Rule Act had been passed five years before.

In February 1920, Mr. Lloyd George announced a measure to set up two Parliaments in Ireland. The disorder on both sides grew rapidly. The 'Black and Tans' were let loose on the country, and the Lord Mayor of Cork (McCurtain) murdered by police. In April a hunger strike of political prisoners was declared and was backed by a General Strike declared by Irish Labour. Society was paralysed for a couple of days. At first no one in England would believe that illegal outrages could possibly be committed by their own forces on ordinary people in Ireland, innocent as well as guilty—and no wonder. It was a ghastly story, but one to be matched in every war, I fear, for violence breeds violence. There were about 50,000 regular troops in Ireland, and as far as I know they were not guilty in this matter of *illegal* outrages, but the English ex-soldiers recruited into the Royal Irish Constabulary and the *ex-officers* recruited as Auxiliaries at £1 a day with rations and uniform to assist the R.I.C., became violent at once. They were all armed, and began shooting people, burning villages and houses, and so on. General Crozier, who was in command of the Auxiliaries, did his best, but finally resigned because he was not allowed to enforce discipline. He and Mr. H. W. Nevinson, who was sent over to Ireland to investigate conditions by Mr. Massingham, editor of *The Nation*, have proved the Irish accusations against these forces up to the hilt. Finally, the reprisals were made *official* by Mr. Lloyd George's Government (1920).

General Crozier's words are: 'I resigned from the R.I.C. on account of the condonation of crime by politicians, in the Trim Case, of armed robbery of defenceless women by the police. . . . The Assize judge eventually awarded the unfortunate women compensation, to be paid by the ratepayers.' He further asserts that the Restoration of Order Act opened the floodgates of crime by doing away with arrest and searching of houses by *warrant*. This opened all houses to criminal raiders of both sides and ordinary criminals disguised as Crown forces or as Sinn Feiners, and allowed the secret service of the military and the 'Intelligence Officers' of the police full scope to wax fat. One police gang was the richer by £10,000, stolen from a bank at night, in the execution of duty.

'Æ.' reported to the American Commission of Inquiry: 'The co-operative movement in Ireland has gained world-wide recognition as one of the sanest and most beneficent of national movements. Its membership included men of all parties and creeds in Ireland. . . . Many thousands of Unionists were able to join with their Nationalist countrymen in an all-Ireland movement for their mutual benefit. Over one thousand Societies have been created with an annual turnover now exceeding eleven million pounds. The creameries, bacon factories, mills and agricultural stores created by co-operative societies are a familiar feature in the Irish countryside. Up to the moment of writing, forty-two attacks have been made on co-operative societies *by the armed forces of the Crown*. In these attacks creameries and mills have been burned to the ground, their machinery wrecked, agricultural stores have also been burned, property looted, employees have been killed, wounded, beaten, threatened, or otherwise ill-treated.' He goes on to say 'that if barracks have been burned or police have been killed or wounded . . . and if the armed forces of the Crown cannot capture those actually guilty of the offences—the policy of reprisals, condoned by spokesmen of the Government, has led to the wrecking of any enterprise in the neighbourhood whose destruction would inflict injury and hurt the interests of the greatest number of people, whether innocent or guilty.'

Mr. Healy quotes the terrible total of damage done under the ' Black and Tan ' régime, and assures us the figures were never gainsaid :

7,684 arrests.
2,412 deportations.
26,602 raids, often accompanied by looting.
682 armed assaults by police and soldiers.
2,205 sentences.
532 courts-martial.
75 deaths.
53 suppressions of newspapers.

Added to which there were the burning of towns, hotels, creameries, places of recreation, Carnegie libraries and business premises. The English Government had in the end to pay £4,000,000 to the Irish for damages done through the wrongful and illegal acts of the Crown Forces.

I give these facts here because they are in themselves an explanation of the increased distrust of England and the determination to sever the connection between the two countries that was characteristic of Constance's action from this time on. These things only strengthened her original conviction that an Irish Republic was the one possible cure for her country's troubles.

In 1920, Constance was again arrested and tried by Court-Martial. Under ' The Restoration of Order in Ireland Act,' she was accused of ' being associated in organizing the killing of soldiers, and of drilling men, carrying and using arms, and training volunteers.' It must be remembered that this was when the ' Black and Tans ' and Auxiliaries were restoring order by killing, looting and burning. At the moment it was they, not she, who were doing illegal actions. Nevertheless she was sentenced to two years' imprisonment with hard labour, and was in prison till autumn 1921.

A Treaty between Great Britain and Ireland was signed by delegates in London, 6th December 1921. The treaty was approved [by 64 votes to 57] by the Dail in January 1922, as an alternative to the 'immediate and terrible war' threat.

The unhappy split in the Republican ranks was intensified by this vote. Mr. de Valera, who had been President of the Republic since 1919, resigned. The General Election of May 1922 was an agreed Election, that is to say, a Panel was agreed on between the two parties for which all were to vote. It was understood that the Treaty was not to be an issue at this Election, which aimed at the appointment of a Government to carry on the nation's business and the averting of civil war. The agreement was not carried out by the Pro-Treaty Party. The Republicans lost seats, among which was Constance's seat. She took her stand with Mr. de Valera.

Ever since Easter Week the strain and hardships of Constance's life had been terrible. She had no fixed home, and for most of the time was either 'on the run,' or in prison. Mrs. Skeffington wrote of it:

'After 1916 her home at Surrey House, Dublin, was raided and wrecked by British Military: pictures, lace and valuables were looted. The crowd came later and finished the business, until a friend intervened and had the place padlocked. Many of Madame's possessions found their way as souvenirs into soldiers' and officers' kits and were given to their friends. A hand-press was found there too and smashed up. A manuscript of an article which Madame was writing (or reading for some friend) on Catherine de' Medici caused anxious query among the soldiers. "Who was this woman? A Sinn Feiner?"

They were only partly reassured finally when told that the lady was dead for several centuries.

From that time on, Madame never had a home of her own. She was "on the run"; raided, imprisoned or travelling for the moment, and held merely two furnished rooms as her temporary place of abode. Her large pictures and few personal belongings, silver and the like, she stored in the houses of friends. Though she loved beauty, and possessed even then, out of many wrecks, some exquisite pieces of old furniture, valuable pictures, first editions, autographed copies of verses, etc., all that she had was literally at the disposal of her friends. I never knew a person with less sense of property or less attached to possessions. Her linen and other effects went as a presentation to St. Ultan's Hospital, founded for babies of the poor, by her friend, Dr. Kathleen Lynn, who had served with her in the Irish Citizen Army, and had been deported after 1916. I have seen her when someone admired a vase or a picture say, "Do you like it? Take it," and literally force the thing upon an embarrassed acquaintance.

I had this story from a woman friend arrested and put into Kilmainham Jail with Constance Markievicz. This woman was a member of a rebel women's group founded by Maud Gonne, of which both were members.

She was in an adjoining cell, when one morning, by the friendliness of a wardress, she was allowed to get a glimpse of her neighbour. Constance was sitting on her plank bed, looking radiant. She asked her for the loan of a comb, and when it was handed to her (a pretext to get her inside the cell) she said, "Oh, Perolze, did you hear the news? I have been sentenced to death!" This with such a radiant smile of rapture that it sounded as though she was announcing some tidings of great joy. Later, she was to see the insides of many jails, Mountjoy, Aylesbury, Holloway, Cork, again Mountjoy. She was to be twice court-martialled, and conveyed once in a battleship with no female escort over to England. Aylesbury was the hardest experience. A convict, a "lifer," alone among the most hardened criminals, with murderesses and worse; wearing convict clothes with the broad arrow, shut away from the world. She was put in the kitchen to help with the cooking, and was given the hardest, most menial tasks. But even here she won friends, and her good spirits and comradeliness broke down barriers. "Chicago May" tells in her *Memoirs* later how she learned to know Countess Markievicz, when both were serving life sentences, and what a good sport she was.

Madame was what is known as a good prisoner, that is, she did prison work and kept the rules. She never hunger-struck in protest until at the very end, in 1923, when a sympathetic strike was initiated. While in Mountjoy and Cork she did gardening for her health's sake, and helped to lay out the Governor's garden and border-beds. She was an enthusiastic gardener, and she had a "lucky hand." Most of her friends, rich and poor, still have plants that Madame planted for them: Madame's rose, Madame's lavender bush or rosemary, Madame's rock plants bloom still and are remembered for her.

She also helped in the prison library, helping to catalogue and make selections. She was in prison for three Christmas times running, 1916, 1917, 1918, and used to say plaintively, "I wonder if I will ever be out for another Christmas?"

In Holloway she and another woman interned for Mr. Shortt's German Plot in 1918 were accorded special treatment, being internees, not regular prisoners. They had cells set apart on a special landing, with separate bathroom for themselves and took exercise separately. They sewed, embroidered, wrote or painted all day. They were refused letters or visits, however, and saw no newspapers.

When therefore, one August morning, they saw a cell being got ready for some new inmate of their corridor, they were full of curiosity and conjecture as to who it could be. "Well, I hope it's Hanna Skeffington," said Constance, "for she'll tell us all about America." (I had just returned, and having broken the passport regulations by crossing from Liverpool to Dublin without a permit, was arrested in Dublin and sent to Holloway "for the duration.") She was right, and soon afterwards I arrived. I had been hunger-striking since my arrest some days before, and I continued to fast, though Madame advised me to discontinue, for she feared I would be forcibly fed. I was not weakened yet, however, and we walked and talked all day together and exchanged news. We had not met since 1916 in the College of Surgeons. After two days I was released, and conveyed to a hotel in London. The others were held for many months afterwards.

Madame, who loved the fresh air, sunlight and freedom, must have suffered a lot from prison. It must have shortened her life by many years.

Madame ran a Roneo paper, writing, printing and circulating it herself, during 1922 and 1923. She was a good cartoonist, and many of her sketches and lampoons were reproduced in the current Republican press.

She always had by her a pad on which she drew pen-and-ink or pencil sketches and portraits. She had the gift of seizing a salient feature, and would dash off sketches of her colleagues round a Sinn Fein Committee table or at an Ard Fheis or public meeting, in court or at a court-martial even. Many of these are preserved, some are excellent likenesses of friend and foe. Her sketches of Eire or Banba or Dark Rosaleen were conventional.

Her favourite recreation of late years was to take out her little Ford car (a second-hand "bargain") to the mountains, take lunch along and her sketch-book and paint all day.

She loved to fill her little car with children and take them along too, packing in her little dog, Shuler, and rattling off, a very noisy band. In town, whenever Madame saw a friend, she hailed you and gave you a lift. She seemed a reckless driver, but really was quite safe. She got a lot of fun out of tinkering with that little car, which always seemed to be on its last legs. She carried through a whirlwind campaign in it, driving it and stopping in villages or outside chapel gates after Mass to address crowds in the last election of 1927 before her death. She broke her arm in two places cranking it, got the arm set, and went right on with her meeting as if nothing had happened. "Just fix this up for me," she said to the local doctor. "It's lucky it's only my arm, I can still talk." This car too was used to collect logs and turf and coal in 1926 when there was a fuel famine in the city. Madame carried up bags of coal to the tenements—a regular Santa Claus, they used to call her when she breezed along.'

Constance gave her reasons for declining to agree to the Treaty in a speech she made in the debate on the subject in the Dail in January 1922. Even those who do not agree with her opinion must surely feel that it shows a noble spirit and one worthy of all honour. She had no thought of herself. It was her considered judgment that only the Republic as visualised in 1916 would cure Ireland's ills.

'Looking as I do for the prosperity of the many, for the happiness and content of the workers, what I stand for is James Connolly's ideal of a Workers' Republic, a Co-operative Commonwealth. . . . Can any Irishman take that oath honourably and then go back and prepare to fight for an Irish Republic, or even to work for the Republic? It is like a person going to get married plotting a divorce. I would make a Treaty with England once Ireland was free, and I would stand with President de Valera in this, that if Ireland were a free Republic I would welcome the King of England over here on a visit. But while Ireland is not free I remain a Rebel unconverted and unconvertible. . . . We have been told that we didn't know what it [the Republic] meant. Now I know what I mean—a state run by the Irish people for the people. That means a Government that looks after the rights of the people before the rights of property, and I don't wish under the Saorstat to anticipate that the directors of property and the capitalists' interests are to be the head of it. My idea is the Workers' Republic for which Connolly died, and . . . a real treaty between a free Ireland and a free England, with Ireland standing as a free sovereign state. I believe it would be possible to get that now; but even if it were impossible, I myself would stand for what is noblest and what is truest. That is the thing that I can grasp in my nature. I have seen the stars and I am not going to follow a flickering will-o'-the-wisp.' [1]

In the summer of 1922 Constance made a tour of the United States with Kathleen Barry, sister of Kevin Barry, the medical student hanged in 1920 on 'the

[1] From the Official Report of the Debate on the Treaty between Great Britain and Ireland, signed in London, 6th December 1921. Public Session of Dail Eireann, Tuesday, January 3, 1922.

charge of complicity in the shooting of a soldier.' It was a kind of triumphal progress. One paper, in saying San Francisco was happy to be her host, added, 'The world always pays the tribute of high respect to the men and women who stand unswervingly by a principle . . . the high places in the history of the human spirit are the places where uncompromising idealists held their sway for their respective periods. . . . The world always bows before something precious.'

In addition to her comradeship with her fellow-countrymen in the U.S.A., she took the greatest interest in the industrial conditions, the Trade Union movement, and the condition of the Indians. She thoroughly enjoyed the people and the scenery, but she felt the constant publicity a strain. I remember her description of one house she stayed in, where the only possible way to get quiet was to climb a garden wall so high that no one else felt like tackling it. There she was left alone.

Early in that year she stayed with us in London for a longer time than she could usually spare. She was addressing meetings in different places near. We knew at the time that her arrest was likely because of the trouble in Ireland between Republicans and the Free State authorities. However, she was not interfered with, but the night after she left, the leaders of the London Branch of the Republican Party were arrested. A meeting she was addressing in the Midlands was raided by police, but her friends got her out by a back way. She went through the tour arranged, speaking in Manchester and many other large towns, and then settled for a time in Scotland. Her great desire was to secure the removal of the Oath for members of the Dail. When the attack was made on the Four Courts in Dublin in 1923, she saw her last bit of fighting, then was 'on the run' once more, and finally was arrested on a lorry in her old constituency where she was holding a protest meeting, and was taken to prison in the North Dublin Union Internment Camp. She went on Hunger Strike for a fortnight about Christmas, because this had been agreed on for all prisoners. The leaders called off the strike when two prisoners had died. She was afterwards released with the others. Her own description of the Hunger Strike is contained in one of her letters. She assured us she did not suffer, but I think her general health suffered severely from the life she led, with all its hardships and anxieties, and its bitter sorrow for the disunion that had crept into the old Republican Party. Still she continued to work with all her strength to the end of her life.

All these years life for Eva, too, was very difficult. We had to carry on all our own work in addition to striving to help Irish people.

In September 1914 we had undertaken the visiting and relieving of German women and children and the few older men who were not interned. Various agencies carried out the relief work with money supplied by Government and also by friendly people, but regular visiting was essential. The distress was heartbreaking that first winter. Later the Germans were sent back, or if English by birth were allowed to remain here provided they could support themselves.

In 1915 and 1916 we went up and down the country speaking as members of the Women's Peace Crusade, supporting the efforts of those who sought to end the war by negotiations, not by further slaughter. In 1916 we also worked for the No-Conscription Fellowship, for we were both extreme Pacifists. Many of our friends were imprisoned for refusing Military Service. Many were court-martialled, constantly tried by tribunals or deprived of posts. This added to our prison visiting experience. Other dear friends, of course, were in the trenches and there was the constant anxiety about them too. Eva overworked herself incessantly and was terribly anxious about Constance always. We both got seriously ill for a time and in 1920 had to go to Italy to recuperate. For part of the time we stayed with our friends George and Margaret Gavan Duffy. The former was Sinn Fein representative in Rome. While we were there, Constance's friends became very worried lest violence should be done to her under the 'Black and Tan' rule. At one time when she was in prison in Ireland, they were not satisfied with her treatment. They therefore begged Eva to secure an audience with the Pope, to tell him of Constance's imprisonment and ask him to bless a rosary to be sent to her in prison. It was not easy for a non-Catholic to carry out this plan. However, we went to an ordinary audience at the Vatican. When the Pope entered the chamber, everyone knelt. As he passed round the room giving them his blessing, each person kissed his ring. When it came to our turn, I am ashamed to say I was so absorbed in anxiety that I forgot my part. However, Eva was calmer, mercifully, and speaking in rapid Italian she got in the whole story of her sister's danger and asked him to bless the rosary. The Pope listened carefully to all she said and gave the blessing. His long pause appeared to alarm his attendants and some of them came hastily down the room. I caught sight of an Irish chamberlain in a resplendent uniform and with a cocked hat under his arm, coming along with a surprised look on his face. However, as he was a friend, I thought he was probably not too perturbed. What remains in my memory is the sad tired face of Benedict xv. as he walked towards us. I felt profoundly sorry for him, for the world's burdens must have weighed heavily on his shoulders. I was not surprised to hear later of his illness and death.

We received the greatest kindness from the Gavan Duffys and other Irish people in Rome. Many interesting hours we spent at the Irish College. The Rector, Monsignor Hagan, an able and determined man, was seriously ill at the time but was always ready to talk of Ireland, as were other Irish priests and monks including the Father General of one order, the Prior of a well-known Irish Monastery in Italy, and a learned Jesuit, studying at a famous Library in Rome. All were friendly to us and their conversation, as one would expect, was both interesting and racy. It was a unique experience.

When later we went on to the North of Italy, we did not realise, perhaps, how strange it must have seemed in places where she was not known that Eva should be receiving letters stamped as from an Irish prison. At any rate, on one occasion, we quite unintentionally caused some trouble to a patriotic and innocent Englishwoman whose name resembled Eva's. The day after we had left a certain hotel, the police arrived, and finding our rooms empty, searched everything, beds, sofas, cupboards and fireplaces. Nothing was to be found but perfectly harmless scraps of letters. So they insisted on interviewing the lady of the suspicious name. She was naturally greatly annoyed. We did not even know of it until, two years afterwards, I went to the town for a night, and calling on her was utterly taken aback to be asked for an explanation. There was nothing to explain, I could only apologise profoundly. I suppose some bright young detective on the look-out for promotion thought he saw in us a means of securing it.

We returned to Hampstead and took up work again. Eva wrote and published two more volumes of poetry and two of prose. But her health was undermined. She refused to lead an invalid life, though suffering desperately at times, and in 1926, after a short but severe illness heroically borne, she died. 'Her memory will always be enshrined in the hearts of those who loved her, and her work,' as Constance said, 'has left a spiritual inheritance of love and peace to those who can understand, that will never die.' Constance had not realized quite how fragile she had become, and it was a terrible shock to her. She came over and stayed with me. She looked to me very ill, but denied that anything was wrong with her. It was then that we had the conversations to which she refers in her last letters. I was deeply struck by what she said, and I felt her so full of love and wisdom. It seemed to me that she had learned so much more from the life for which people blamed her so severely, than most human beings learn from lives that are considered most praiseworthy. She had the inner vision as it were, and could see truth. We sat for hours while she copied in water-colours a sketch of Eva that she had done in oils twenty years before. And as she worked, she told me of her early life, of Easter Week and that last night in the College of Surgeons, and of how life changed for her from then. She spoke with deep feeling of all Eva had done for her, and finally of her own certain hope of immortality. We parted with great reluctance, and she planned another visit soon. But, alas, it was not to be. When I saw her next she was dying in a hospital ward. She had unfortunately not told her friends about the operation for appendicitis until it was over. Then I received a letter saying everything was satisfactory and she was getting on well. I answered that I would go into the country with her as soon as ever she was well enough to move. But almost immediately there came a message on the wireless summoning her family. I went to Dublin next morning. Her daughter was with her, and no one else was allowed to see her. The moment I did see her I knew there was no hope. A second operation had been performed and she was terribly ill, but brave as ever and perfectly alert mentally. She smiled a welcome. 'You know, Eva has been by my side ever since I came in here, and now you are on the other side I am quite happy.' In spite of constant sickness she continued to speak of people and things. I felt her surroundings too hard for her, and asked in distress why she hadn't told us before the operation, so that we could have found a good Nursing Home for her. She said, 'Oh, I thought nothing of the operation, besides if the hospital is good enough for the poor it is good enough for me.' There were about six people in the ward, they looked poor as well as suffering. Nothing could exceed their loving sympathy. They would hardly speak lest they should disturb her. As I passed in and out from the screened corner, they would just smile and whisper an inquiry. A little old lady who was discharged as convalescent came round the screen to say good-bye. 'Please God I'll meet you again in Dublin, but if not there, in Heaven, Madame dear.' As night drew on the Matron told me that they did not think Constance would live till morning, and I might stay with her. Outside in the rain a large and silent crowd stood, hour after hour, praying. Inside in the Hospital Board Room sat a group of her friends. The Matron of the Hospital [a Protestant institution] had lent the room to them. They were mostly Catholics. Here, too, all were praying, hoping still, they said, for a miracle. As I went through the hall once, someone thrust a little bottle of Lourdes water into my hand. 'Do take it to her,' she begged. I asked a Catholic nurse to sprinkle it. Constance smiled her thanks to the giver. For hours I sat there watching; Dr. Lynn, her own doctor, came in constantly, and about 4 A.M. saw signs of a hopeful change. Other doctors were called in and I sat with her friends in the Board Room where we talked of their belief that their prayers would bring her back to life. At last the doctor came, announcing a wonderful improvement. 'Constance says you are to go home to bed at once,' she added. Her friends were overcome with joy and I heard the word 'miracle,' and so it seemed for the time. As I went back to sleep, every person I met outside the hospital rushed to me and made the same inquiry—the people going early to work, the driver of the taxi, the hall porter and the maids at the hotel. Next morning I returned to the hospital and the surgeon said, 'It's a miracle, but I think she will recover. I never expected her to live out the night.'

As I went about the town doing some errands for Constance, people I had never seen came up to me to ask about her, men, women, and children. 'Ah! what would the people in the slums do without her,' one woman said with her eyes full of tears. 'She's given up everything for us and she thinks what's good enough for us is good enough for her. Please God she'll get better.' The tram guard who handed me a ticket asked me anxiously, 'Will she get better, do you think?'—though how he knew who I was I cannot guess. It was very touching. Everyone talked of her. A friend told me how some time before during a coal shortage Constance had collected all kinds of fuel in her little car and taken it round to the houses of the poorest, sometimes climbing up staircases with a bag of it on her back. Also how a few months before, during the General Election, after breaking her arm in two places in cranking her car, she had had it set and with a merry jest gone on to speak at her meetings, without a pause. But I got the impression that she had worn herself out, and I think she knew it. She had been returned again for the St. Patrick's division of Dublin, and when she walked to the Dail with Mr. de Valera and other deputies to attempt to take their seats without taking the Oath, she said to a friend, 'Some day the Republicans will walk down and be admitted. But I shall not be there then.' Even in the hospital she said, 'I sometimes long for the peace of the Republican Plot.'

In the afternoon, after my night vigil, her husband and stepson arrived from Warsaw. She was absolutely delighted to see them, and they were with her at the end. I was an intimate friend of Constance and Casimir, and I know that it was life, not their own choice, that separated them. Casimir was kept in Russia by the World War, which swept individual lives apart everywhere. He was wounded, then desperately ill, and ruined by the Revolution. Finally he escaped to Poland and began to work for the rebuilding of this, his own country. Constance, drawn into the Irish Rising, for the rest of her days had no more private life. Such is fate. Casimir twice went to Ireland for brief visits to her. With his son, he rushed to her when he heard of her illness. As I sat by her after their first visit, a parcel of lovely roses was brought in. She would not even let me undo it, though her weak hands shook as she opened it, and took out a card with a charming inscription of greeting from them. 'Look,' she said proudly, 'don't they know how to do things?' And she talked of them and of the old days, with affection. I should not speak of these private matters but that certain people have taken the opportunity of biographical notices to invent stories of a quarrel. To Constance and Casimir these things no longer matter, but it is right for those who know the truth to speak.

He stayed with me after the funeral, and showing me a bundle of his old love-letters which he had found in her desk, he spoke with strong feeling about these lying writers and added, 'In all the years there never was an unkind word between us.' He felt her death deeply. He himself became ill in 1931, was an invalid for many months, and died in 1932.

The morning after Casimir's arrival in Dublin I was obliged to go to London on business for a few days, and I said 'Good-bye' to her, full of hope and cheerfulness, but alas, not twenty-four hours later, I had a telegram to say she had passed away.

Almost the last words she uttered were, 'But it is so beautiful to have had all this love and kindness before I go.'

My brother and I returned to Dublin for the funeral. Once more the streets were crowded by her friends. We went to the Rotunda Buildings on the Saturday night, where people were waiting in silence to say 'Good-bye' to her. It seemed an endless stream through that little room where the coffin lay amid a mass of flowers, watched by Fianna boys.

The drive to Glasnevin on Sunday morning through those poor streets of her constituency was pathetic. Wherever one looked there were people united now in sorrow and affection. Within Glasnevin cemetery were her special friends in hundreds. Before the coffin was placed in the vaults where it was to await final burial next day, Mr. de Valera made a simple and beautiful little speech in Irish and then in English.[1] I give my brother's account of the funeral, written the day after, also articles on Constance taken from *The Nation*, an Irish weekly, as I think they describe as well as words could so moving a scene.

[1] Given on p. 118.

'MADAME'

The pages of Dublin's history are bathed in colour: red for the violent death, blue for the lips of poverty, gold for the heart of love. Last Sunday was all gold. The blazing sunshine fell on the streets, mile after mile lined with an endless crowd, waiting in patience to honour the memory of a friend. Madame was being borne toward her grave, and over 300,000 waited to see her pass.

A short week before, the dark night was full of prayer. Desperately ill, after a second operation, she lay in a public ward of a hospital at the point of death: a Protestant hospital, which gave its Board Room to six Catholic women, that they might pray till dawn. Outside were groups of hopeful, hopeless human beings, children and women and men who would quite literally have given their lives to save her who had given up her life to them. Singing, praying, they waited for news. Towards morning, it seemed a miracle had happened: she was alive again, though still in danger. A few days of happiness and hope, and then the end.

The end? There is an immortality on earth. The memory of Countess Markievicz will live in the children who loved to see her and whom she loved; it will be cherished by those who were starving, those whose rents she paid, those to whom she carried sacks of coal on her shoulders, for whom during the Strike of 1913 she cooked and toiled, the out-of-work, the broken, the hopeless, to whom she was at once Hope and Bravery and Beauty and Romance. Feeling again the glow of her vitality, drawing life from her smile, taking heart from her cheerfulness, for them Sunday—in spite of sorrow—was a golden day.

During the recent election she broke both bones of her lower arm with the starting-handle of her ancient car. All she said while they were being set was: 'Glory be, it's not my jaw: I can still talk.' And with her arm in a sling she went on to her meeting and made her speech. During her illness she bore all the misery and pain without an impatient word, cheerfully, smiling and with a sense of humour, making things easier for those who nursed her. The other patients loved her: for her and them there was no difference of class. 'She thinks what's good enough for us good enough for her,' they said. Yet even they did not know why she was there: when the doctor asked her where she would go for her operation, she replied: 'To the cheapest hospital: I am a pauper.' She had given all she had to those in need, till she had nothing left for herself.

Artist to the tips of her fingers (she painted beautiful things in prison) she loved truth for its beauty and beauty for its truth. She had a fierce intolerance of a social order which permitted poverty, with all its ugliness, misery and squalor. Increasingly her chief aim was to help the poor in her constituency. For her, politics, rebellion, prison, the death-sentence itself, were no more than incidents, by-products of an industrial struggle. In England she was known as a 'rebel countess,' 'inconsistently refusing to take her seat either in Westminster or in Dublin.' In Ireland all this seemed the merest logic, the reasoned consequence of a belief in freedom as a remedy for intolerable destitution.

Before the funeral her body lay in the Rotunda Buildings, and hour after hour a double line of human beings streamed slowly by, paying their last respects. Through the evening, far into the night, early next morning, they came and saw and passed, more than

100,000 friends. Many had bought or sent wreaths and flowers. Flowers are expensive in Dublin: she had eight lorry-loads of them. One dear old country woman came with three fresh eggs: she had promised to give them to Madame when she came out of hospital: they were hers. There was nothing the people would not have done for her. Dublin has never seen a greater show of affection, adoration.

REGINALD E. ROPER.

The articles 'Death of Countess Markievicz' and 'A Patriot at Rest' are from *The Nation*.

DEATH OF COUNTESS MARKIEVICZ

Madame has died in the public ward of a hospital among the poorest of Dublin's poor. Remembering the ease and delicate pleasantness to which she was born, such a death seems pitiful; but remembering her own choice of life's values, which things she cared for and which heedlessly let go, there seems something in it right and inevitable: it was the logical conclusion of her life.

It was a marvellous thing, the winning of such a woman to the hard service of Ireland. She inherited, by birth and circumstance, all the ease and all the finer pleasures that the civilisation of the modern world provides. In her youth she had famous beauty and famous powers in the hunting field; and she had a vivid intellect and wit. If the life of sport and social amusement did not satisfy her, another world was open, for the deep and ardent sense of beauty which made her sister a poet made a painter of her. She lived the joyous life of an art student in Paris for a while, and knew the keen delights of intellectual comradeship and friendly rivalry in the service of art.

It could be imagined that Ireland's literary renaissance and the adventure of rebellion might appeal for a time to a daring spirit and an artist's mind. But the long strain of apparent failure, the loss of friends, the impoverishment of life, the spoiling of the life of peace—real hardship, real danger—would not these prove too severe a test ? Would not regrets come, and nostalgia for the green leisure of gardens, or the pleasant distractions of rich cities, or the achievements of an artist, or the joys of the hunting field ?

But that was not what happened. Something different from a mood of adventure drew this woman into Ireland's cause, and in her life there were no complexities, no hesitations or half-measures or regrets. One strong impulse flung every lesser thing aside—all was simplified and unified in her by a lasting, single passion of pity and love. To the people of Ireland she gave herself, and she held nothing back. It was a giving of which the lavishness cannot be measured or described. It is symbolised by the circumstance of her death—the hospital ward, without privacy, without beauty, and the ceaseless loving care of the nurses, and the prayers of the throngs of people who stood all night long outside.

She was happy : no one who lived or worked with her can doubt that. None of the hardships of Ireland's service were spared her, but none were too great for her spirit to endure. She came through all with a gay bravery that never flagged. Nothing that the enemy could do daunted her, nor did she ever yield to disillusionment or let her faith in the people fail. She never wasted a thought on mourning over defeats, or in bitterness or despair, but was ready for each fresh enterprise, brimming with enthusiasm and hope. Admiration for her own sacrifices she would not tolerate. There was no sacrifice, she maintained. She had been offered one kind of life and she had chosen another. She had chosen the work that interested her and the life she preferred; one could claim no merit for that.

This peace of the happy warrior, she had, and also, in a large measure, the vivid joy in everyday things which some who have suffered long periods of imprisonment seem to retain in spite of trouble and time. A sunny morning, an amusing encounter, a friend's poem or story that she could praise, a clever dramatic performance by the Fianna boys, the discovery of a lonely glen, or an afternoon snatched from political work to go sketching in the mountains—such things were enough to fill her with the eager, garrulous happiness of a child. Even in the last days in hospital, sick to death, she was made happy by the visits of her friends and their presents of scent and flowers, and the plans they were making to take her away to the country when she grew strong.

Was she sometimes tired? The claims on her compassion and her help were unceasing. Her days were a rush and whirl of urgent work; but it seemed as though she loved it all and could not be happy at rest. It was startling to hear that she said, in hospital, to a friend: 'I long sometimes for the peace of the Republican Plot.' Did Ireland take too much from her and give too little? No matter now; Ireland received, freely and gratefully, all that she had to give, and that was what she desired. Losing her life, she found it; in suffering, she found happiness, and in battling for Ireland, peace; and in death she has won the immortality of a nation's love and praise.

DOROTHY MACARDLE.

The Funeral

It is with profound sorrow we announce the death of Countess Markievicz, the noblest soul that served the cause of Irish liberty and common Irish humanity in our generation. A week ago we rejoiced in the thought that our very dear friend had passed the critical stage in her illness, and we were happy to give the good news to our readers. On Thursday night, at nine o'clock a change set in, and Count Markievicz and his son, who had been at the Countess's bedside practically since their arrival in Ireland from Warsaw some days earlier, were summoned. At midnight, the Countess became unconscious, and at 1.30 A.M. she died. She was attended by Fr. E. MacSweeney, C.C., of Westland Row, and all the last rites of the Church were administered to her by him. We are informed that everything that medical skill could accomplish was done for her by her three medical attendants, Sir William Taylor, Dr. Kavanagh, and Dr. Kathleen Lynn. Grateful thanks are due to the hospital authorities of Sir Patrick Dunn's, and to the nursing sisters for their kindness and assiduous attention to their much-loved and distinguished patient.

On Friday night the remains were taken from the Hospital to St. Andrew's Church, Westland Row, in which Church a Requiem Mass was celebrated on Saturday morning. Fr. E. MacSweeney, C.C., was the celebrant.

After the Mass the remains were removed to the Rotunda Buildings, where the 'lying-in-state' took place. Irish Republicans desire to express to Mr. Kay, the lessee of the Rotunda, their gratitude for having placed the buildings at the disposal of Madame's friends without charge. The use of the City Hall, and later of the Mansion House, for the lying-in-state was applied for, but the Town Clerk wrote that, by order of the Commissioners, the use of either building was refused.

When the remains were taken on Friday night from the hospital to the church, and from the church to the Rotunda, they were borne on both occasions on the shoulders of present and past members of the Fianna Eireann organisation, of which body Madame Markievicz was the foundress and President. On both occasions the signs of deepest sorrow one witnessed in the streets were most impressive. Thousands and thousands of the poor of Dublin, the workless, the clothesless, and the hungry, young and old, walked in the processions or lined the roadways as the cortege passed. Never was there—even in Dublin, famed for great and imposing funerals—a more striking tribute of profound sorrow and sympathy or love for the dead one than was given heartfelt expression to by the common people on Friday night, on Saturday, and again on Sunday, when the remains were carried to their final resting-place in Glasnevin Cemetery. The thousands who stood in line for hours on Saturday and all Saturday night and on Sunday morning, to view the remains, and then the hundreds of thousands who marched in the funeral procession or lined its eight miles of route, assembled simply to testify their great love for a highly-gifted and valiant woman who had thrown aside everything worldly people prize so that she might devote herself wholeheartedly to the liberation of her motherland and the upliftment of its down-trodden people.

The funeral on Sunday was of enormous dimensions. All the Irish National, Republican and Labour organisations with which Madame had been associated, were fully represented :—Sinn Fein, Fianna Eireann, Inginidhe na h-Eireann, Cuman na-mBan, Fianna Fail,

Transport Workers, Workers' Union of Ireland, Labour Congress and Trades Council, etc., etc.

Count Markievicz and his son arrived at the Rotunda a few minutes before noon and had a last look at Madame Markievicz before the final closing of the coffin on Sunday.

Before the coffin was closed, Father Ronyane, O.C.C., Rome, recited the Rosary, in which all present joined.

The route of the procession was via Parnell Street, Capel Street, Parliament Street, Dame Street, George's Street, York Street, Stephen's Green, Grafton Street, College Green, Westmoreland Street, O'Connell Street to Glasnevin.

At Glasnevin, Father Fitzgibbon, C.C., Chaplain, headed the procession to the vault in the O'Connell Circle. When the coffin, borne on the shoulders of Fianna Fail and Sinn Fein leaders, including Mr. de Valera and Mr. Arthur O'Connor, and boys of Fianna Eireann in uniform, was placed in the vault, the De Profundis was recited by Rev. Gregory Clery, O.F.M., and later prayers in Irish were recited by Rev. T. W. O'Ryan, P.P., Rolestown, Co. Dublin.

Mr. de Valera's Oration

After the chief mourners had visited the remains, a bugler of the Fianna sounded the Last Post, and then Mr. de Valera delivered his oration in both languages.

Speaking in English, he said :—' Madame Markievicz is gone from us ; Madame, the friend of the toiler, the lover of the poor. Ease and station she put aside, and took the hard way of service with the weak and the down-trodden. Sacrifice, misunderstanding and scorn lay on the road she adopted, but she trod it unflinchingly.

' She now lies at rest with her fellow-champions of

the right—mourned by the people whose liberties she fought for; blessed by the loving prayers of the poor she tried so hard to befriend. The world knew her only as a soldier of Ireland, but we knew her as colleague and comrade.

'We knew the kindliness, the great woman's heart of her, the great Irish soul of her, and we know the loss we have suffered is not to be repaired.

'It is sadly we take our leave, but we pray high heaven that all she longed for may one day be achieved.'

A PATRIOT AT REST

It is with a heavy and grievous heart that we mourn the death of Countess Markievicz who was laid to rest in the Republican Plot in Glasnevin on Monday last, the 18th inst.

Beannacht De ar a hanam dilis.[1]

We had hoped, but in vain, for her recovery. Overwork had rendered her unfit for an operation and illness of a serious nature. Her passionate heart has obtained the rest she was unwilling to allow it in this world.

Dublin will be lonely for the Countess—its Countess. Heroic figures like Constance de Markievicz make Dublin unique among the capitals of the world. Without them it would be nothing. They make Ireland's history a page of romance to thrill the reader of distant and disinterested lands.

Born into a family of the landed gentry of Ireland, which was more than usually English in its traditions and outlook, Constance Georgina Gore-Booth grew up with exceptional gifts and accomplishments. Her beauty found a wealthy and graceful world at her feet. A good painter, her talents brought her into

[1] The blessing of God on her dear soul.

the more definitely artistic world. She discarded the social attractions of London for the more artistic charm of Paris. She returned in her maturity to her own Ireland where a sincere life led her from among the artists of Dublin to mingle with the patriots and the people of Ireland.

Constance de Markievicz's superb logic and courage led her to perform deeds that the vast majority of us only prate about doing. Ireland must be free ; a blow has to be struck for her, she goes openly into battle ; she shoots and is shot at ; she is condemned to death ; she has the luck to be spared her life and is sent to prison. With the vicissitudes of political struggles, she is released ; she continues the fight for Ireland in all the phases it incessantly assumes. Logic and courage such as hers are so rare that people who cannot emulate her in either, try to dispose of her as eccentric. Courage is a danger to a materialistic world, and logic is troublesome.

The consistency of her Christianity and eventual Catholicism and her ardent charity led her to live among the poor. Her funeral on Sunday last was the funeral of a queen who reigned in Irish hearts but especially in the true hearts that beat beneath the ragged sleeve.

Born to comfort, and luxury even, she chooses to die in the public ward of an hospital among her truest, dearest and now most bereaved of sorrowing friends. Born in a castle—a stronghold of English landlordism and ascendancy—she lies in an Irish Republican's grave, cared for by loving Irish hands. And the people miss her a little less now that she lies so close to them, than they did in the stormy days of her exile in English jails.

Constance de Markievicz is a pure gold link in our chain of great patriots who were born of foreign stock among the Gaels of Ireland. Wolfe Tone opens the list. Erskine Childers was recently admitted to his enduring foothold in it. The last illustrious place is filled to-day by one who has been described as the bravest woman in Europe.

Readers of *The Nation* will cherish for ever her contributions to the paper.

From among hundreds of Resolutions passed by public bodies I choose the Resolution of the Workers' Union of Ireland for quotation.

'The Executive Committee desires to express its keen sense of the deep loss that the common people of Ireland have suffered in the sad and untimely death of Madame de Markievicz.

Madame de Markievicz was not alone a great soul, she was a valiant fighter and thinker. If the supreme sacrifice was ever necessary, she was always prepared to pay it. She knew that no country could be free so long as its people were living in misery, and suffering from hunger and want. Knowing this, she ever strove to lead the movement for an independent Ireland along the lines of greater freedom—the emancipation of the workers and peasants of Ireland.

Ireland can ill afford at this time to lose women like Madame de Markievicz. In the hour when poverty and hunger are on the daily increase ; when thousands flee from Ireland's shores to escape unemployment and the misery and hunger that follow ; when the dogs of war are straining their leashes, the death of Madame de Markievicz comes to the people of Ireland as an immeasurable loss.

We can best pay tribute to her life and work, and honour her more in death, by working to the end that the dream of Madame might be realised—an Ireland free in the complete sense—in a word, work for a Workers' Republic of Ireland.

The Executive of the Workers' Union of Ireland.'

The above resolution was passed with all standing, and all further business adjourned out of respect to the memory of Madame de Markievicz.

Some of those who never really knew Constance and Eva regret that what might, in a worldly sense, have been ' successful lives ' were spent, so they suggest, in Eva's case, in the pursuit of ' a vague Utopia,' and in Constance's case, in ' conspiring among the ignorant.'

But this is the judgment of the unwise. Of Eva herself and of her work for the poor and for the reform of industrial and social wrongs, just as truly as of her contribution as poet and mystic, the best appreciation is to be found in the words of a fine review of *The World's Pilgrim* (her book of imaginary conversations) contributed to the *Manchester Guardian* by the well-known critic and writer C. P. He says: ' What gives the dialogues the force of truth that is great, is the equipoise of intellect and universal sympathy that controls them, a sort of strong gentleness that has room for satire, but a satire so benign that it becomes a grace. . . . Michelangelo conversing with the spirit of Pheidias calls himself the world's pilgrim, seeking for the hidden springs of life and force. Eva Gore-Booth, both as poet and mystic, may be said to have found them.'

Of Constance, let it be always remembered that for the sake of her ideal of freedom, she who loved life and beauty, learned

To be rich in poverty,
Without sunshine to be gay,
To be free in a prison cell.[1]

[1] ' Broken Glory,' by Eva Gore-Booth.

She shared all she had with the poor, working for them, living and dying with them.

> Nay, on that undreamed judgment day
> When, on the old world's scrap-heap flung,
> Powers and empires pass away,
> Radiant and unconquerable
> Thou shalt be young.[1]

Constance and Eva Gore-Booth are in truth among those who 'ribbon with gold the rags of this our life.'[2]

> They shall be remembered for ever.
> They shall be alive for ever.
> They shall be speaking for ever.
> The people shall remember them for ever.[2]

ESTHER ROPER.

[1] 'Broken Glory,' by Eva Gore-Booth.
[2] 'Kathleen ni Hoolihan,' by W. B. Yeats.

POEMS OF EASTER WEEK

By Eva Gore-Booth

EASTER WEEK

Grief for the noble dead
Of one who did not share their strife,
And mourned that any blood was shed,
Yet felt the broken glory of their state,
Their strange heroic questioning of Fate,
Ribbon with gold the rags of this our life.

TO CONSTANCE—IN PRISON

Outcast from joy and beauty, child of broken hopes forlorn,
Lost to the magic mountains and parted from all flowers,
Robbed of the harvest moon that shines on far-off fields of corn,
Bereft of raindrops on green leaves, bright wrecks of fallen showers.

Nay, not outcast, whilst through your soul a sudden rapture thrills,
And all your dreams are shaken by the salt Atlantic wind,
The gods descend at twilight from the magic-hearted hills,
And there are woods and primroses in the country of your mind.

Yours is that inner Ireland beyond green fields and brown,
Where waves break dawn-enchanted on the haunted Rosses shore,
And clouds above Ben Bulben fling their coloured shadows down,
Whilst little rivers shine and sink in wet sands at Crushmor.

CHRISTMAS EVE IN PRISON

Do not be lonely, dear, nor grieve
This Christmas Eve.
Is it so vain a thing
That your heart's harper, Dark Roseen,
A wandering singer, yet a queen,
Crownèd with all her seventeen stars,
Outside your prison bars
Stands carolling?

TO C. M. ON HER PRISON BIRTHDAY

FEBRUARY, 1917

What has time to do with thee,
Who hast found the victors' way
To be rich in poverty,
Without sunshine to be gay,
To be free in a prison cell?
Nay, on that undreamed judgment day,
When, on the old world's scrap-heap flung,
Powers and empires pass away,
Radiant and unconquerable
Thou shalt be young.

COMRADES

TO CON

The peaceful night that round me flows,
Breaks through your iron prison doors,
Free through the world your spirit goes,
Forbidden hands are clasping yours.

The wind is our confederate,
The night has left her doors ajar,
We meet beyond earth's barrèd gate,
Where all the world's wild Rebels are.

HEROIC DEATH, 1916

No man shall deck their resting-place with flowers ;
  Behind a prison wall they stood to die,
Yet in those flowerless tragic graves of ours
  Buried, the broken dreams of Ireland lie.

No cairn-heaped mound on a high windy hill
  With Irish earth the hero's heart enfolds,
But a burning grave at Pentonville,
  The broken heart of Ireland holds.

Ah, ye who slay the body, how man's soul
  Rises above your hatred and your scorn.
All flowers fade as the years onward roll,
  Theirs is the deathless wreath—a crown of thorns.

FRANCIS SHEEHY-SKEFFINGTON

DUBLIN, APRIL 26, 1916

No green and poisonous laurel wreath shall shade
  His brow, who dealt no death in any strife,
Crown him with olive who was not afraid
  To join the desolate unarmed ranks of life.

Who did not fear to die, yet feared to slay,
  A leader in the war that shall end war,
Unarmed he stood in ruthless Empire's way,
  Unarmed he stands on Acheron's lost shore.

Yet not alone, nor all unrecognized,
  For at his side does that scorned Dreamer stand,
Who in the Olive Garden agonized,
  Whose Kingdom yet shall come in every land,

When driven men, who fight and hate and kill
  To order, shall let all their weapons fall,
And know that kindly freedom of the will
  That holds no other human will in thrall.

ROGER CASEMENT

I dream of one who is dead,
As the forms of green trees float and fall in the water,
The dreams float and fall in my mind.

I dream of him wandering in a far land,
I dream of him bringing hope to the hopeless,
I dream of him bringing light to the blind.

I dream of him hearing the voice,
The bitter cry of Kathleen ni Houlighaun
On the salt Atlantic wind.

I dream of the hatred of men,
Their lies against him who knew nothing of lying,
Nor was there fear in his mind.

I dream of our hopes and fears,
The long bitter struggle of the broken-hearted,
With hearts that were poisoned and hard.

I dream of the peace in his soul,
And the early morning hush on the grave of a hero
In the desolate prison yard.

I dream of the death that he died,
For the sake of God and Kathleen ni Houlighaun,
Yea, for Love and the Voice on the Wind.

I dream of one who is dead.
Above dreams that float and fall in the water
A new star shines in my mind.

UTOPIA

Cruelty, bloodshed and hate
Rule the night and the day,
The whole earth is desolate,
To what God shall one pray ?

Is there a force that can end
The woe of the world's war ?
Yes, when a friend meets a friend
There shall be peace once more.

For love at the heart of the storm
Breaks the waves of wild air,
And God in our human form
Is life's answer to prayer.

THE POET'S GOD

' What is God ? ' men said in the West,
The Lord of Good and Ill,
Rewarder of the blest,
Judge of the evil will.

' What is God ? ' men said in the East,
The universal soul
In man, and bird, and beast,
The self of the great whole.

I saw the primrose flower
Rise out of the green sod,
In majesty and power,
And I said, ' There is Love, there is God.'

DEDICATION TO 'THE DEATH OF FIONAVAR'

TO THE MEMORY OF THE DEAD
THE MANY WHO DIED FOR FREEDOM
AND THE ONE WHO DIED FOR PEACE

Poets, Utopians, bravest of the brave,
Pearse and McDonagh, Plunkett, Connolly,
Dreamers turned fighters but to find a grave,
Glad for the dream's austerity to die.

And my own sister, through wild hours of pain,
Whilst murderous bombs were blotting out the stars,
Little I thought to see you smile again
As I did yesterday, through prison bars.

Oh, bitterest sorrow of that land of tears,
Utopia, Ireland of the coming time,
That thy true citizens through weary years,
Can for thy sake but make their grief sublime.

Dreamers turned fighters but to find a grave,
Too great for victory, too brave for war,
Would you had dreamed the gentler dream of Maeve. . .
Peace be with you, and love for evermore.

THE PRISON LETTERS OF COUNTESS MARKIEVICZ

MOUNTJOY PRISON, DUBLIN, 1916

[illegible]

DEMOCRATS [illegible] BARONS. [illegible] It was such [illegible]-erent [illegible] few, seeing [illegible]. It was a new life, [illegible] re[illegible] reflect [illegible] though [illegible] the same that [illegible] seeing, [illegible] when [illegible] fighting and you hate [illegible] and I [illegible] think [illegible] wrong. It was so [illegible] of [illegible] other [illegible]

[illegible]

[illegible] lowest [illegible] it is [illegible] by. [illegible] they could [illegible] each [illegible] — [illegible] knew [illegible] hence [illegible] so well and [illegible] with a good [illegible]. There [illegible] for [illegible]

MOUNTJOY PRISON,
DUBLIN,
May 16, 1916.

DEAREST OLD DARLING,—It was such a heaven-sent joy, seeing you. It was a new life, a resurrection, though I knew all the time that you'd try and see me, even though I'd been fighting and you hate it all so and think killing so wrong. It was so dear of Esther to come all that long way too. Susan too, for I expect lots of people will think it very awful of her. Anyhow, you are three dears and you brought sunshine to me, and I long to hug you all!

Now to business. H—— and H—— are agents for Surrey House. They wrote to me *re* giving up tenancy, and very decently secured the house, which had been left open. The house is very untidy, as I had no time to put it straight after the police raid.

My valuables are all with a friend (silver and jewelry). I am rather unhappy about the pictures. I don't want anything thrown away. Egan —— might store those pictures hanging on the walls, and my illuminated address from the Transport Union. He has some pictures of ours already.

Don't store furniture with M——: he was a brute to his men in the strike. You'll want to insist on their bringing proper boxes for the books, as they are awfully careless. The china too wants care. Then there are the acting things. You'll probably want to buy a tin trunk or two, and get them packed with naphtha balls. There are wigs in the bottom of the kitchen press and in the cupboard half-way up the stairs. They want to be put by with care. The linen too, such as it is, wants to have the starch washed out before it is put by. If you could only catch Bessie ——, she knows the house so well and is such a good worker. There are a lot of crewel wools in the big press on the stairs: they want to be put with naphtha balls too. If someone could house the wigs and them I'd be thankful.

On the right of the fireplace in drawing-room is a sort of a desk. The same key fits it and the big brown press upstairs. One of my friends has the key. If you have not got it, pull out top drawer and push down and push lock back where it pokes through. Small centre drawer is locked: there is nothing in it.

Could Susan get my clothes and look after them for me? There is a little brown case with drawing things that Susan might keep for me. I told you that C—— and Co. are trying to let St. Mary's. I think my name should be suppressed and it should be let in yours.

Of course my household bills are not paid. C—— of Richmond Street is my grocer; F——, Rathmines, my baker; K——, butcher, and H——, oilman, are both Rathmines. I owe two coal bills: one to C——, Tara St., and the other to a man I forget in Charlemont St., on the right-hand side as you face the bridge, but close to the chemist at the corner where the trams cross. I owe also a trifle to G—— of O'Connell St. for a skirt, and to the Art Decorating Co., Belfast. But there is no hurry about any of these. Don't pay anything unless you know the bill is really mine, as people have played queer tricks, getting things on credit in my name before now.

You poor old darling. It's such a bore for you. I feel rather as if I were superintending my own funeral from the grave!

There is a very old book of music in the drawing-room. It might be valuable. If you have time, bring it to a Mr. Braid at P——, and ask his advice about selling it. I promised to let him have a look at it, as he says it is unique. I had no time to leave it with him.

I left a green canvas suit-case and a small red

dressing-case with the caretaker of Liberty Hall. I've had them there some time. I dare say Peter's arrested, but he wasn't mixed up in anything, so he may be out. I left my bike knocking round the Hall too.

I miss poor 'Poppet' very much and wonder if he has forgotten me. Poor Mrs. Connolly—I wonder where she is, and if you got him from her. I do feel so sorry for her. She was so devoted to her husband. Also she has four children at home and only the two older girls working. With regard to Bessie ——: what I had in mind for her was to start her in a small way in some work after the War. She is a beautiful laundress. Of course she would want another girl with her to do accounts, etc., but you could let her know that she is not forgotten, and the ten shillings a week is only to keep her safe and happy until something can be arranged. It's much better for people to earn their own living if they can.

Poor Bridie —— ought to get a month's wages, at least. She was arrested with me. Bessie would know where she lives: somewhere in Henrietta St. If you can't find Bessie, advertise for her in the evening paper. I hope you found Mrs. Mallin. I wish I knew, for it worries me so to think of her.

I nearly forgot the little Hall in Camden St. Mr. C—— of Richmond St. is the landlord. If things quiet down, I'd like to go on paying the rent for them as hitherto. A little boy called Smith, living in Piles building, could find out. The landlord, of course, might know. He was quite nice.

I feel as if I were giving you such a lot of worries and bothers, and I feel, too, that I haven't remembered half. Anyhow, it's very economical living here! and I half feel glad that I am not treated as a political prisoner, as I would then be tempted to eat, smoke and dress at my own expense! In the meantime, all my debts will be paid, I live free, and after a time I suppose I will be allowed to write again and see a visitor. I don't know the rules. But do try to get in touch with Mrs. C——, Mrs. M——, and Bessie —— for me. I would be sorry for any of them to be hungry, and I would be sorry too if they thought I had forgotten them, for they were friends.

By the way, the garden seat and tools might be of use to Susan. There are a few decent plants, too, which she could take if she likes, and a couple of decent rose-trees.

Now, darling, don't worry about me, for I'm not too bad at all, and it's only a mean spirit that grudges paying the price.

Everybody is quite kind, and though this is not exactly a bed of roses, still many rebels have had much worse to bear. The life is colourless, the beds are hard, the food peculiar, but you might say that of many a free person's life, and when I think of what the Fenians suffered, and of what the Poles suffered in the 'sixties, I realise that I am extremely lucky. So don't worry your sweet old head. I don't know if you are still here, so I am sending this to Susan to forward.

I hope that I shall live to see you again some day and I shall live in hopes.

With very much love to you three darlings. I can see your faces when I shut my eyes.

CONSTANCE MARKIEVICZ WITH HER DAUGHTER AND STEPSON

Constance Gore-Booth as a child

Eva Gore-Booth as a child

Eva and Constance Gore-Booth

Constance de Markievicz ICA T.D.

(Irish Citizen Army; Member of the Dail

Photo : Poole, Waterford.

Constance Markievicz and her dog

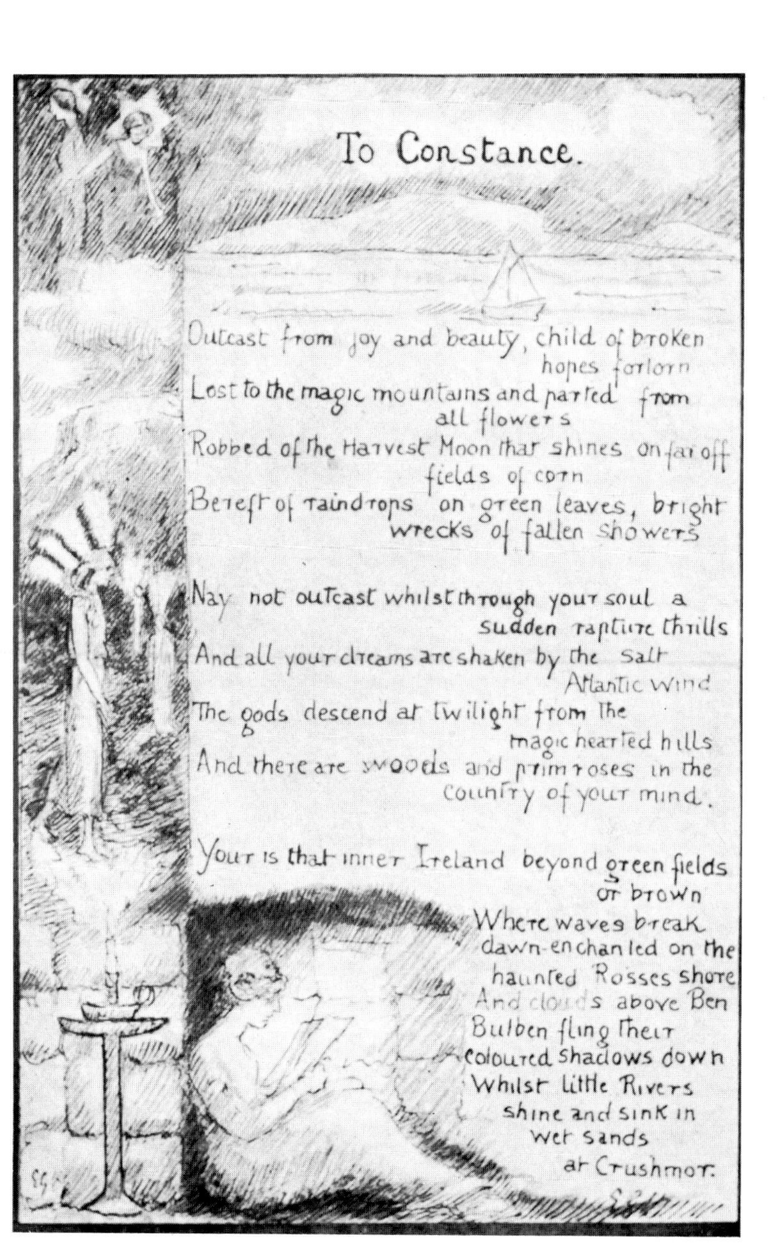
To Constance.
Outcast from joy and beauty, child of broken hopes forlorn
Lost to the magic mountains and parted from all flowers
Robbed of the Harvest Moon that shines on far off fields of corn
Bereft of raindrops on green leaves, bright wrecks of fallen showers
Nay not outcast whilst through your soul a sudden rapture thrills
And all your dreams are shaken by the salt Atlantic wind
The gods descend at twilight from the magic hearted hills
And there are woods and primroses in the country of your mind.
Your is that inner Ireland beyond green fields or brown
Where waves break dawn-enchanted on the haunted Rosses shore
And clouds above Ben Bulben fling their coloured shadows down
Whilst little Rivers shine and sink in wet sands at Crushmor.

Do not be lonely,
Dear, nor grieve,
This Christmas Eve,
Is it so vain a thing
That your Hearts Harper,
dark Roseen,
Crownéd with all her
Sixteen Stars,
A wandering Singer, yet
a Queen,
Outside your prison bars,
Stands carolling.

CHRISTMAS CARD—POEM AND ILLUSTRATIONS BY EVA GORE-BOOTH

Constance Markievicz and Father Scott

Return to Ireland, 1917

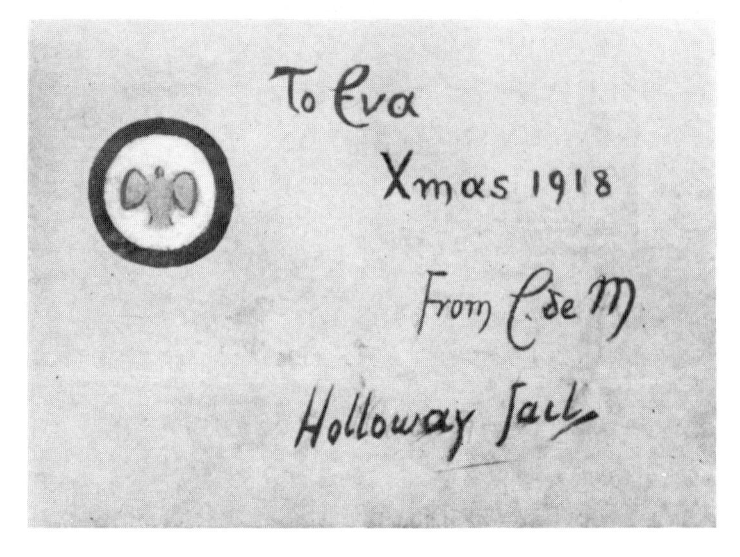

Book cover and inscription painted by CONSTANCE MARKIEVICZ in Holloway Gaol

Photo : J. Cashman.

Countess Markievicz, Mr. de Valera and other Deputies on the way to the Dail, 1927

Photo : The College Studios, Dublin,

LYING IN STATE

THE REPUBLICAN PLOT, GLASNEVIN

Photo : Independent Newspapers, Ltd., Dublin.

MR. DE VALERA, MR. RUTTLEDGE AND OTHER DEPUTIES CARRYING THE COFFIN

Photo : Independent Newspapers, Ltd., Dublin.

Funeral Procession in Dublin

Eva Gore-Booth

UNDATED FRAGMENTS ON UNOFFICIAL PAPER, 1916

Unofficial paper

No date.

I am alas! going into exile. Make a point to try and get in to see me. I believe you could by influence. Do you know S—— ? and is he an M.P. ? He and I were great allies in the Strike, and he might be willing to help. I know he liked me personally. He might get the Labour people to put 'questions,' anyhow.

Remember, I don't mind being in jail, and if it is better for the cause, I'm prepared to remain here. My only desire is to be of use to those outside in the long, tedious struggle with England. Nothing else matters really to me.

I believe that by rights I am entitled to receive and write one letter on moving, so that if you get no letter in a few weeks, write and say that previously, at your visit, I arranged to write to you always. Quote this rule and ask why you have not heard. They would do a good deal to avoid any fuss and to combat the idea that we are being ill-treated.

This is unofficial paper! and written under huge difficulties!

Remember it is only by pushing and sort of discreet threats and making yourself disagreeable that you will be able to do anything for us.

I am going to Aylesbury. I shall be quite amiable, and am not going to hunger-strike, as am advised by comrades not to. It would suit the Government very well to let me die quietly!

Unofficial paper

No date, no address.

You see, the gap has been thrown and I have found a real friend, and it makes the whole difference: both mentally and bodily. She is taking awful risks for me and both body and soul are ministered to. Tit-bits of news and 'tuck.'

I want you to give her a copy of our book, with your autograph. Try to find some person connected with —— that has not too grand an address, who could then just send her a picture postcard with her name and address and to whom she could then write and let her know if she was going into town and call for news. Also give her tit-bits of rebel news, that must not be sent through the post.

Trust her absolutely, and let not your right hand know what your left hand doeth (Esther of course excepted). None of the crew or the family must even guess, for people *will* talk.

You had probably better not try and see her again, as you are both probably under watchful and protective eyes.

At present, anyhow, I see my friend a lot. I am sending you also some things to do for me.

Unofficial paper

No date, no address.

DARLING,—This will go to-morrow, with my love. For God's sake be discreet.

I am alright and not a bit unhappy. I love the book, it is a real joy. They have put the Rose in the triangle on its side, didn't I put it upright ?

Ask me all the questions you can think of.

It makes all the difference having a friend here.

Don't count on my getting out for ever so long, unless a real fuss is made (home and America). I don't see why they should let me go.

You should get ' questions ' asked—on anything you can think of—the company one is in, starvation, etc., and try to make them publish the trials.

You've probably done all this ! I am so in the dark.
They don't want a continuous fuss.

Let me know the Trades Unions conditions for workrooms *temperature*. The Trades Unions should have a visitor or inspector here. They should start jail reform. The people are all poor people, and they should see to them.

I love being in poetry and feel so important ! [1]

Unofficial paper

These questions should be asked me and all political prisoners at a visit :

What do you weigh ? What was your normal weight ?
What do you get to eat ? Can you eat it ?
How much exercise do you get per day ?
How often do you get clean underclothes ?
Are you constipated ? Can you get medicine ?
What temperature is the room you work in ?
What is your task ? How much do you do in a week ?

If they won't let me or any of the others answer, push to get answers by every possible means.

[1] Refers to Eva's poem to her.

AYLESBURY PRISON
August 1916—*June* 1917

AYLESBURY PRISON,
August 8, 1916.

DEAREST OLD DARLING,—The one thing I have gained by my exile is the privilege of writing a letter, but there is very little to say, as I do not suppose 'an essay on prison life' would pass the Censor, however interesting and amusing it might be!

What you have called 'my misplaced sense of humour' still remains to me, and I am quite well and cheerful.

I saw myself, for the first time for over three months, the other day, and it is quite amusing to meet yourself as a stranger. We bowed and grinned, and I thought my teeth very dirty and very much wanting a dentist, and I'd got very thin and very sunburnt. In six months I shall not recognise myself at all, my memory for faces being so bad! I remember a fairy tale of a princess, who banished mirrors when she began to grow old. I think it showed a great lack of interest in life. The less I see my face, the more curious I grow about it, and I don't resent it getting old.

It's queer and lonely here, there was so much life in Mountjoy. There were sea-gulls and pigeons, which I had quite tame, there were 'Stop Press' cries, and little boys splashing in the canal and singing Irish songs, shrill and discordant, but with such vigour. There was a black spaniel, too, with long, silky ears, and a most attractive convict-baby with a squint, and soft Irish voices everywhere. There were the trains, 'Broadstone and Northwall' trams, and even an old melodeon, and a man trying to play an Irish tune on a bugle over the wall! Here it is so still and I find it so hard to understand what anyone says to me, and they seem to find the same trouble with me. 'English as she is spoke' can be very puzzling. One thing nice here is the hollyhocks in the garden. They seem to understand gardening here. There is a great crop of carrots, too, which we pass every day, going to 'exercise' round and round in a ring—like so many old hunters in a summer.

I had the loveliest journey over here. My escort had never been on the sea before and kept thinking she was going to be ill. I lay down and enjoyed a sunny porthole and a fresh breeze. There was a big air-ship (like the picture of a Zeppelin) cruising about when we arrived. I was awfully pleased, as I had never seen one. I do so long to fly! Also I'd love to dive in a submarine.

I dreamt of you the other night. You had on a soft-looking dark blue small hat, and it was crooked. You had bought tickets and three donkeys, and you were going to take Esther and me to Egypt, of all places! When I woke up I had to laugh, but it was wonderfully vivid. Look it up in a dream-book. I have dreamed a good deal since I was in jail and I scarcely ever did so before.

I'd love to show you all the doggerel I wrote in Mountjoy, though I know you'd only jeer—in a kindly way. I love writing it so, and I've not lost it. It's in my head all right!

When is your next book coming out, and the one with my pictures, if it ever does? They were very bad. I can do much better now. I was just beginning to get some feeling into my black and white when I left Ireland. I made quills out of rooks' feathers that I found in the garden. They are much nicer than most pens: you can get such a fine, soft line.

My darling, I repeat—*don't* worry about me. I am quite cheerful and content, and I would have felt very small and useless if I had been ignored. I am quite patient and I believe that everything will happen for the best.

One thing I should enjoy getting out for, and that would be to see the faces of respectable people when I met them !

I don't like to send anyone my love, for fear that that most valuable offering would be spurned. I expect, though, that Molly has a soft spot for me somewhere. Very best love to Esther and to Susan and all the 'rebelly crew,' if ever you come across them.

Do go to the Transport Union Headquarters if ever you go to Dublin. They'd all think you were me, and they would love to see you and you could tell them about me.

Send me a budget of news and gossip, when you can write, about all my pals and my family, and anything amusing at all.—Yours,

CON(VICT 12).

AYLESBURY PRISON,
September 21, 1916.

DEAREST OLD DARLING,—I wonder if you expect this. I was always a rotten correspondent and hated writing and now it is such a joy. I could go on babbling for ever, though there is nothing to write about. I did love seeing you and Esther so. By the way, I hope she got her hat all right. Yours was very nice. You don't know what a picture the two of you made, all soft, dreamy colours.

(Moral : always visit criminals in your best clothes, blue and grey for choice, if it's me !) [1]

I am now going to see if anything arises out of the minutes—*i.e.* your last letter.

[1] We used to borrow every bright thing our friends possessed, to wear when we visited prisons.

First, tell O. M—— not to get into my boat, unless she has the health of an ostrich. I often think how lucky it is that I am here rather than you! Give her my love. I would so much have liked to see her, and have since found out that I may have *three* visitors! But I *must* give their names.

Puzzle—how find out for next time, so as to give their names? *You* may answer this, but it's very hard to tell now who will be able to come here in January!

Is *James* W—— Lady Cecilia's husband? I know several of that name. He was a dear and awfully nice to me when I was young.

I have been dreaming again. A school of village boys, perched on high, high stools at enormous desks. You the schoolmarm, in blue. Boy turns round, in a blue holland pinny with shorts, bare legs and socks and E——'s head *and a beard!* It seemed quite natural! He had been writing x's on a paper divided into squares, two on the top line and three on the bottom thus:

x x
x x x

Thank Susan and Violet a thousand times for settling the house. It must have been an awful job. I'd love to write to Susan. Tell her how I am and that I often think of her the right side of the bars in Dublin.

I wish that for your next visit you would try and get a statement of accounts from J——. I want to know what bills are paid. Some might easily get left out otherwise, as people would not know where to send bills. Find out if he did anything about Christmas cards. I wrote him about some drawings I had done. I hope Mrs. M. is getting her £1 a week all right. Give all the crew my love. Tell Andy Dunn to go on singing. P—— will know where to find him.

I often think of the 'click' and the refugees and our kitchen teas. Tell Andy too that later on we'll try to get someone to teach him, and ask him to give my love to Mr. N——, if he will accept such a gift from a felon!

By the way, convicts can have photos, so send me yours, I always forget to tell you this—and Maev's.

Talking of dreams—*fix* five minutes in the day and think of me, I will think of you at the same time and we'll do it as often as we can. Tell me what hour when you write.

Don't hurry to answer this, as news may come of Casi.

I send my love to all my friends in the Transport Union and the Co-op. Tell them that I am often with them in spirit, and that I have nothing but happy, pleasant, busy memories of them.

Mr. F—— is a friend there, of course he may be in jail!

So many of my friends I know nothing about. Mr. —— O'B——, too, I'd like to be remembered to, and oh! so many more!—and I don't even know if they're alive!

Where is Bessie —— stopping? Give her my love. I think she would be very wise to go to America. Give her a letter to 'John Brennen' if she goes. 'John' would remember her, and would, I am sure, like to see her, and she would be something from home for Bessie.

Do you know what the other Gifford girls are doing? Tell P—— to give them my love and to M. C——. She and P—— are great pals.

By the way, did you remember about the blue serge dress? P. has the trunk. The key, a small one, was in a red leather bag left in Liberty Hall. The second key was left in a house that was burnt. My lace, with a lot of household gods are in the trunk. The dress is at the bottom.

I wonder if 'Mr. P.' has forgotten me? I often think of his nice brown eyes. Do you remember how Reginald played with him at Manchester?

I am not sure which Mr. Power you mean. Is he 'M——,' and very good-looking and a friend of Violet's?

I am now going to lapse into verse! I want you to criticise. Tell me something about metre and what to aim at. I am quite humble and I know I'm not a poet, but I do love trying.

High walls hang round on every side
A cage of cruel red,
The sickly grass is bleached and dried,
As brick the flower bed.

The fierce rays of the sun down beat,
The burning flagstones scorch our feet,
As in the noonday's blighting heat
We walk with weary tread.

Upon our cheeks a blessed breeze,
And in our weary ears
The rustling talk of happy trees
Glad that refreshment nears,
A softly soothing, gentle drip,
Wee drops for grass and flowers to sip,
God's chalice for the moth's grey lip
Or angels' happy tears.

Of course, I know it's only jingle!

I loved the metre of the dedication you read me out. Trying to do a thing oneself makes one appreciate anything good much more. Write me a verse or two in your next letter and tell me how to get to work! Don't tell me to wait till I am blest by the 'gift'!

Don't worry about me. I am quite happy. It is in nobody's power to make me unhappy. I am not afraid, either of the future or of myself. You know well how little comforts and luxuries ever meant to me. So at the worst I'm only bored. With so many thought-waves of love and kindliness coming over to me, how *could* I be unhappy? Indeed, I feel very privileged.

You remember 'They shall be remembered for ever.' What we stood for, and even poor me will not be forgotten, and 'the people shall hear them for ever?' That play of W. B.'s was a sort of gospel to me. 'If any man would help me, he must give me himself, give me all.'

I love hearing about all the people you write about. I remember Clare A——'s mother so well. She was very beautiful and I used to love looking at her. I hope some day to meet C. A. and Ottoline M——. I remember her so well, though I never got to know her. I'm longing to see her.

Tell Miss Reddish I often think of her and of Mrs. Dickinson and all the others, and of the great election we fought and won. Tell Mabel that her sick soldier never came to Dublin. I wrote to him to (I think) Tipperary. I remember Mr. McNeil now quite well; he is awfully nice.

Fancy G—— doing the Grand Tour again! Please give M. £1 of my money for her birthday and ditto for Christmas.

I am so glad about the book. I hope that it will go well and it is a great joy to me to think I may help to sell it, and that my little gift of drawings may be worth something to my old darling.

There are the most beautiful cloud effects here, East and South over big old elms. They are really wonderful. Did not know that England produced anything so heavenly! Oh! for the Dublin Mountains and the soft twilights and the harvest moon on cornfields! I must write a poem about cornfields.

Love to you and Esther, all rebels and felons, comrades and friends!

AYLESBURY PRISON,
December 29, 1916.

DEAREST OLD DARLING,—I was waiting and wondering who ought to write first, and now I've got St. Ursula from you and can contain myself no longer.

Mr. Gavan Duffy interviewed me yesterday and we talked my trial up and down. Of course, I forgot to ask him about Casi and Staskow's things that were lifted by the police! But no matter. He seemed very capable and careful, and he took copious notes.

Do the following lines fit onto the poem I sent you before?—and do they improve it?

> We're folded in a sheet of rain.
> Clasped to the heart of things
> My spirit slips the yoke of pain,
> And one with nature sings.
> 'I am the cloud that floats so free
> The boundless space, the deep blue sea.
> Of Heaven and Peace I hold the key
> And poise on golden wings.'

I am not quite sure if it's sense. Words are such odd things—they suddenly become alive and mean all sorts of things on their own and not what you meant at all. And they simply run away with me and I can't manage them at all.

I have begun another poem, but one is so hustled here one can't do much. But I love trying and trying to put things into verse. It seems to show one so much of the beauty and the secret and symbolic side of life that one never dreamt of before.

All that has happened to me seems to have opened to me such wonderful new doors. I seem to pass through it all now as a dream. Day by day slips by and I am not unhappy. I just live in a sort of expectant peace and feel so very close to *you*.

Christmas day has come, and more and more beautiful cards. They seem to me to be symbols of the wonderful love and friendship that is waiting for me and fighting for me outside.

I am blest with such a number of warm-hearted, true friends. If I had not got to jail, perhaps I would not have found it out. You see, there is compensation in everything.

Your beloved letter has just come, such a joy. But still no card of your own design.

Brownie is a darling and a real friend. Give her my love and tell her I'm afraid her key was lost. Doesn't that sound mysterious ? She is not one of the 'crew,' but just a dear friend of Casi's and mine, gay and warm-hearted.

Talking of keys, do write and ask Ella Y—— for mine. I lent her nearly all my keys and she never gave them back. She wanted to open something. On second thoughts, *don't*. I'd sooner lose the keys than fuss her, and in any case, they are probably lost, and *I* certainly don't want them !

My head is quite turned with the reviews you sent me ! Those poor rough scribbles ! If ever I get out I'll do a lot more. I've learnt such a lot since.

This is a real jail pen, *vile*, and I couldn't make it do what I wanted in the drawing at all.

Don't make yourself miserable, darling, about me. I am often afraid that you are much more unhappy than I am. I feel a quiet, peaceful, a 'nunc dimitis' sort of feeling.

All my life, in a funny way, seems to have led up to the last year, and it's all been such a hurry-scurry of a life. Now I feel that I have done what I was born to do. The great wave has crashed up against the rock, and now all the bubbles and ripples and little me slip back into a quiet pool of the sea. I am getting even more sentimental than you—in spite of the Censor's cold and unpoetic eye!—but that's how I feel, quite peaceful and calm. Tell me about W. if you think of it and Maud Gonne. Give my love to the doctor, M—— and all of them. I *love* Susan's verse on my card. Wish her a very happy Christmas, with my love. I got three copies of that one, but none of the others.

I had a really lovely dream the other night: try and interpret. A wonderful crimson sun rose in the corner of my cell, slowly passed up and along and stood over my head. It was followed by a gold one and that by a blue one, and they all gave such wonderful lights, and when they passed over my head they left a wonderful opalescent glow of colours that mix and yet keep their own peculiar qualities. It is difficult to explain but it was wonderfully beautiful.

Still more cards came to-day. Such a joy. I inquired about yours, and it came, but I cannot have it until the Home Office has been consulted and approved! My curiosity is most vivid! What *can* you have put on it?

I am so glad that the 'Aonach' went off so well, and love all the news about the Hall. M—— and the dear doctor are splendid. Good luck to them and to M—— and the paper. My soul feels flattered and I'm longing to see you again. It will be quite soon now. I hope it will be all right about Clare A.

Some of my 'army' sent me cards. I never had so many in all my life before. Mrs. M—— R—— sent me such a lovely one. Try and meet her. She paints lovely fans (New English Art Club) and knows Mrs. D——. She is awfully nice.

Now, darling, the limit is approaching and I must be bidding you good-bye. Give my love to Ireland and all her children, my comrades, and to my 'Poppet' and to his foster-mother. I loved the card they sent. Just room enough to tell you how beautiful I think 'dew-pearled cobwebs.' Your words are like colours and lines—so restrained, vivid and pure. I love the end of 'Maeve' so. The peace she found was, I think, rather like mine. But I've gone a step further, I don't need hazel boughs and mystic streams. I've found it in jail.

Don't say 'How conceited!'

The wandering winds of Christmas time,
The twinkling of the stars
Are messengers of hope and love,
Defying prison bars.

The birds that fly about my cage
Are vagrant thoughts that fly
To greet you all at Christmas time—
They wing the wintry sky.

This is supposed to be a Christmas card! for you and all friends. I have already got 46 and love them, such beauties. But I have not got the one you said you were drawing yourself.

You, Esther, Reginald and Beatrice C—— sent me a picture gallery. But who sent Monna Lisa? Thank G—— for her two and Maeve. They were so pretty and such nice poems. Tell M. I wish I were on the boat (picture) with her! However, I am quite cheerful, for Christmas has brought the world of Art and life and hope into my cell. I have all the cards arranged upon the bed and they are the greatest joy.

AYLESBURY PRISON,
January 29, 1917.

BELOVED OLD DARLING,—For goodness sake do take care of your dear old self and don't run any risks. This English climate is so awful that I wonder how you get along at all. Every day for months it seems to freeze. I long for our more considerate and gentle climate, that always gives you a peep at the blessed sun and a soft warm drizzle. I see the sunrise every morning, and it is most beautiful and quite worth the trouble of walking out to see it, though I need hardly tell you that it is not my will-power that guides my weary legs! As I knew you were not coming, I was not disappointed at not seeing you. Esther and Clare were like a bottle of champagne to me, they brightened me up so. I thought Clare lovely and rather like her grandmother, whom I knew quite well. It's such a joy to look at pretty things. I thought my 'Poppet' looked so fat and well; I longed to hug him!

I *loved* your card. As you say, the idea at the back of yours and mine was somewhat the same, but yours was far superior. I loved the group of children round Roseen. You had a wonderful feeling in it all—movement, proportion and design were all excellent. The tone was very nice too. I feel so proud of it being done for me, and of being in three poems. My head is getting very swelled indeed! I like your new poem very much, especially verse three. Your poems have a magic effect on me. They transport me away to beautiful lands of dim sunshine and pearly waves, where beautiful, stately people drift gracefully about. They are all like you and have wild aureoles of golden hair and long white fingers!

I'm awfully interested in astrology; do try to read Maeve's fate in the stars. Nobody seems to remember my birth-hour exactly, so you will have some trouble there! Couldn't you work back from some other date in my life, such as my wedding day? I was late and was only just in time to get married that day. Or twelve o'clock, Monday of Easter Week?—which I think was the moment we started on our 'divine adventure.'

Please give the old Miss T—— my love. How sweet of the poor old dear to want to see me. And E——. I don't understand from your letter whether the shop is still going in Liberty Hall. Which room do you mean by the 'old band room'? The band changed rooms so often! Give my love to E—— and tell her I got her card and think of her often, and Miss C——, who is interned with her. I got very funny and instructive cards from both! I really did love my cards. I never enjoyed any Christmas presents half so much. I did enjoy seeing the photos of M. and the children that Esther brought. Please give her my love and thank her for thinking of it, it was a great pleasure to me. I want you to write and thank little Ronan K—— for a card he sent, also old Mrs. Pearse. The boy is probably at St. Enda's School. It was awfully nice of them to think of me.

I am getting off this letter as quick as I can as they have taken to reckoning your next from the date it goes, not from the date you get your sheet of paper, which, if you delay writing, allows them to rob you of a certain number of letters in a year. I delayed a fortnight over the last, and that fortnight is lost to me in letters.

[12 *lines deleted by the Censor.*]

I'm afraid that my writing has got rather bad. Send me some Sligo news.

I am still reading your 'Maeve.' I think Connaught

should be spelt 'Connacht.' Someone else has probably told you this long ago! but you asked me. I do love Maeve's last speech, but it would be very difficult to make a stage success of.

I long to give you a lecture on writing a verse play. It could be done and a success made of it.

I wish we could collaborate. Aren't I getting conceited? But I feel I understand audiences and stagecraft and play-producing :—by this, I mean the whole process—from author to the meanest super. I include all these as material that goes to produce a dramatic performance, and they must all pull together. You can't play organ music on a Jew's harp, and *you* give your penny whistles organ music to play.

Some day I may get a chance of trying to explain. I can feel it so well, but can't do it myself.

I am longing to know how you are, but am not anxious about you. I *was* for two days some time ago, but then got into my head that you were better, and now I feel confident that you are getting on alright, though it may be slow. But don't hurry to get up, as you love me.

I've been writing

[12 *lines deleted by the Censor*.]

With best love to all my darlings.

'Beyond earth's barred gates' every morning at 9.0 I seek you there.

AYLESBURY PRISON,
February 27, 1917.

DEAREST OLD DARLING,—The sun is shining, the sky is so blue and the horrid red walls make it look bluer still, and I seem to see it shining through your golden halo and touching up your blues and greys, and then I think 'perhaps she is in a murky English fog' and I grudge it being able to touch you and envelop you in its embrace. And then I think: 'perhaps the same fog will blow over here, and will have us both in the same grip'—and so I wander on, quite drivelling.

I loved your last poem and letter. If you can think of it, do bring Mrs. Meynell's poem next visit. I am burning with curiosity: I think I told you, but can't be sure.

Please tell 'C——' not to publish any *unpublished* poems of mine without asking *me* (through you). Anything once published they can do what they like with, but there are one or two I don't want published yet awhile.

I was so glad to hear of K—— the old darling. I'm sure he's a rebel in his heart. He's one of the people I should really love to see. He and I were so very sympathetic always. Tell him I was so glad to get a message from him and give him my love. He always feels like part of the family.

The greedy starlings are making such a row on the window-ledge, fighting most rudely over the remains of my dinner.

This morning a wedge-shaped flight of wild geese flew over us as we were exercising, making their weird cackling cry, and they brought me home at once. Do you remember the wonderful monster, supposed to be a cow, that Joss concocted, to stalk them from behind or within, and how they fled shrieking for miles at the sight, and how unapproachable they were for weeks owing to the fright they got? The Trojan horse was nothing to that beast.

I have just been reading your letter again and can't help wishing that I were Percy's cow or pig!

Who is the D . . . at Barrington? I can't read the name, and where is Street?

Give Father Albert my love and tell him I often think of him.

Lord MacDonnell was an old friend, also his wife and nice daughter. He always impressed me as a very straight man, although he was a politician! I liked him very much.

Give Emmy my love and tell her I would have sent her a gilt-edged invitation card, but the censor won't allow me! I'd love to see her, don't let her *not* come if she *says* she is coming. Once she gets a pass she must come!

I was glad to hear of Mrs. M——, and so interested to hear that the boy is learning to draw. Perhaps I shall be able to help him, some day. Who knows?

What a lot of letters I am letting you in for, you poor old darling. It would probably upset Mrs. M—— very much, seeing me. It would bring it all back to her. They were such a devoted pair. The last things he said to me were about her.

If you are writing to any of the Hall crowd, tell them I got their cards. The Co-op. girls sent a joint one, and the N—— sent me one each. Tell them to remember me to Mrs. N—— and ask for news of her husband.

Now I'm going to write out a poem, about another jail-bird—a thrush. It's true!

He sang the song of the waking Spring,
The song of the budding tree,
Of the chrysalis cradling the butterfly's wing
And the waking to life of each earth-bound thing
That the sun comes out to free.

He sang of himself and of five blue eggs
Black-spotted and warm and alive,
Of baby-birds hopping on uncouth legs,
Of worms lying cool by the sheltered hedge.
Oh! how he would live and thrive!

He sang of the sunrise, all azure and gold,
He laughed at the prison wall.
The joy of his song made him happy and bold,
He forgot that life could be cruel and cold,
That each shadowy nook could a foe enfold.
His wings could defy them all.

In the air was the rapture of dawn and Spring
But the glittering sun was cold.
The wind from the west, with its sweet salt sting,
Was quenched from the north with his haste to bring
Clouds discoloured and lowering
Which down on the day he rolled.

White on the world the snow-flakes fall
And cold and death have their sway.
They beat on his wings in a smothering pall,
And close at the foot of the prison wall
Which loomed above him so endless and tall
Frozen to death he lay.

Away into space the storm-clouds float
And the earth is again awake.
Cold from his heart the snow-flakes float,
The reviving sun kissed his soft-dappled throat,
But it never will throb to another note
Nor thrill with a sparkling shake.

He will never build the nest of his song
Nor sing to his brooding mate.
Was he right to rejoice or was he all wrong ?
Do hope and faith but to fools belong ?
Is courage all a mistake ?

No effort is lost though all may go wrong
And death come to shadow and change.
He gave his best, and simple and strong
Broke the darkness which lasted the winter long
With Spring-time's triumphant melodious song,
A melody wild and strange,

> And the air had thrilled to his morning song,
> The ripples of life and glee
> That floated, all rainbow-tinted, along,
> Striking a note that rang true and strong
> On the strings of Eternity.

It's very long, isn't it? and they say that 'good things are done up in small parcels.'

I love your birthday poem so much. You've missed your vocation. You should be a Poet Laureate. I will make you mine!

I am sure no one had so much poetry written about them *spontaneously* before, while they were alive. Ordinary kings and queens have to pay for it, so they get rubbish.

Pegasus, being thoroughbred, will not stand a spur—even a golden one.

I wanted so to talk about Blake and about horoscopes the other day, but of course forgot about both! I wish I'd known Blake. I would love to argue about light and shade with him. He was all wrong—strange for such a great man. He took the superficial view that shadow is to soften and conceal. It never seemed to dawn on him that bad draughtsmen may use shadows for this: but a Master, such as Rembrandt, has as true an outline as Flaxman, and each shadow is a definite thing with a shape, as much so as an arm or a leg. But I must not write lectures on Art or Blake! I have no room and you no time to read.

Take care of yourself, you blessed old dear. I am very well, and luckily for me escaped my usual bad cold, which generally gets hold of me in January. The frosty weather always agrees with me.

Last night I dreamt I was walking on the cliff beyond John's Port, with a ripe cornfield with poppies on my right, when a great khaki-coloured snake rushed out of the corn and slithered down the cliff!

You didn't tell me if you found any meanings in the colours of the winds.

Molly B—— is a great girl. I wish I could write her some songs. She sings with such go and has such a nice voice. Give her my love and tell her I long to hear her sing again and I often think of the times we had together.

Give Susan my love. It's awfully good of her to help Bessie. By the way, if Bessie marries, I promised her £10 to set up. If she married, it might help things, so ask Susan to let her know I have not forgotten. I don't even know if she wants to marry!—and remember, in setting her up, I don't mind a few pounds more or less, *but her mother must not live with her*. She's a devil.

Please ask Joss to give Maeve £1 to buy an Easter egg.

You are so encouraging about my poetry, and a little bird tells me all the time that it's twaddle, and I laugh at myself and go on and inflict it on you.

Now I am arriving at the 'wall' and so must pull up.

I hope you like being a 'respectable friend' (see preface to this letter).

AYLESBURY PRISON,
May 14, 1917.

DEAREST OLD DARLING,—When I came up to my cell after seeing you I found this old blue sheet, the bird's own colours! so I begin at once.

I loved your drawings. They are quite wonderful. You have a wonderful gift for line and a great imagination. All you need is the knack of wagging a pen and that is practice. You want to go on and *on* and *on*. Your figures have such grace and life. Do bring more next time.

Did I ever thank Reginald for his Easter card with

its tri-colour messages ? I *loved* it, and those cards of good pictures are such a help to look at.

I want you to send the following messages to Father Albert : he was such a wonderful friend.

[11 *lines deleted by the Censor.*]

I neglected this epistle to the 'Birds' Nest' all Sunday, for I suddenly got a craze to work out Clare's book-plate and it came out much nicer. I've started Esther's too, and I've got some more ideas for it and it is coming out better than I expected. I am going to do your birthday card all over again. I was really rather seedy and that is really why I went off into that wild smudging that you saw. I cannot wag a pen monotonously unless I am very fit, and I am feeling fine to-day.

I have some of Gertrude's primroses, some roses and carnations in my cell and I talk nonsense to them and they are great company.

Suddenly I heard you shouting to me this morning. I wondered so what you were trying to tell me, for I couldn't hear. One's imagination plays one such odd tricks.

Last night I dreamt too, such a strange beautiful dream. I was in an artist's house. He was a sculptor —German or Norwegian I think—and everything was very, very old, simple and massive. The windows were long, low slits with tiny panes, like some palaces in the time of the Huns and Goths, and the only picture there was of a girl, all in blue, with a mushroom hat of iridescent blue feathers, yellow-gold hair and a pale face. While I was looking at it, the figure suddenly looked down at a paper lying in its lap, and I realised that it was you ! There were such lovely lilies growing in carved stone jars in that house and through the windows the sun shone on trees and a river.

I am still reading Blake diligently and I like the two you quoted immensely and I too was struck by the prophecy. Do you know 'the Song of Liberty?' It ends with :—

'Empire is no more and now the lion and the wolf shall cease.' I wonder if that is a prophecy too? I don't understand anything else in it from beginning to end! Tiriel, Har and Heva etc. also puzzle me much.' I suppose they are really only fancy names for quite commonplace articles.

I have just been given F. Albert's gifts, so please say 'Thank you a thousand times' and tell him I love the beads in my own rebel colours!

No one who has not been in jail can realise what a joy it is to get a coloured picture post-card!

The *Life of S. Francis* too looks awfully interesting.

I am already looking forward to your next visit in the flesh. They are like flashes of sunlight.

Your letter still smells delicious. I have it here under my nose.

I wonder so who is acting 'tail' and who 'dog' in Dublin now.

The younger generation of rebels will have a great chance now of building up and doing things for the country. I have great faith in the young.

These last few days the trees have simply flung out their green leaves. They did it at night, so that I should not learn their secret!

The one thing I am learning here is to watch everything closely, whether it is trees or blackbeetles, birds or women.

The sparrows are delightful—like men at their best.

Someone once said 'the more I know men, the more I love my dog,' and I think I rather agree. Dogs don't lie: I don't suppose birds do!

What's G—— doing over here ? and what's happening to Muncaster ?

It's tragic, the way things break up and change. He spent his whole time for such years building up that place, and now I suppose the next man will either alter everything or let the whole place drop to pieces. I should like to have seen it again. It must be rather awful for G——.

Dusk is coming on and the B.B. will have finished pecking at her evening meal by now and is probably preening her feathers and wondering what I am doing.

Again, another day ! and I don't know why I have delayed so long over this. Laziness and dullness I suppose, but really, if you come to think of it, I have nothing to talk about, only vague nonsense.

The Chapel was a treat this morning, with the smell of the lilies. How I love the smell of them ! I think they are your flower.

(Saturday) I have just seen the Governor. Miss Emily N—— wants to visit me. Of course I'd love to see her, but I don't want her visit to interfere with you. (I wish people would go to *you* about visiting me and let *you* arrange. I'm so afraid of someone getting your pass—by accident.) It's so impossible for me to arrange and I only want what and who is convenient to you.

Naturally I am delighted to see any friends.

There is only a week now till I see you. You probably won't get this till afterwards.

I have written one more verse to the B.B. It ends in the middle of a sentence. Here it is. Next verse not done enough to send.

> Then my soul strikes the magical key-note
> And the circle of wonder is born
> When all beautiful thoughts that are free float
> In a vortex out to the dawn,

While the air grows heavy around me
As the Presence encloses my soul
And I know that my Blue Bird has found me,
That together we rule and control.

(I *am* sorry for the Censor !)

By day I dream all sorts of vague ideas and theories about sounds, all sounds being musical notes. Echo will only call back to you when you pitch your voice on certain notes. Certain notes are re-echoed by dogs, who howl if you play to them on the violin or piano or sing them. There is a certain pitch that carries best in every different Hall. I think that there is a lot of natural magic in sounds.

That's an awfully nice photo of you drawing. I wish Esther were in the room too.

The ' brown wind of Connaught ' is blowing. He will kiss you for me and ruffle your curls at sundown. He passes here on his way from Ireland.

There is a small sycamore tree here in the garden. It's not very ' paintable.'

I am having an egg for breakfast !

Alice Milligan's card was prophetic, only it's not a ' duck ! '

They say there was another air raid. I hope you were not alarmed or deafened.

AYLESBURY PRISON,
June 9, 1917.

BELOVED OLD DARLING,—How short your visit always seems and how much must always remain unsaid, unless the powers that be provide me with a brand-new and absolutely clean and unwritten tablet for my poor old memory !

I meant to have asked you where the meeting was that you could not go to, and where Dr. L. spoke.

I also wanted to tell you to ask Susan for a motto to illustrate for the book-plate she probably has, but I'd love to do her a motto.

Now don't work and worry yourself to death about me, you old blessing. I am wonderfully content and I know that all is going well with Kathleen and that there is nothing I can do in my own country that others can't do as well.

The hours slip by, like rosary beads of dragons' teeth, with a big glowing opal bead to mark the rhythm—your visit.

Don't I drivel ?

It is really very curious that you should write a poem on and give a lecture on S. Francis. For I have been thinking of him a great deal and thinking out pictures of him. I could find out very little about him here, then F. A. sent me his life—' out of the blue ' as they say—and then your letter came.

I have copied your poem and decorated it already. It's very beautiful, the poem.[1]

Did I ever tell you that ' Squidge ' sent me a card ? I want you to give my love and thanks to her.

I am so interested in little Doyle's horoscope. You must make it out for Janey, his mother, for me to give her if ever I get out ! Perhaps you may drift across

[1] The poem referred to is one called ' To Dora Sigerson Shorter.'

THE SAD YEARS

You whom I never knew,
Who lived remote, afar,
Yet died of the grief that tore my heart,
Shall we live through the ages alone, apart,
Or meet where the souls of the sorrowful are
Telling the tale on some secret star,
How your death from the root of my sorrow grew,
You whom I never knew ?

Mrs. Shorter died after Easter week 1916.

them, but I am sure she would be most interested in it and would love to have it signed by you and dated, to put by until he grows up. You have hit one nail on the head in it in a wonderful way.

What you poetically term my 'ascetic way of living' certainly has great compensations. I think that something I might call the 'subconscious self' develops only at the expense of your body—of course with the consent and desire of your will. To develop it, it is necessary to cut yourself off from a great deal of human intercourse, to work hard and eat little, and as your subconscious self emerges, it comes more and more in tune with the subconscious soul of the world, in which lie all the beauties and subtleties you speak of.

I think, too, that any friendships worth having have their roots on this plane: and, too, that this is the secret of the monastic orders and of the hermits and philosophers from the beginning of the world, especially of the Eastern mystics.

It used to puzzle me so when I read of girls—like Maud's sisters—becoming Carmelite nuns, and I could never see either the sense or the use of it. Since I have been here I understand it absolutely, and I know that for people with a vocation the compensation far outweighs the things you give up.

You ask me if the flowers last. They are wonderful. One lily—I threw it away on Monday—lasted one month and two days. I think it knew that I loved it. I am always going to keep a flower or leaf in water from one visit to another.

I am glad that I am President of so many things! I should always advise societies to choose their presidents from among jail-birds, as presidents are always such a bore and so in the way on committees! I always rather liked taking the chair, for the fun of bursting through all the red tape : and when remonstrated with, I could always corner them by saying, 'ridiculous *English* conventions ! Surely an *Irish* Committee is not going to be bound by them ? ' Now they'll be able, on all the committees in Ireland, to waste all their precious time tying up their minds and other people's in red tape. Notices of motion about rubbish taking the place of the divine inspiration of the moment, and then all that twaddle about amendments and addenda and procedure of every kind ! I wonder whether you would get dignified and shocked ? It is such years since we served on committees together : not since we went out to force a Suffrage Bill through Parliament. I have no ambition to have a vote for an English Parliament, and don't suppose I would use it. I don't think that Parliaments are much use anyhow. All authority in a country always seems to get into the hands of a clique and permanent officials.

I think I am beginning to believe in anarchy. Laws work out as injustice, legalised by red tape.

You have such a lot of real good news and interesting gossip in your letter. You always manage to tell me about the things I most want to hear about.

The Fianna news was very cheering, and isn't the Doctor splendid ?—when one considers that her paying patients must almost all be in the enemy's camp ! I call it awfully plucky and fine of her to come out in public the way she does. It's wonderful too the amount she does for the poor. I feel so proud of having introduced her to the real Ireland. One has such wonderful luck sometimes. If another doctor hadn't suddenly lost her mother, I should never have met ours.

I think my handwriting is getting awful. I think the sort of work I do is bad for writing.

Do you ever hear of Mrs. Connolly and her daughter Ina, great friends of mine? Ask for news of them, next time you write to the doctor or any of them. Ina was a splendid girl. Ask too if the 'Feis' has come off yet.

Do you remember the verse labelled 'Introduction' at the head of Blake's *Gates of Paradise*? Judges ought to take it to heart.

I am already beginning to get excited over your next visit and to wonder whom you are going to bring.

I wonder if any of my visitors will ever get into jail themselves? Take my advice, and *don't you*, for you are not strong enough. Some people it would be very good for. I am sure that six months of it would do P—— a lot of good!

I saw a lovely moon the other night, and in my mind's eye began to play billiards with it. I rolled my mind into a great ball and cannoned off the moon into the B.B.'s window. If you think of it, the moon is the apex of so many triangles.

I would have loved to hear your lecture on the 'Peace of St. Francis.' You can tell me something about it, if you've room, in your next letter.

It's so funny to me to realise that I never wrote letters until I got into jail! and it's really quite an amusing game! You're so awfully good. I sometimes find it on my conscience that I give you so much to do. I must be an awful nuisance. Don't wear yourself out, that's all.

Did you ever visit the catacombs in Rome? The old paintings must be so interesting. I have just been reading about them. I have always longed to go to Rome. That and the Pyramids and perhaps the Parthenon, which you would almost have to pass; I always feel I know these places quite well.

This morning, when the flutter of wings came, at nine o'clock, I was peeling swedes. They, you may not know, are a kind of turnip largely eaten by sheep! We have been eating so many lately that I feel I shall soon begin to 'baa-baa.' But they are very good indeed. You should try them, though perhaps as a veg.[1] you already know them.

Now, darling, the limit is reached and there is no space for love which would require a very big one and remembrances to all friends. I hope Esther will be coming again soon. I long to show her the book. I know she would understand.

[1] Vegetarian.

HOLLOWAY JAIL
DURING INTERNMENT
1918—1919

HOLLOWAY JAIL,
June 8, 1918.

DEAREST OLD DARLING,—How I long to see you. I am getting more and more bored and inquisitive here! What is the meaning of it all? We wonder more and more. Is it political or military? Anyhow, it is not to their credit and will certainly rebound on our oppressors. Myself, I think it is about the best thing that could have happened for Ireland, as there was so little to be done there, only propaganda, and our arrests carry so much further than speeches. Sending you to jail is like pulling out all the loud stops on all the speeches you ever made or words you ever wrote! I've been reading the Billing trial. What a show-up for England! What a judge, what a jury and what a crowd! I wonder what a 'competent authority' would think of the merits of that and of our 'German Conspiracy'? It's really comic opera.

We are only allowed foreign papers here, which is one of the mean and petty ways of a great Empire to tease its imprisoned rebels, as there could be no practical reason for not allowing us the Irish papers. We are not allowed Labour papers either, even English ones!

Mrs. Clarke only got news of her children to-day. She is in a fair way to break down, as she has been fretting so about them and neither ate nor slept. She simply lived for them and is one of your ideal mothers.

Now I want you to write to the Dublin Military Authority. They have sent my attaché case, having removed all letters and papers and *my cheque-book*. Now they did not steal Mrs. Clarke's letters nor Maud Gonne's, so why mine? Manuscript poetry, letters and notes of my own (typed and in copybook) for lectures and speeches. The notes are on Ireland's Geographical Status and her claim to Sovereign Statehood and on various industries and history. I can't say anything nice because of the Censor's prying eyes. Much love to you and much dislike to him!

June 22.

I am radiantly happy! Don't be alarmed. 'Stone walls do not a prison make,' etc.! I've just got the result. Such a victory! Our arrests did it! for we were not at all certain; in fact, most doubtful of results. Ireland is always true to those who are true to her. Putting us away cleared the issues for us, so much better than our own speeches ever could.

Send me your stories to read when they come out. I am longing to read them. I don't think I have any talent that way myself. Could you send me the *Herald*, the *Dreadnought* and the *Socialist* (through the Censor)?

Thank Reginald for his book. I had procured the *Programme History* for him and had begun a letter to him, when I was 'took.'

I am quite well-off, for a wonder, so you can buy me any book you think, and also some stockings with thick soles. I passed yours on to Mrs. C. who came with nothing but what she stood up in. Water-colours too, and etching materials. I wish I knew how long they meant to keep me, so as to know what to get in. The whole thing is really laughable. My companions I think of as 'Niobe' and 'Rachel,' as they are the two most complete and perfect—though now, alas! mournful—mothers that I ever met! It's really very bad luck on the kids to lose *both* parents.

I loved 'Mrs. Fits, the rubbish woman.'

I have just got a bundle of Irish papers with all the back news, through the Censor! Do you think he read them? So funny! Just at present I wish I could challenge King George to mortal combat, box the Censor's ears, ask many questions of Ll. George in the English Parliament, publish a newspaper in America and kiss you! etc., etc.

July 19.

I have not heard from you yet this week. I wonder if yours has been stopped by that wretched Censor? There seems to be no method in his madness at all.

I am so glad that you are out of town. London is such a horrid place. Sight, ears, smell, morals and sense of beauty are offended at every moment in this most odious town. (Is this politics?)

You once asked me about Kingston. Give him my love if you see him again. Tell him to get to see me if he can. I dare him! Of course I'd love to see him again. I'm very interested in Greece, and you will be surprised that I like your play very much and I would like to act it.

Please write to Miss D——, Limerick, and tell her that her sister is better. She is a great friend of mine and has been very kind to me and I would like you to know her.

Dulcibella is such an angel, she never forgets us. She sent us raw onions this week. I ate one as big as an egg, and quite believed, for one awful moment, that I was in Aylesbury again and had stolen it!

How long are they going to keep up the pose that they are afraid of our seeing even infants?

I wonder so what will happen to W——, also to George and his cousins. The present popular howl must be very disagreeable to the ears of many alien cousins, who have given their whole lives and energies to the country of their adoption.

W.'s alien father was such an old dear, too, and his native mamma a real crawling old snob. Perhaps you have forgotten W. I often laugh when I think of him.

There is no point in my seeing a solicitor. What can he do but spend my money ?

There is no German Plot, and it is more satisfactory to sit tight than to appeal to law or the want of law that put one here.

July 31.

Got your letter dated 29th. Censor is mending his manners ! and apparently doing a day's work for a day's pay !

I wish I had your book. I would illustrate it, just for fun. Send me a couple of those reproductions—coloured—of Florentine pictures, Christmas cards on brown paper mounts, to copy costumes from and I'll do you a picture for your play.

To-day's *Irish Times* twice alludes to Ireland as a 'Domestic Question.' Liars !

Greek History is very blood-thirsty. Everything I ever read pales before it.

So excited about your new poetry book. My head is so swelled ! I shall soon have to wear a new hat.

After all, darling, you may call yourself a pacifist, but I never inspired you to immortal verse until I had fought in a Rebellion !

Do you read the *Irish Independent* ? If not, do so, for this last fight of the children to play innocent games is too funny for words.

So glad you wrote to Madge. I am giving myself the pleasure of augmenting your birthday present, as my bank-book has just come and I am quite wealthy !

Spend it on a spree or take a holiday or otherwise amuse yourself.

So glad you agree about solicitors.

I'd very much like to see Kingston. . . . We used to be great pals. Mrs. G. has been very tiresome and odd. I don't wonder at B——. I think she must be annoyed and jealous at not being arrested ! It is so tiresome trying to write telegraphically !

Old Mrs. Murphy makes me unhappy. Does she want a few shillings ? D . . . the end of the page !

August 22.

It was a real joy to see your lovely old face grinning behind its specs again ! I wonder, is the realm tottering ever since ? Lots of paints, etc., come. A1. and the brushes are a dream. One tube of oils by mistake. When you return it, you can get it changed for ' Saturn red.'

Your poems are the pick of the basket (anthology). I simply hate poems in slang. Cockney accent makes me stop my ears. War certainly does not inspire great literature. *You* always get away from the obvious, from local colour, the exact date, time and place and take root in eternal truths.

So one can always, if one is in touch with the eternal, and the roots of things. One can always pick you out and appreciate you. But those fools who depend on lost h's and a battle in Flanders are too dull for words.

I wish you had brought me some drawings to look at. The worst of prison is that it is such an ugly place.

Please agitate to get the papers that were stolen out of that attaché case.

Fancy G—— still doing the Grand Tour ! I was so soon fed up with the intense respectability.

Did Clare get my letter ? How I wish *I* were painting a corn-field with a white cottage.

September 3.

Your last letters have come in quite decent time and are such a joy. Do take care of yourself, stay in bed and *don't worry* about me. I put up 1 lb. last week, and am *not* going to hunger-strike, but get fit and strong.

I'm painting a lot and using this jail as a rest-cure! As far as I am concerned you can be quite happy, for I really wanted a rest.

The bottled jellies were lovely and the grapes charming. I have hung three bunches up on the bars of our cage, where the sun shines through them.

That cheque I sent is *for you*, with my love. I will send another for the fur coat. Let me know about how much. No hurry.

It's Miss Daly who is trying for a visit, *not Mrs.* We are so glad that you can put her up and look after her.

Two lovely little Florentine picture-books arrived from Clare. A great joy. And papers, etc., from Patricia.

People are so kind. Mrs. C. is much more comfortable the last few days. I had been getting a bit anxious, she is so frail. She has a wonderful spirit, and we joke away. We yelled over your last letter, with the big 'D' (omitted). Don't go to jail as a proxy: it would kill you, and one Irishwoman is better than a dozen Englishmen, even conscientious ones!

There are wasps here. One walked up my leg yesterday, but we parted amicably. They never sting me and I never kill them. We are affinities. Perhaps I was one in my last incarnation!

September 11.

You don't say anything about your health in the letter just received and I feel anxious. Esther does not look too well in the photo either. It's awful for you two dear old crocks that somebody else's detestable war keeps you out of Italy. But why don't you go to Ireland for a bit ? At least you'd get food there. You'd have great fun, too, as everyone would mistake you for me, as before. And then you'd get everything you'd ask for and much more. Dulcibella's home is so lovely. I always wanted to take you to Glendalough.

M. G. has been very ill with a rash, but she is on the mend and up again. We were most anxious for some days.

We were frightfully excited about the Peelers' Strike. Why don't the jailers do ditto ! and by way of sabotage, destroy the jails ? Did Clare get my letter ? By the way, you might send me an old picture post-card, as they don't count as letters, and would be a help to painting. I'm working quite hard and doing quite a big thing and improving a lot. Jail is so hideous, which is a bore. I've done Deirdre and Maeve and more horses. I love the two wee books of pictures. They are a great help. I look forward to your book so much. Write my name in it before you send it to me.

October 8.

Letter just come. Give my love to Janey and tell her she must come to see me if ever I get out, and that I thought of her at the time of the S. Patrick's pilgrimage. I was in here at the time.

The coats came on appro. Bad value. The green one nice, but *must* have the fur below the knees, and it's a little too short too. The weather is warm, so there is no hurry. I don't think —— is a very good place. But perhaps it is, on consideration. I have not shopped there for such years. I don't like ' coney seal ' anywhere, at all.

My ' baby ' wrote to me. He has been very ill, poor little fellow.

I am making a border for your ' Dora Shorter ' poem, it's very nice.

Your p.c.s are very nice.

Don't let 'Squidge' or anyone else see me under the present absurd regulations. As you say, it's *my* funeral, and I'm dancing at it! A little patience, and won't we talk! I feel quite capable of talking not only the hind but all four legs off that belted ass, the British Empire.

Do you remember O'Shaughnessy's poem, 'And three with a new song's measure?'[1]

Mrs. C. is better again, thanks to a filthy bottle, a painted chest and being rolled in cotton wool for a week. One of the few times I've known a doctor to be of any use.

How's your health? I hope electric treatment is right. Watch it carefully yourself.

October 18.

We *must* take what you call an 'absolutist' stand here, and giving an undertaking cuts the ground from under our feet. Living up to your principles is always damnable, but it is particularly necessary just now. Madge could explain, if you wrote her. We are going on all right.

Mrs. C. is really a little better at last. For the first time since we've been here, she seems really to be on the mend.

My weight goes steadily up and I'm getting all 'round and rosy.'

We got some lovely marmalade left at the gate. I think it must have been Patricia. If you come across a pot of raspberry jam do send me one. Mrs. C. and I make puddings out of spare bread and put marmalade

[1] One man with a dream, at pleasure,
Shall go forth and conquer a crown;
And three with a new song's measure
Can trample a kingdom down.

in and are thinking a change would be nice! Aren't I a greedy pig?

About visits, we are asked, beyond the jail rules of having a wardress present at visits, 'to give undertakings in writing not to talk politics and our visitors not to carry messages or make reports.' Under these conditions we refuse visits. Is that clear?

I do love your letters so. We roar over them.

I'm painting away here and will have quite a lot to show you.

October 21.

So glad to hear you are a bit better. How I wish I was there to fuss over you. I wonder where you are? My imagination visualises you and E. in resplendent raiment and on verandahs and in wind-swept pinewoods and in comfortable, civilised beds. . . .

When you come back, if it is not too much bother, I want you to send anything you send here *to me*. It's so exciting getting things, but if it means a lot of arranging, don't bother. But do if you can. You are such an old darling.

Cloaks no good. *Must* have one long enough. The authorities have supplied me with shoes, stockings and a costume, so for a jail-bird I'm not so badly off! Health splendid.

Such an interesting packet of newspapers came from P. L. on Saturday. She's really an angel and I'm most grateful.

Mrs. C. much better. She really has a hero's soul. She makes the best of everything and is an ideal jail-bird.

Your p.c.s are such a joy. I have finished copying out your Dora S. poem, with border and caps., and I'm longing for you to see it.

The world seems to be more topsy-turvy than ever.

What hypocrites people are! Do read P. C. O'Hegarty's *Unconquerable Nation.* I wish I could get it for you, but the Realm might totter if I tried.

I'm glad you think there is a chance of our being let out. I suppose it will suddenly strike them that we are less powerful out than in, and then out we shall go!

In the meantime, we are quite cheerful and resigned and we don't worry.

December 4.

I do love your post-cards. I wonder if you are better. Are you doing any election work? Don't overdo it. I see that M—— is out and I am glad. He is a hero. If the whole situation were not so tragic it would be laughable. The English election is like Alice in Wonderland or a Gilbert and Sullivan Opera. The *D. News* and the *Chronicle* are a treat.

Thank God we are not a materialistic nation! Anyhow, it keeps you out of a lot of trouble. It seems to me that the Germans, in the far end of things, will have really won the war, as they have gained a victory over themselves or, rather, materialism.

Did you see some absurd yarn in *D. News* about a cypher letter and Sinn Fein? I wouldn't be a bit surprised if they don't start a new 'plot' to keep us in! It is so easy to get a poor fool to carry a letter for a few shillings.

You sent me such a lovely picture of a rock garden, I longed to be there. It's such a bore not knowing how long they intend to keep you. There is nothing to help us calculate. I suppose we are just a card in their hand and will be played when it suits them. It's hard on Mrs. Clarke. I'm thankful to say she is better again, but I don't think she'll be really well until she has her operation. My weight is 9 stone 9½ and am very well. So M. went home! Had she leave? I wonder if she'll be sent back. It's very mysterious why they ever took her, but they are, luckily, sometimes very stupid.

January 6, 1919.

We are still revelling in your gifts.

Do you know J. A. Hobson? I once met him and liked him so much. Since reading his last book I want to meet him again. Do try to get in touch with him. It's all true what he says and I want to ask him a score of questions.

Wilson seems to me a very dark horse. I hope they won't get him assassinated. The Elections were very cleverly rigged. The English people seem to be both foolish and unprincipled. I don't think our people would ever rise to cries of 'Revenge!' We conquered by telling them that each one of them must learn to carry the cross for Ireland, and that without pain and self-sacrifice our country would be lost. Do you remember Yeats' 'Kathleen ni Hoolihan,' 'If you would help me, you must give me yourself, give me all'? That's what the elections mean for Ireland, and something great for Ireland must come out of it.

Your letter was very good, but I was sorry that you omitted Rachel, who is the most suited to the job of the lot. Do you know S. Moberly's prophecy? I've just illuminated it and it's fine. I ring the changes between broad and soppy brushwork and fine, light illuminating. Wait till you see all I've done. I've written several things too, but don't get on, as I simply can't tear myself away from my painting.

It is such a puzzle to me why they keep us. English spite, I suppose. Perhaps they are going to wait until they have made the 'world safe for Democracy'! It's certainly not safe in Ireland just now. We pray that Wilson does not lose his head and his soul, wallowing in drawing-rooms and getting his eyes progged out with the spikes of crowns !

January 17.

Fur coat is beautiful, so snug and warm. I got the thread from Limerick at last. Do write to M. She sent me things and I can't spare letter. B—— need not worry. I'm not thinking of taking her back. But she has good points and knew every detective in Dublin by sight. Thank women candidates for telewag. How soon is civilisation going to be fed up with the fat Englishman ? I see that they have great new schemes for the betterment of mankind, and that helpless coloured people are praying to be under their beneficent rule. Anyhow, they are incubating baby Frankensteins all over the globe and scattering dragons' teeth, even among their own democracy.

I see no more reason for our release than I saw for our jailing, so don't delude yourself with hopes. Some day someone will have an Idea, and we shall be free. The only pity is that Englishmen have so few ideas ! They can do sums and say long prayers and bully their way through life, and that's all. They certainly don't like idealists or people who are ready to support the principles they teach.

If you have a friend who does not mind shopping, get them to see if you can still get big model engines, signals, rails, etc., like Bug had, driven by methylated spirit. Any boy would understand. Who told you about Mrs. C. ? I can't read it. She is so fretted at being away from her boys. I can't make out why they keep her. She is not sleeping now and is so feeble.

It's so puzzling, why they keep some and let others go.

In some ways it is a blessing that they are so stupid. I often laugh when I read the papers.

January 22.

Thank you for the things. You sent fixative but no blower. Thank Esther for hers. I know Hobson slightly and want to meet him again. You might buy me his new book. I want to read up Imperialism and earlier Peace Conferences and anything about Empire building and theories about internal construction of a State. I would buy any good books that might be useful to pass on. I want to get together a little library of Economics and Welt-Politik. Is there any hope of there being a white rook among the birds of prey engaged in tearing up carcases?

Did you read Miss Brodrick's letter in the *Daily News*? It's quite good. The English must be so bored that the only result of having put us in here has been to put them in a false position before every honourable person and to give the young people at home the chance to develop themselves and to learn to do without 'leaders.'

I don't believe in leaders myself; I had just time to fix up my end before I was 'took' and it has had great results with regard to the women.

Could you order the *Dreadnought* and *Herald* regularly for me? They sometimes come and sometimes miss.

Do you ever see our Labour paper? Tell me if you don't and I will get it sent you.

Why do you put your letters in two envelopes? Is it to support trade?

This awful weather does not agree with Mrs. C.

It is not too warm here at all. She is so fragile. Can you tell why she was arrested at all? I never knew such brutality. She led the life of a semi-invalid.

The lily you sent was such a joy to us and the altar-flowers were lovely.

January 30.

I do hope you are minding yourself this awful weather.

Mercifully for us the Police Strike did not come off, so there is still a stoker who stokes, and we are not too bad.

K. C. in bed with a bad cold.

Hanna S. could have been an M.P. *if she had wanted to.* A seat was offered her. She is not altogether an S.F. I think, and I *know* prefers to work from the Women's platform. I quite agree with your estimate of *her*.

Do try and worry out why that December letter of mine was held up for so long. I had certainly put nothing in it that I thought would be delayed.

One thing I am quite grateful to that diabolic Censor for: he has taught me a lot of useful things, caution, for one. If one had more paper and a less obvious Censor, one might have been tempted to be indiscreet. Not about policies. I shall always stand against 'secret diplomacy,' not in pompous speeches and newspaper articles, but by speaking out myself.

Saying things that might get others into trouble is all that I fear. It is awful to think that even Art is conquered by militarism. Think of any one wanting to paint awful war scenes, when they could paint reapers or the sea.

Connolly was such a prophet. He said war was

going to be between the Fat man and his Black flag and the Workers and their Red flag and now it has come. He also saw victory for the Red.

I am growing pessimistic and wonder how *they* will abuse power when they have got it.

Did you see the latest Hun atrocity in Ireland? St. Enda's school! I am filled with wonder at the patience and discipline of the people. So few retaliations, for which I am thankful.

February 6.

Yours and E's presents are such a joy. I have hung the garment where I can see it when I am painting, it is such a gorgeous colour.

Write Carlisle. Tell him where I am and if he can get me out I'll lunch with him at the Carlton! or anywhere else.

I get such funny letters from the ends of the world, and I begin to understand why M.P.s employ secretaries.

My election was a foregone conclusion. I must know most of those who voted for me. The Transport Union is strong, ditto S.F. Everyone had to concentrate on the 'doubtfuls.'

Isn't Dev. great? That's *not* his portrait in the *Daily Mail.*

I'm afraid they will hold the rest of us all the longer now, out of spite.

Don't come up here this awful weather. I shudder to think of you out in it. I don't go out much. It's not the sort of weather for a jail!

Yes, get Hobson's book, and what about Bertrand Russell's?

Ask for my watch here next call, it is losing.

I'd love a run to John's Port or up Ben Bulben.

Do you remember when we went up years ago, on my birthday, in the snow and mist, and how grand and mysterious it was?

I heard from Kitty the other day. Very good news. Uncle and the other relations turning up trumps.

I've got the menu of the Historical Banquet for you, with a lot of signatures on it. Mr. W. P. sent it.

My cards are so nice in the album.

If I ever get out I shall have such a queer lot of parcels.

What hypocrites the Allies are, and us in jail for doing what they boastfully pretend to have done!

Anyhow, I think the old tin kettle must burst soon. Democracy must learn something out of all this, and then——?

We are really so sane in Ireland and it really would be 'safe for democracy' if the Armed Forces were withdrawn.

Aren't we a patient and long-suffering people?

February 14.

Here I am, all alone in this Englishwoman's home! Luckily, I always find myself good company. Of course, I miss K. very much, but for the first time in my life I was thankful to see the back of a dear friend. Give her a good 'scholding' and a hug from me and tell her the tea-pot's broken, but *not* by me this time! I've no one to bully now, and she needs it. Tell her to stay in bed or rest up. Weren't you shocked when you saw her? and they dare to talk about German atrocities, the hypocrites! But it will all react in the end.

I am almost sure it was St. Hubert. I think it must be a misprint. I am now doing 'Heroic Death.' It is rather nice.

Illuminating is great fun, for a change. You can get such nice colour. I wish I had looked at any in my life.

Have you heard where Dev. is? What a gossip you are having!

Do you know a girl called Evans on the Vote? She wrote me such a nice letter, and is publishing, or has published, one from me.

So glad you saw Mr. S. It's not much good holding meetings about Russia, for nobody minds talk nowadays.

It wasn't talk blocked conscription: it was the astounding fact that the whole male population left at home and most of the women and kids would have died rather than fight for England, and they simply did not dare exterminate a nation.

Our contempt of money and our taking death and jails as all in the day's work must puzzle the British more than a little.

You criticise our election organisation! The enemy says it was 'efficient,' 'perfect,' etc. It was practically nil!

So everyone butted in, women and children taking a very prominent part.

I believe it brought out a lot of women speakers.

February 24.

I was informed this morning that my last letter to you was kidnapped en route. I am puzzling my head as to why. It was such unimportant blather that I had not made a note of its contents. I always do so if I sail near the wind or if I write 'acid tests.' Kathleen too, having just had free intercourse with you makes it all the funnier. They are all like a comic opera.

I suppose it was spite and that they want to break one's spirit. The only thing that I remember in it was that I asked you to write to Molly O'Neil and explain that I simply could not write to my friends and not to mind not hearing. Maybe they are afraid of my sending messages to her!

Isn't K. C. a dear? So patient and so unselfish. Her only thought was not to give me trouble, as if any little thing I could do for her was trouble! I do hope she'll lie up. She is really very bad and will only kill herself if she runs round. I quite forget that she is not here and I start talking with her occasionally.

It is so funny being alone, and never seeing anyone with whom one has common interests of any kind.

At Aylesbury we had a certain community of hatred that gave one mutual interests, and the mutual sport of combining to pinch onions, dripping or rags! Doesn't it sound funny and mad? but it kept one going.

I can't be bothered about exhibiting. I'd have to go through so many forms and would probably not be allowed to do so, even if I asked humbly for leave.

If you have anything of mine fit, I don't mind your sending, but *don't sell.*

February 26.

Did K. give you a cheque? I got such a nice letter from another sister, saying how kind you were. I was so glad that you were able to repay them a little for all their goodness to me. Their house was a home to me, when I was 'running' round that part of Ireland. They fed me up and looked after me, and I just came and went as I liked.

Will you send someone (*not* a duchess !) or go to see Annie L——, Ward C. Mental Hospital, New Southgate ? She is an old Aylesbury comrade and used to be called Dyer. Give her some money to buy little extras, with my love, and tell her why I can't write and where I am. It's near here, I believe. Write if you can't go. Mr. W. P. who attends to my correspondence in Dublin tells me she wrote twice to me.

'Colour' is such a joy, so are the gaudy ribbons you sent. They help me with my painting. Colour is like everything else. It depends on the relationship of the many to each other, the air, life, etc., for their beauty. Alone, a colour is meaningless : merged in the waves of life and light and combined with other colours, it equals the one composed of the many, assumes emotions, which it can convey to you : it acts, has qualities and personalities. This sounds odd but it's true, and it is only as people grasp this that they are of any use in the world.

Do you think Nellie has ? J—— has not. Charlie has, in his own line.

Thank Clare for things yesterday, and oh ! *do* thank Mrs. McKenna. It was *misery* not knowing the time.

What's happened to C—— ? I wonder if the Censor will object to this ? He certainly is an awful fool. I'd love to tell him so, but find some relief in writing it !

December 12.

I haven't heard from you for an age. I think the Censor is an evil person. One of my letters *re* election was stopped and he just pinched it. Evidence, I suppose, of a new 'plot' ! I was actually allowed a big bit of paper to write an Election Address on ! I wrote one in such a hurry that it is probably not sense! The *Freeman's Journal* is putting all sorts of rubbish into our mouths. It's so fair to shut us up and not let us answer! Luckily the Irish people do not believe the daily papers, especially the *Freeman*, which is reported to be run by English gold—I mean—Treasury Notes!

By the way, buy me Coles' new book. Brailsford and Hobson have been such a delight. I am studying them over and over again. Please thank Miss M—— for the lovely dressing-gown. I was just going to write out for one.

Who is 'whimsical Winnie'? I love her.

Did you see that one of us died at Usk? It was not in the English papers. Do you get the *Independent*? I told them to send it to you. We are so lucky here. Usk is evidently very hard. However, it is quite good for the Cause to die in Jail, and I'm sure he did not grudge the sacrifice.

I was wishing that you were not a pacifist the other day. It would have been so funny to have impersonated me in Dublin, but they would have thought they had gone mad when you (or I) began to speak, and rainbow-tinted words on the beauties of Peace began to fall from your (or my) ruby lips! I drivel.

Such beautiful white lilac came.

By the way, what has happened about the flowers for the church?

HOLLOWAY JAIL, UNDATED

1918—19 ?

As [illegible] our extraordinary [illegible] have given us leave [illegible] write three letters a [illegible]. It sounded [illegible] until I got the [illegible] noticed! A very Engl[illegible] mercetty [illegible] call it [illegible] you and our common enemy the Censor [illegible] is no German [illegible]

[illegible]

[illegible] I love all the local gossip [illegible] such a clever old darling, and on the thun[illegible] have been such a comfort. We share everything. [illegible] delicious.

Undated (1918-19 ?).

At last our extraordinary captors have given us leave to write—three letters a week. It sounded generous, until I got the paper supplied! A very English generosity I call it. Let me tell you and our common enemy the Censor that *there is no German plot*! Very likely you won't be let know this, for I believe myself that it is all a political game, and that the English Government *wanted* a German Plot. Further than this, the whole affair is a mystery to me, why I was kidnapped, etc.

Our policy was very open and simple: to try and get the Powers to bring up Ireland's case at the Peace Conference (as Lord Salisbury brought in Greece), and with all this talk about Freedom of the Seas we have a great chance.

By the way, I wish you'd worry the Irish Government for my attaché case: it has some oddments in it that I prize and some notes about Ireland's claim to Sovereign Statehood that will no doubt interest the English, but they will be disappointed if they expect plots! There were some manuscript poems, too, that I had no time to read.

I was always disappointed myself, when I saw the headings of 'Plots,' and found it related to cabbages and potatoes!

Talking of newspapers, they won't give us Irish ones: nothing but foreign ones, with no interest but the war news.

What is the point of it all?

I love all the local gossip so. You are such a clever old darling, and all the things you sent have been such a comfort. We share everything. The 'sparrow grass' was delicious.

I think my cheque-book is in my attaché case. When I can get at my money I will send you some.

Do you mind (I know you don't) my keeping your cool things for the moment ? It is so hot here.

Poor Mrs. Clarke will never stand this. She frets for her boys and she has never got over the shock of her husband's and brother's murders. She nearly died and has been very feeble since.

Now this wretched paper will hold no more.

Please thank Esther, Reginald and Clare for all they sent us.

Poor Poppet ! Fancy arresting *him* !

Don't worry about me : I really wanted a rest. I had the German measles just before I was seized !

Undated.

Just seen alarmist reports from M. Do try and calm her ! We are far safer here than outside, as we are all to ourselves on a landing and exercise alone. I believe there are a few cases among the few hundred persons shut up in here.

Please write a reassuring note to Madge D. People get so excited when they read these exaggerated pars, in the shrieking Dailies. Please thank Reginald for things, and I do so love the cards. His little book of etchings was a joy.

I've heaps of pickles and anchovy—enough for a couple of months. I am getting fat. Gone up a stone.

I often long to see you. Isn't the whole thing a miserable bit of petty tyranny and spite ? So English !

Send me in a common scribbling block and an exercise book, when you've time. No hurry, as I've still got paper.

The red chrysanthemums look so lovely in my cell.

Aren't the small nations of the world having a fine old

'beano'? It does make me laugh. We can't be kept out of our own for ever, if only the wave rolls on! Do you remember Blake's prophecy? Do write it on a card for me some time.

Did Shawn ever show you some doggerel of mine I think he had?

My letters seem to grow very dull, but these sheets are not inspiring.

I sent cheque for the boy to go for change of air straight to Dublin.

Undated (1918-19 ?).

Beloved Old Darling,—I do hope you are better. It's awful to think of you ill, and me so chirpy myself. Thank God you are not here. Your last letter was lovely and I could see that you were really better.

With regard to this new visiting scheme of the Eng. Govt., I did not like to worry you until I knew that you were better, so I did not tell you definitely; but I would not like anyone to submit themselves to such an indignity just for me. No, *no*, NO! Either sign, or see me with a wardress present, according to jail rules; but once we Irish rebels pledge our word we are to be trusted, and to be watched and spied on after one's word is given is more than I would put up with. It is a nuisance but unavoidable, and one is not looking for a bed of roses! One does not expect honourable treatment. People always 'judge others by themselves.'

We are all right. M. G. is better. K. C. is not so well; she suffers so, but has such a wonderful spirit. She never complains but makes the best of everything.

I want you, when you are well, to arrange for someone to bring flowers for the Church, *at my expense*, enough for two posies for the two vases on the altar. You would probably find a Catholic girl in some Irish

Society who would undertake the job. Flowers to be left at the gate ' for R. C. Priest.'

I have got my vote registered all right, in spite of Unionist objectors, Censor's delays, etc. This was part of a batch of good news from the ' western Front.'

Undated.

DEAREST OLD DARLING,—I do love your letters so, they are such a cheer. The cards are a glory. That head of Christ by Leonardo is one of the wonders of the world. Those copies of *Colour* that Esther left are an inspiration. I've hardly let them out of my hands. They are such a painting lesson, when one can't get much nature. Canned fruit is A 1. It and Dulcibella's vegetables keep me alive. Bless you all, you kind and charitable people. Tell Gertrude I would love cigarettes ! I feel that I forget to thank you half enough. Mrs. C. loves the fruit and she finds it so hard to eat enough. M. G. has a splendid appetite, luckily. I do a little cooking, too, and make ' savoury messes ' over a gas ring !

Fancy you meeting ' Miss Holland '—old beast—how we hated each other ! and do still ; but I guess Ludwig would have loved even me, if she could have seen into the future ! I wonder if she is alive, and if she has made her former pupil out ? Good luck to her and hers.

By the way, how often does J—— pay money into the bank for you and me and *when* ?

Kitty seems to be flourishing. I'd love to see her. So sorry that I can't see you at present. You'll understand my attitude, I know, and be patient. It's very slow here and everything seems to be going at a great pace outside. Empires and Governments seem to be rather like the Gadarene swine just now.

Many thanks for Litvinoff's book. Poor Russia !

I often think about my Polish relations. Poor Casi hated wars, revolutions and politics : and there he is —or was—in Kiev, or in the Ukraine.

Undated.

I will buy the thing I made Mrs. M. but don't let her know that it's *me* buying it. Just say that you can sell it for £1 and don't say to whom. Don't send her more money than that : it would be like dropping water through a sieve ! but I'd like just to give her that. I'm afraid she is too old to work, as she never had to, and you must learn young. She has a sister, who, she says, is comfortably off in Manchester or Liverpool.

Don't take Mrs. G. seriously : she is rather 'touched' and she is always seeking someone to hold her hand, take her shopping and do all her errands for her. She can never find even a friend, because she is so absorbed in 'number one !'

I'm painting away and quite content. It's great fun trying to do water-colours. We have been moved into a more comfortable lodgement : the realm will be endangered if I say more !

I'm so sorry you are in the grip of the 'flu. It's almost as bad as being in the grip of the English !

I've heaps of books still and some of them will take a long time to read.

Do take care of yourself and don't overdo it.

By the way, according to 'information received,' the *men* are allowed larger sheets of paper for letters and two sheets !

Trust the English to always make a point of worse treatment for women.

By the way, shall you 'stand' for Parliament ? I

wouldn't mind doing it—as a 'Shinner,' as an election sport, and one does not have to go to Parliament if one wins, but oh! to have to sit there and listen to all that blither!

Undated.

Many thanks for your two, which came through quite quickly for a change.

I am glad you got mine about the better distribution of food so quickly.

How mad the world seems to have grown! What do they all want? Do you think they will go on fighting and lying and talking hypocrisy until a great plague comes to sweep all their armies away?

Poor Democracy! So much is being done in its name.

I do hope you are taking every precaution. We are safer here from infection than anywhere else, so don't worry about us. We are warmed with hot pipes and well ventilated, and there is nothing in our conditions to effect our health.

Please send me tooth-paste, a box of sweet soap, a sponge, and some Jaborandi hair tonic.

If you consider that I cannot get a fur coat for the money I sent, I will send you another cheque.

Isn't it absurd to lock up doctors for nothing just now?

Just had such a gorgeous box of sweets from Ireland. Blackball, chocolates and all sorts of luxuries. Please thank whoever sent me fags.

I'm afraid I don't see much chance of our liberation. I don't know why they put us here, so it's very hard to make a guess what the tyrants will do with us.

By the way, has anyone had the imagination, patience and perseverance enough to make a map of the land where the Czecho-Slovaks and the Jugo-Slavs are born and bred? They interest me enormously. They are rather like something Alice found in Wonderland!

Undated.

Many thanks for things.

Poor Staskow! I'd hate him to be killed or wounded. He did love life. He was attached to the Russian Volunteer Fleet at Archangel and was interpreting. When you get back, try and find out through any and all Russian agents. Russia must be an awful place to be in.

The Censor has no method. The letter you wrote on receipt of the cheque was delayed until after I had got the next you wrote!

We are now only to write on 'domestic and business subjects!'

I would like to remind the sweet rulers of this Empire that they have constantly affirmed that 'Ireland is a domestic question!'

Poor old G——, how frightened she must be crossing! I don't think the peas were from her after all.

So glad that you will be seeing Hannah. Give her my love.

I was so interested to read some of Hobhouse's experiences, and thought of the time I kissed you at Aylesbury, and the row, and of *how* the Realm trembled! But *I did it!*

I'd love to read your pacifist novel. How do you manage love-scenes? Have you a collaborator? I feel that I could help!

You old darling!

What an epidemic of plots there seems to be! They don't seem to have put anyone in jail over this last. I get more and more puzzled. Why this secret imprisonment?

Undated.

We cannot accept the new scheme they have offered us for visits, as I don't see how one could possibly keep the promise one is asked to give.

They want us to promise not to talk 'politics.' To-day life *is* 'politics.' Finance, economics, education, even the ever-popular (in England) subject of divorce is all mixed up with politics to-day. I can't invest my money, without politics; buy clothes without politics. Art is all political, music is battle tunes or hymns of hate or self-glorification, and so I simply do not know what they mean when they say we must not talk politics.

What the Censor let through is no criterion. He did not like some of the Christmas cards sent me, I find!

So I refuse to keep the promise I don't understand.

I never deliberately said I'd do a thing without believing I was capable of doing it yet.

'An Exile's Dream of Ireland' I would like for the picture.

I don't like making capital for myself out of being in jail!

I see an awful account of Kathleen in to-day's paper.

It was cruel, cruel putting her in here.

I do love the purple chiffon Clare sent me. It's a joy on a dull day.

I'm quite fat and well and working quite hard at painting; 'Colour' is such a help.

I think I am safer here from 'flu than anywhere else. Do take care of yourself.

Clare looks so lovely on the postcard.

I fear I am an awful plague. I feel so bad when I hear of you up here on bad days and at unholy hours. I wish I could give you some of my strength.

When I read of Dev.[1] I thought of O'Shaughnessy's

[1] 'Dev.' is always Mr. de Valera.

poem ; the lines beginning 'One man with a dream.' Mercifully, there were three, not one.

Undated (1918-19 ?).

The Censor stopped my last to you. Said it was political. I did not consider it so. I discussed the morals of politicians and my own future !

I am drawing a lot. When you have time, send me some small rough boards or a rough block, very rough ; neutral tint, cobalt, brown, and pink in tubes, and some very fine pens—crow quill—or nibs ; some blue darning silk for stockings, sweet soap and a hand looking-glass, round if possible, with a handle which folds over, so that I can stand it up for my face and hold it to look at my drawings. Also some nice cold cream.

Ivy was not contraband, and I loved it and the home news.

I hope Kathleen's health did not suffer from her return to town. Poor old G—— ! I think some vegetables must have come from her. Very grateful.

Poor Kitty ! Judging from the papers, the War enables people to get divorced quite easily. I wish her luck.

Pickles are excellent, but smaller bottles would be more suitable. So sorry you did not see Janey. Give her my love and do try to see her. I'd hate to think she went back to the old game. Do send me English Labour papers occasionally and an odd picture one. The books are a great joy. I loved the pictures in Savoy and will take great care of them all for you.

I am reading H. N. Brailsford. He seems to be a man after my own heart. I wonder if I would be after his !

A dear little photo of you and E. in the flat is with me.

‘ON THE RUN’

BLACK AND TAN PERIOD

(Probably all 1920)

[illegible] so—I was so glad to hear from you. What on [illegible] is the meaning of [illegible] move [illegible] such [illegible] country selection? [illegible] always describes him [illegible] a Man of [illegible] admirable [illegible]. Irvine is quite [illegible] most people [illegible] not have [illegible] I fear that [illegible] to see [illegible]

[illegible]

[illegible] Sweatman [illegible] and [illegible] goods on the market [illegible] politically the [illegible] is organised to [illegible] Irish [illegible] and trade to hold their own against English, German, or any other foreign industry [illegible]. It gets

Undated.
'ON THE RUN.'

DARLING,—I was so glad to hear from you. What on earth is the meaning of their latest move? It's such a funny selection. Old Kelly always describes himself as a 'Man of Peace,' and it is an admirable description. Irwine is quite unknown to most people.

Was it not lucky that I was away? I hear that Mrs. C—— asked to see the warrant and that the detective in charge said there was none. She then asked what I was charged with and they said they did not know. They had orders to arrest me and that was all. There were some police and a lorry-load of soldiers and they searched the house to her amusement. She made them look everywhere and waste a lot of time! If you see Cecil, you might try and find out with what awful crime I am charged this time! It's enough to make any one curious.

I've a sort of feeling that it may mean strained relations with America and nothing more. We have created a delightful situation in America for the enemy, thank God! G——'s return with his tail between his legs is rather significant. It was wonderful, when you come to think of it, how few were caught. Of course we are on the run most of the time, and no one who respects themselves lives much in their homes.

Wasn't it a shame to stop the Aonach? It was just a fair and nothing more: you hire a stall and sell. Shopkeepers and industries count on making a nice few pounds, and manufacturers hope to get Irish goods on the market through it. It was political to the extent that it is organised to help Irish industry and trade to hold their own against English, German, or any other foreign industry or agencies. It gets customers for the shops that are willing to put themselves out in their efforts to help their country's struggling industries. Of course this is treason, as the enemy wish all Irish men and women to emigrate or starve. M—— attributed all the trouble in Ireland to the stoppage of emigration during the War.

I believe the English are trying to goad us into another rebellion, so as to murder a large number of intelligent and brave patriots. Everything that is done points that way, but I hope that the country is too well in hand for anything of the sort to occur. The people are wonderfully steadfast, under the most ridiculous persecution and provocation. No one knows at what moment they may be arrested on some vague charge, and any house may be raided at any moment. The police are employed entirely as an army of occupation, and I believe that there are several gangs of English thieves making themselves very busy. This does not of course get into the papers, but our own crowd are constantly held up and robbed, both in their houses and on the streets.

One of T——'s sisters married Sean M—— the other day, and as they were going home one night last week from her people's house in Brunswick Street to Queen's Square, they saw two soldiers and a civilian hold up a man with revolvers. They ran! The robbers had white handkerchiefs over the lower part of their faces. Next day they found that quite a lot of people had been stopped and relieved of their watches, money and jewelry. This is an everyday occurrence just now, and invariably some of the assailants are soldiers. It is generally supposed that Barton the detective was shot by one of these gangs, as he was employed for years in hunting down the cross-channel thieves, but of course it's put down as a 'Sinn Fein Outrage.'

No one can see any sense in the motor-permit Order,

except to cripple Irish trade. Motors have been very little used by us, except in Elections: we have not the money! Of course, S.F. traders can be hit that way and their businesses ruined. All this fuss may be to upset our organisations for the elections, and to prevent our people in the slums learning the intricacies of P.R., but I don't think that the enemy will gain much. The situation appeals to the imagination of the people, and they love the excitement. They are not afraid and they have a great sense of humour. It gives them endless joy when they outwit 'the Hun,' and vast and pompous military raids result in the arrest of two harmless pacifists.

How is your health? I hope that you are none the worse for your exertions during my visit.

I am going to keep quiet for a bit and then dodge them and go about as usual, as there is much to be done.

'SOMEWHERE IN IRELAND.'

BELOVED OLD DARLING,—I have succeeded in getting *Ossian* at last: it was evidently second-hand, as it was cut. P. S. O'Hegarty has been looking for it since before I was on the run. Awfully funny things are happening, and we manage to have many a good laugh. The enemy raided Mrs. F—— and found only two women in the house. They tried to terrorise her into telling them where her husband was. In the middle of the altercation the lights went out. It was a penny-in-the-slot machine. The officer ordered her to put in a penny. She refused point-blank. 'Put it in yourself,' she said, and she watched them relighting the gas. They went away empty-handed, the officer saying that they would get him in spite of her.

'On the Run.'

A thousand thanks for your letter and lovely gift, which actually got to me in time! I was delighted and overjoyed and surprised. It's wonderful to have a birthday 'on the run.' It's an awfully funny experience. Mrs. C. will tell you some of it.

I spoke five times for various women in the elections and had some very narrow shaves. At one place I spoke for Joan, and they sent an army, just about an hour too late. At another, I wildly and blindly charged through a squad of armed police, sent there to arrest me, and the crowd swallowed me up and got me away. The children did the trick for me.

Of course I don't keep quiet, and the other night I followed some of the Army of Occupation round about the streets. They had a huge covered waggon, and they seized some fellows and put them inside and searched them. They charged the crowd with bayonets too, and children were knocked down and terrified and women too.

Shawn and some boys were held up by detectives last night when they were leaving the public library. One of them said he thought there was a detective watching the people reading, when two men stepped past them and poked revolvers at them through their pockets, in the American way, and said that they were talking of them, and demanded to know what they were saying. Of course they just humbugged, and the two men finally moved away.

'On the Run.'

You were an angel to send me such an interesting parcel. Thank you so much, and Esther too, for the book.

I sent a hamper between the two of you. I hope

you got it alright. I had to get someone to choose the contents, as I was taking no risks before Christmas, as I did so want to have one at liberty. I told them to put in a turkey for Esther and other carnivorous friends!

It is awfully funny being 'on the run'! I don't know which I resemble most: the timid hare, the wily fox, or a fierce wild animal of the jungle!

I go about a lot, one way and another, and every house is open to me and everyone is ready to help.

I fly round town on my bike for exercise, and it is too funny seeing the expression on the policemen's faces as they see me whizz by! There are very few women on bikes in the winter, so a hunted beast on a bike is very remarkable.

Things are going ahead alright, so it does not much matter. People are subscribing to the Loan, in spite of, or perhaps because of, the fact that it has been made a jailable crime by the enemy.

I wonder how you are getting along and how you spent Christmas. I had *two* Christmas dinners at the two extremes of Dublin and had quite a cheery time, everyone congratulating me on not having been at home!

Poor Alderman K——! No one can understand why he was taken. He is a pacifist and he was never mixed up with anything violent. The housing of the poor and building up industries was his line. His nickname, given to him by himself, was 'the Man of Peace.' Some of them think that a 'plot' is being fabricated to prove that everyone who has been keeping rather quiet was engaged in secretly conspiring to shoot policemen! But I think that this is too absurd a lie, even for Ll—— G——, M—— and Co.! You can write to me at any friend's address or at Liberty Hall. I always keep in touch when I move around, and my letters get to me alright.

No date, no address.

DEAREST OLD DARLING,—I was much relieved to read the list of things that S. wants! It does not look as if he were in any great straits to live! I had quite a happy laugh when I read the list of 'frivolities' that he wants. Evidently he can't be in serious want, or any real danger. Such a blessing! I doubt if one could get all he wants for £20! Of course he has no idea of prices. Do you think that anyone could be found to bring him sweets? Stockings, handkerchiefs and sweets and tobacco are the only things that would be practical to send. There is no use sending hats, gloves or shoes on chance. I can't get at any of his things at present, and I think it really would be folly to send him things like English novels just now. I fancy that the camera, handbag and footwear were all stolen. The clothes were all too small. He exchanged his cabin trunk for mine and it has vanished. Of course I will send him things in place of them in time, but just now seems rather a bad time. When I was on the Continent, English cameras were a great nuisance, for you could not get plates to fit and it would probably be better for him to get a French or German camera. Would not the person who takes clothes bring a business letter (open) just to tell him these things?

I am sorry, too, that there was no woman in the Albert Hall. I suppose that Mrs. Skeff. could not get away. She is President of the Court of Conscience, Mrs. Clark of the Children's Court, and Mrs. Wyse Power Chairman of the Public Health Board, so the women have done well in the Corporation. It was very difficult to get women to stand for Municipal honours. It was part of our policy to run women. I could not get any woman to stand in either of the wards in S. Patrick's. I got Mrs. Clark, who of course headed the poll, and

Mrs. M'——, a stranger to them: but the Committee, mostly men, worked hard for her and it was given out that they had selected her because I was not qualified to stand myself, and more than all she is pleasant and has a good personality and the right kind of brains. But most of the people who got the votes got them because they were known personally to the voters, and men as well as women who were on our ticket did not get in, not being known.

Shawn is working hard to get into College, and Maeve herself is very busy. She seems quite fit and well and is looking lovely, though thin.

It is rather wearying when the English Man-Pack are in full cry after you, though I get quite a lot of fun out of it. Even the hunted hare must have a quiet laugh sometimes. You don't know what a joke it is sometimes to speak at meetings and get through with it in spite of their guns and tanks and soldiers and police. I had some very narrow shaves. The other night I knocked around with a raiding party and watched them insult the crowd. I was among the people and I went right up to the Store Street Police Barracks where the military and police lined up before going home. Night after night they wake people up and carry off someone, they don't seem to mind who. Some of the people they took lately did not belong to our crowd at all. When they could not find Mick S——, they took his old father, aged 60, and his baby brothers!

Mrs. C—— had a very funny scene with them. They found a pair of socks in her old room and asked whose they were in a most insulting manner. Of course she gave it them hot! She wound up by saying that even Sinn Feiners occasionally put on clean stockings, when they still continued to believe that they were not her husband's. Of course I can't tell you how people escape and where they all are because of the Enemy's accursed spies who open our letters.

We all have very cheerful news from Dev. and we feel sure that we are at the end of the British tyranny over here.

CORK JAIL

June 14—*October* 18, 1919

CORK JAIL,
June 14, 1919.

DEAREST OLD DARLING,—Clare has just written that you are ill and I am so sorry that I just got arrested, for I know how that will worry you. But you needn't bother, for I am in excellent health and spirits. I am here for advising girls not to walk out with the police and a few other remarks of that sort. The whole thing would make a very funny story for a magazine!

I'm afraid the green brooch was not very nice, but it was the nearest thing I could get to what I remembered of the old, but it strikes me as having too much silver and too little pattern. Some day we'll find a better one.

I have been *so* busy since I was back in Ireland and had a lovely time. Spent two days among the mountains with Bella and saw and hugged 'Mr. P.' He was like a stunned person when he saw me, I thought he was going to faint.

Certainly animals are more human than some people, especially English politicians.

This is the most comfortable jail I have been in yet. There is a nice garden, full of pinks, and you can hear the birds sing. I have heaps of friends here, who send me in lots of very good food—in fact—*all* my meals. Our people are such darlings. In Dublin my meals were sent in, and at Mallow, when they made sure of the police being able to identify me and changed and improved the warrant, a girl gave me a teapot of lovely tea and some cakes to keep me going.

I wonder if G—— realised she was talking sedition when she used to abuse Maggie C—— for walking with a policeman, years and years ago. It was a terrible crime in her eyes, and she sacked Maeve's first nurse for doing ditto! I wonder what her present point of view is! Someone ought to warn her of the risks she runs!

I can't help laughing all the time. Anyhow, I'm alright, so don't you worry.

I got in at the psychological moment, if I mistake not! and I'm glad.

I'll write again soon, so take care of your dear old self. Do write me a line if you can. I know I'm a selfish devil to ask you.

Love to Esther and all the love of my heart to yourself.

CORK JAIL,
June 21, 1919.

DEAREST OLD DARLING,—Just got yours and so sorry to hear that you are ill.

I'm fit and flourishing. I have lots of friends here and saw Miss McSweeney to-day. She is writing to you and will keep you posted. She is a dear.

The joke about my identity is this: the two policemen who recognised me and swore to it being me who made the speech had never really seen me. I spoke at 11.40 P.M. There were a few rough torches and a huge crowd. In the background cringed the police. After the meeting, I transferred my hat, coat, and a long blue Liberty scarf you gave me years ago, to a girl. These police, who swore they knew *me*, followed *her* round Newmarket, while I looked on and laughed. So you see what liars they are!

We showed S—— a lot of life while she was over. I like her. She's a sport, and brave as brave.

I wonder if your Donnelly is anything to do with the publisher who married Nellie Gifford. I got a card from her to-day from America.

Kitty [1] seems to be having a great look-in just now. Everyone seems to want her. I think she will get

[1] Ireland.

her divorce all right in the end. No one can say she is not entitled to it.

One of the last good works before getting lifted was to help organise a scheme for raising money for the starving Hun babies. I am wondering how many more will get arrested over it! We ought to get a good deal of money over it anyway, for people over here, being poor, are very generous.

I got lovely roses yesterday, and such heaps of strawberries and cream too. Friends are so good to me. If you want to be really appreciated in Ireland, go to jail!

By the way, have you done any more horoscopes lately? and can you tell me how often I get to jail? and shall I be hung in the end?

I feel quite cheerful and happy. My arrest came just at the right moment. Also I wanted a little rest and change of air!

The climate here is lovely and the situation perfect, on a hill, facing the south.

When they motored me to Mallow to be tried, they headed the procession with an armoured car, and several tons of soldiers and police, armed to the teeth, in other lorries. It was Gilbertian. Mallow was in a state of siege. The only thing they hadn't got was an aeroplane.

Now goodbye, darling, and good luck to you.

Take care of your precious self and don't hurry back to London. Was the evening dress a success?

CORK JAIL,
July 9, 1919.

DEAREST OLD DARLING,—Just delighted with your letter. I did not get the tale about King Billy out of C. K., I got it in a novel and ran it to earth in

Haverty's *History of Ireland.* Another rather sweet and almost prophetic yarn is about Henry II. Before he finally appropriated Ireland (mentally at least) he sent a messenger to the Pope to ask permission to crown his son John as King. The Pope permitted this atrocity, but sent Henry a crown of peacock's feathers, tied with gold wire, to perform the ceremony with! You could write a poem about that.

You are right to a certain extent about Mitchel: he was certainly not a Bolshie, but that made it all the more wonderful that he took such risks and went in so whole-heartedly for the Revolution. He was a queer mixture. The oddest thing about him was that he was against the freeing of the black slaves in America. Of course his reason was that the English were on the other side, and the reason why the English Government were so keen on Emancipation was that slave labour, being unpaid, enabled the Americans to undersell the English tea-planters (Jamaica, etc.). The English originally established slavery in America. He had wonderful instincts about politics. He prophesied the War with Germany, and his ideas for Ireland were far better than those adopted. He was one of the Divine Ancestors of Easter Week. I think they all failed because they had no policy. They were all writers and theorists, but could neither organise nor frame a policy. Fintan Lalor had ideas, so had Davis, but they never seemed able to evolve a policy or an organisation to work their ideas. Perhaps the country was not ripe. I agree with Lenin that if the conditions are not there, no sort of propaganda will hasten or impede it. Pearse was rather like the '48 men in that, but thanks to Tom C—— and Sean McD——, the organisation was there, and Connolly had the brain, so that when the moment came they were able to grasp it. Pearse wrote beautifully and spoke beautifully, and they say he wrote his speeches and got them off by heart. He was the only *orator* I ever listened to : he had a fine delivery, a beautiful voice and a poetic and sincere way of putting things, and what he said was always interesting and made you think. Connolly was quite different. He was no orator and had a bad delivery, but he never made an uninteresting speech. He had more force and more world-knowledge and everything he said was worth remembering. He was so practical too. They often seemed to me to be a complement to each other.

. . . Just been interrupted to have a visit : a Miss Freeman—an American girl—was one of them, and she knows you. There were three visitors and only a quarter of an hour for visiting, so not much time to talk.

I can't read what you have written : 'I, etc.,' that Max has put to music. I forget the 'old woman of Beare.' Could it be Ireland ? I'll borrow Pearse's work and read it again.

Famines are potent weapons. I would like to read Mitchel's account of the Coalition Government before questions about Russia and Central Europe are put.

Have you ever read *Knocknagow*, by Kickham ? It's not the famine but the eviction of later years, and it is very interesting. Did you ever hear of the Glenveigh evictions in 1861 ? It makes one's blood boil to read : a high watermark of cold-blooded cruelty !

Thanks for Georges and Ransome. I agree about the style of the Georges. You feel that he is trying to impress you with the amount he knows and that he is not sure enough of his facts to be precise. Ignorance camouflaged by stupidity. However, he is supposed to be a genius. Chesterton now : he doesn't give you many facts, but he has ideas, though he spoilt the book in the end by using his marvellously ingenious mind to try and sum up the book against the Hun! He only began seriously towards the end of the book, so it's a failure. Even he found it hard to deny that most of modern England is a copy of things German. If you are writing on religion and start with the theory that the English Protestant Church is a German Mission!—and so it is and beer-drinking and old-age pensions and conscription and the Socialism that may eat them all up! If I were the Kaiser I would make a bee-line for London! It would be glorious before one died to teach the English how to try a King! 'L'appetit vient en mangeant.' I would defend myself and ask for a public trial and for Labour to be on the Bench. Why do the wrong people always get the opportunities? People would not hate the Kaiser if they saw him and saw that he was only a sad and dignified old man, and not a Minotaur. So glad to hear about Maev. What do you think of her playing? Is there any inspiration in it?

Now goodbye. . . . What a letter I have inflicted on you!

CORK JAIL,
July 5, 1919.

DEAREST OLD DARLING,—Your letter was most interesting. Thanks also for the books. History is more thrilling than any romance, and so cynical! Do you realise that King Billy of great and glorious memory who fought Popery in Ireland was financed by the Pope? King Billy formed the League of Augsburg to check Louis XIV. and to break up the alliance with the English Charles. Billy tricked everyone and collared the swag! I have remembered something about Mrs. Fitzherbert and Ireland. The law about Catholics would have been repealed and she would have been accepted as Queen, but this would have involved

Catholic Emancipation being conceded to Ireland. There was trouble between Pitt and Fox over it and Mrs. F. and Ireland went to the wall. I am much more sorry for Mrs. F. than for the Queen! The Queen always had her Queenship to which she attached great value, and Princesses never seem to marry for anything else. I dare say she was like ——. The whole case seems to me to be somewhat similar!

To go back to style: I suppose I am very Irish for I love Mitchel. Some of his phrases simply bring the tears to my eyes. He always rings true to me, though I don't as a rule like early Victorian rhetoric; but he always seems to me to put a colour and a glow on things that make you see them with your heart.

A book, the wording of which amuses and pleases me, is Chesterton's *History of England*. It is so human and so unexpected and is all written from such an utterly different convention to the ordinary History and there is a great deal of truth in it. Of course he has a style of his own. The modern curt style is, to me, very often telegraphic. We rather like adjectives and symbolic things over here; our speeches are often rather rhetorical but that again is quite different to writing. I know it was a common sneer in England at one time that we could not talk of Ireland in Plain English. It was always 'Kathleen ni Houlihan' or some other unpronounceable name, and her 'four green fields' gave great offence too. Now I like all that. Another person whose writing I liked was Oscar Wilde, but as a rule when I read books I just read to get ideas and facts in a great hurry and only disliked the style if it was too obscure and long-winded, so I have really thought very little about it. It has sometimes seemed to me that nowadays people are rather like me, and that the ideas and facts count more than the workmanship. You can find an analogy there in painting but it is all very complex. Correctness is not either truth or beauty and there is always the intangible something that is both, if you can attain to it. Early Victorian artists made a great struggle for absolute correctness in a very scholarly way; to us it is often awfully dull.

To go back to History. Has it ever struck you that in the early days of parliaments when 'burgesses' sent from local councils composed those parliaments, when so much land was common and when religious communities looked after education, sick, poor, etc., that England was on the high road to Bolshevism? I am trying to write that up. It is very interesting work. English Politics are so different to Irish but very interesting too.

Why is the *Daily H.* backing Ll. George in a subtle sort of way?

. . . . . .

CORK JAIL,
July 16, 1919.

DEAREST OLD DARLING,—Don't you bother about Maunsel but see about the poems yourself. M—— G—— married a publisher. I will write to have their address sent to you to-morrow. So then write to him, use my name, give him names of books and ask him to copyright in the States at once. Somebody may pirate them: you will have to come to an arrangement with him. He is very nice and quite straight. If the copyrighting costs anything much, I'll be responsible. You are sure to make a lot of money if no one has stolen them already. Anyhow, try at once. Ask D. to be your agent. Now do this at once like a dear.

Fancy W—— trapesing round after Kings, with a dyed head. I had to laugh about I——, he was a socialist when last we met.

You did not tell me what you thought about M——'s music. Is there a spark in it? I never care for mere technique. I suppose she is in a state of being wildly amused and interested in life. Gossip never bores me, as it is life. To me it is full of character and history.

Yesterday was the first month of my imprisonment. The enemy celebrated it by putting a barbed wire entanglement under my window. I wonder so why. They are so funny! The Cork people are awfully good to me. They send me in three good meals, cooked already per day, and lots of oddments and all the papers. I feel very proud of being Irish. Our people are so loyal and so affectionate.

I often wonder what England would be like if they tried to impose the Police rule that they have imposed here! Our people are wonderful, under the most frightful provocation. Comparing the English and Irish papers day by day and the way our rulers rule us and the way they rule England is an eye-opener to anyone.

Talking of papers, thanks for *Colour*. I will keep it for you as I know you get it regularly. It is very amusing, though I don't always admire their taste. They seem to get hold of lovely things. They never seem to have any reason for admiring things: I can't get to the bottom of their ideas—if they have any. Are they, the people who run the paper, a Club? or where do they get the strange pictures they publish?

Do send me your article on religion when it comes out. Have you been writing much poetry?

I had a letter to-day from those in St. Patrick's who have been working on the register and they say that if there is another election I should get a still greater majority! You know they passed the P.R. Bill to try to damage S.F. It's going to work out just the other way. Can't explain here, but you watch. The last thing I did was to hustle the constituency to work the register for the municipal elections—to have things ready. Everybody is so ready and eager to work. I have one great girl in my constituency: she is actually President of the S.F. Club. My getting locked up has done more to bring women out into the open than anything else. The shyest are ready to do my work when I'm not there.

Now goodbye, darling. . . .

CORK JAIL,
July 22, 1919.

DEAREST OLD DARLING,—I wish you could do something about poems and M. You are mad ever to give that vague 'American rights.' You might try the play. It would not do any harm to write to D——. His wife is a great friend: she was out in Easter Week with me and is a brick. She ran a kitchen, which is just as important as holding a gun.

England seems to be in an awful state, much worse than Ireland. No one will have any control over anybody if they go on much longer, and there will be terrible things happening. If a revolution comes it will be much worse than Russia, for people are so congested. There are no big open country districts, with stores of food. I don't fear a revolution here as many are so disciplined—not that silly compulsory thing which is automatic and breaks down—but disciplined voluntarily, which is quite a different thing.

I loved your poem. Have you written much lately? I am so sorry about 'Broken Glory.' Are you sure that the agreement is binding? Can't you break it, if you get no money? Did you ever get anything out of it? I got £20 for one poem, without American rights. Of course it was not real poetry, only doggerel!

But some of your real poetry would have a very large appeal because of the subjects.

I am very interested in family gossip, always.

There are three cats here who all play together: father, mother and the ugliest kitten you ever saw: it's just like Mr. Balfour—figure, eyes and all. But they are rather superior to an English family, for they don't get cross. Imagine an English paterfamilias following a ball round a field, and what would happen if his young hopeful ran away with it. This old cat never minds.

Thackeray is very dull, so colourless and no point of view except the ordinary child's history one. Whose is the best history for reference purposes? I am getting very interested in it, and one history leads to another. You can't understand the why of things unless you see all round.

Now bye-bye, darling.

CORK JAIL,
July 28, 1919.

DEAREST OLD DARLING,—I am so sorry to hear that you have a cold that I must write again at once. I hope you are taking care of yourself. Colds in summer sound so awful. I wish that you were in the country.

. . . . . .

Do you know anything about the Act of Supremacy? Was it ever repealed? and do English Bishops swear allegiance when they are ordained? and parsons? I am always coming across it in histories but they only refer to it and don't tell you what it was or if it was ever repealed.

I have just had a visit from two friends. I do wish you were in Cork. It's so warm and mild, with just a nice sea-breeze coming in. It would do you a world of good.

The moths here are so lovely. They come fluttering in through the bars at night, every shade and every shape: such big ones all splotched over with orange and red, great white soft things and wee ethereal ones, all opalescent and shimmering, moonlight colours. One I got to-day was like the waves of a pale, twilight sea. Another was like a creamy shell. I try to save their lives.

Is there any chance of your coming over to Ireland this Autumn? I am so sorry for you, being hunted by post-impressionists. But I don't believe you can be evicted for a year at least.

Now, darling, I must stop this. I have just had a visit from two such nice young men from the neighbourhood. The Cork people spoil me dreadfully. Such fruit and flowers all the time.

. . . . . .

CORK JAIL,
August 2, 1919.

DEAREST OLD DARLING,—So delighted to hear that you are better and that you are contemplating going to the play. Mind you write and tell me about it. I saw a very silly English review of it.

Do you know R——? He's very nice and a Republican. I never knew it till I met him in the Clare election cheering Dev. If you like the play, you should write and tell L. R. to go and see you: he's very nice.

Of course there are endless possibilities in the economic situation in Ireland. The difficulties are not from us but from the English enemy. You can't even open coal-mines or sell butter or export anything without being faced up with bayonets. Every Board in the country is run by a man whose salary depends on his putting English interests first. If they build piers, they build them in the wrong place. The education in the schools is hopelessly inadequate to Ireland. Since the War all kinds of new regulations against Ireland's trade and commerce have been started. In the case of fixed prices, Ireland always gets less for the same or even superior goods. The old Sinn Fein organisation started on this, but you can do so little with an enemy in occupation of your country. Directly we get the Republic into working order we shall do a lot.

Is the *Daily Herald* trying to please everybody? They seem to love Ll. George and the King! To me it seems so odd that with all the genius the English have for compromise, no Labour leader can find a compromise that will make the workers of different sections work together or evolve a policy that will carry the country.

I am so glad you are going to Miss Neild. It will be heavenly in a garden after London. Cork is very warm and very dry. We don't seem to have any rain, though you often see thunder clouds rolling round the prison. The rain often seems to miss this.

That blockading and starving the enemy's children is an old trick of the English. I have just been reading about Carew in the reign of Elizabeth, who destroyed harvests with machines and killed cattle with the avowed purpose of starving women and children.

It's a real pity for me that you are not in the neighbourhood. I had three visits last week. One of my visitors has been arrested since.

Such good news from America. Much better than you see. Nothing is allowed to be printed, but we always hear from travellers.

I think it is a very good sign that Canada wants a representative in the U.S.A. There are many signs that the tide has turned at last and that we are on the incoming wave, if only we can stick there. It's awfully hard to hover in the air—as it were—and do nothing. But if we can do it we must. Now goodbye.

CORK JAIL,
August 14, 1919.

DEAREST OLD DARLING,—I am so glad you are out of London just now and I hope you will remain so. It sounds so heavenly to lie on a sofa in a garden and just enjoy flowers and sun and air. It's hot enough here just now, but luckily for me it is never really oppressive in Ireland.

Don't you mind what Cassidy said in Drogheda.

In some parts of Ireland we would welcome a Labour candidate, and no one with 'Westminster' on his programme would get a chance outside a few counties in the North and Waterford.

Anywhere where S.F. is not it would be a great advance on the right road and would mean an additional shrinkage of Carsonism.

It seems to me that England is gaily riding to ruin, unless there is some wonderful secret policy somewhere. I can't see where it will all end. The futility and brainlessness of all leaders in every camp. With the exception of a few clever 'doctrinaire' socialist people who can state a case—they seem to be devoid even of common sense. The only way for an unorganised majority is to rush them in to doing things and to *tell* them what to do.

Everybody seems to be splitting hairs about 'direct action' and other phrases, while one bit of liberty after another is taken from them. Lloyd George puts off and throws sops to Cerberus and every clique in England follows suit.

I get rabid, this hot weather, you perceive!

N—— was in Dublin before I came in here, and I told him what I thought of them all! These Englishmen get very much surprised at what we say to them. They think themselves such God-Almighty fine fellows and they can't understand that we don't admire words: they are so good and so cheap here that we only admire deeds and the willingness to suffer and deny yourself for a cause.

Norah Connolly came to see me to-day; she was delighted with Drogheda. Do you know that we, Cuman na-mBan, have already sent £500 for the starving in Europe?—mostly collected in pennies all through Ireland, without permits? Every collector risked jail! Mind you, it was entirely a rank-and-file collection. Just the girls. I call it so splendid.

Mrs. Skeffington has been awfully knocked about. She interfered with the police who continued to hammer an unconscious man with clubbed rifles and she was clubbed over the head. She lost a lot of blood and will have to keep quiet for a bit. You probably saw it in the *Independent*.

I have nothing to say to-day. It's too hot to think, except about you, darling. Write and tell me how your health is and how everyone is going along and would there be any chance of your getting over here in the Autumn (I don't mean to jail!) but to the Republic.—Bless you, old darling.

CORK JAIL,
Sunday, August 17, 1919.

DEAREST OLD DARLING,—Many thanks for the *New Age*. Labour is very complicated over here and it is very difficult to expound on four censored pages! In the first place, it is supposed to be non-political except on Labour issues and as yet has not debated the question of abstention. Even the 'Transport' contains some who are not Sinn Feiners, though the bulk of Irish workers are with us. Sinn Fein is composed of both Labour and Capital, mostly of course Labour, but there are some 'rotten' capitalists in it. They would use S.F. to damage Labour if they could and to boost themselves. The Unionist and Redmondite crowd would in their turn use Labour to bust S.F., and Carson would use each to break up the other! So far, Labour and S.F. have acted loyally towards each other. Their disagreements have been open and without any spleen, and as long as they continue to do so, they will both be for the good of Ireland.

All sorts of mysterious people are trying to make mischief in a very clever way: sometimes by getting a Trades Union to believe that S.F. is anti-Labour, sometimes by declaring that S.F. is Bolshevism! but so far it has not mattered. It is a bit difficult to side-track Irish people and we just go ahead. I belong to both organisations, for my conception of a free Ireland is economic as well as political: some agree with me, some don't, but it's not a sore point. Easter Week comrades don't fall out: they laugh and chaff and disagree. It annoys the enemy considerably. Of course no Labour leader would get in in place of a present S.F. member unless he forswore Westminster. It's so obvious that I don't think anyone would try. I feel equally sure that any Labour man who pledged himself to abstention would be accepted by S.F. in a Labour constituency and not opposed. S.F. is not a solid, cast-iron thing like English parties. It is just a jumble of people of all classes, creeds, and opinions, who are all ready to suffer and die for Ireland, and as long as it remains that, there is nothing to fear from Labour.

I enclose a funny cutting from the *D.H.* in case you did not see it. You know the author. I simply roared over it and would like to congratulate E. S. It would be an excellent idea for a scene in a play. Did you see L—— R—— in the end? Norah Connolly is in Cork and has been to see me twice. She is very well satisfied with the Congress.

Can M—— prevent you publishing a complete edition yourself? Try and get his leave, don't say for where, but just vaguely to publish, and then write to my friend. I'd put the Easter Week ones in one chapter and those to me in jail in another, each with a little explanation and write a short account of what *you* saw in Dublin that time: say something about Skeffy's ideas on pacifism and war and I believe it would go like hot cakes. I am sure you could find some of our crowd going across who would look after it for you. I don't mean political envoys! But there are always people going and I could help in this even here. Some of the priests are very interested in literature, and they are always going across.

Anyhow, get leave to bring out a book as soon as you can, and then we'll try.

I know an American poetess—Teresa Brayton. I believe I could get hold of some people to review it too.

I forget if you know Colum. who is there; and Ernest Boyd, a journalist, and a friend have gone lately.

Anyhow, we must get a hustle on now. I must talk to Norah about it too. I am sure my drawings would sell a few copies.

Now good-bye, darling. How is Esther? You have given me no news of her nor of Clare.

CORK JAIL,
August 23, 1919.

DEAREST OLD DARLING,—I was delighted with Strindberg's poem. Please thank Reginald.

If I ever get out of this, I might get over, if there was no chance of getting you across to Ireland.

I had been thinking of going to Bella ; it's so lovely there. Couldn't you come too ? I'm sure she'd love to see you and I could look after your food, but they have lots of hens and garden things. Glendalough is close and it's so beautiful. The lake is grand and then the sun most obligingly sets in the right place and the ruins are awfully attractive.

One place I always long to bring you to is New Grange, near Drogheda—it's most inspiring. A great mound as big as Lissadell House: you go in by a narrow passage and come to a huge chamber: great pillar stones roofed over with slabs—flat. Here and there dim chisellings are to be seen—circles and spirals. It's like something out of a dream. No one knows its history.

Norah Connolly just been again. She is going to write to you about publishers in America, and says that you would do better with a more regular publisher than my friend, who is more of a printer, who publishes occasionally.

You will see that Liberty Hall is raided and that they have arrested the caretaker! I simply yelled when I read it. Do you remember how someone carried off his wife's photo ? You got it in the end—and another English soldier stole his dog. I think that the police must have brought the gun in with them. They are very given to that sort of trick, and I know that the Committee would have made a row if anyone had brought in a gun.

Did you ever read a book called *Human Nature and Politics* ? It is awfully interesting—by Graham Wallas. Every would-be leader of Revolution should read it. It is the sort of thing that comes instinctively in Ireland, and though we never philosophise about how to run a movement, we do it by faith or luck or instinct.

There is such a nice dog here—a 'Poppet,' only bigger and black, but so friendly.

The soldiers are nearly all so small and so young that you feel they ought to be at school, instead of idling about with iron hats and fixed bayonets. It's an awful life for a young man; I don't expect any of them will ever settle down to a quiet life again. They all want to be demobilised, but if they were they'd hate it, and there is not enough work already, so Lord knows what they'd do. I suppose they'd starve and that there would be a revolution!

I think one of the reasons why they are making wars is to dispose of revolutionary man-power. They have made an awful world of it, and in the meantime Dev. is in America and the oppressed peoples are joining forces.

There's a vicious crop of dragon's teeth sprouting in many lands.—Much love, I must stop.

CORK JAIL,
August 30, 1919.

DEAREST OLD DARLING,—I ought to get out on the 16th October but that means nothing, and I would never dream of counting on it.

If I do get out and am not re-arrested on the doorstep, I will wire to you. English law in Ireland is but legalised oppression. Police law is very comic, if you consider: they accused me, they gave evidence against me, their magistrate condemned me, and they are allowed to garrison the jail with guns in their hands to see that I don't get out. It would be awfully funny if everyone was allowed to guard their own prisoner.

The gas has gone on strike here to make a little variety! but they have let me have two candles, so I can see alright without hurting my eyes.

. . . . . .

The labourers' strike here has been won hands down.

I rejoice in the bad weather when I think of Denikin sticking in the mud of the Ukraine. Armed cars, lorries and tanks—in a clay country without roads! A motor car is useless there except in the summer—there are no bridges and the fords are often impassable. It's all deep sticky clay. The lightest carriage takes four horses to pull it, and can only crawl. You never saw such a country for getting about in in the Autumn! There is nothing for aeroplanes to attack and it's hardly worth an Englishman's or a Cossack's while to attack small villages of thatched mud cottages. So maybe Lenin will win through after all. God speed him! and poor Russia. I wonder so on whose side C—— is.

CORK JAIL,
October 1, 1919.

DEAREST OLD DARLING,—Your letter just arrived—such a joy, as I thought we were cut off.

Fancy you painting cupboards! It sounds quite well, though it did give you a headache. There is something quite poisonous in some of those made-up enamels. I once made myself deadly sick painting a bath.

I thought there was something queer about the strike too. But it may be that Thomas could not put it off any longer because of pressure from the rank and file.

Do tell me more about Wilson. I don't think the enemy would mind my knowing that! I think that his patent is very nearly up in America. I hear lots of news from there.

Dev. is simply splendid. He's not made a single mistake. So straight and honest.

That's another thing about this strike: the people may take control and everything go with a rush. I have not at all the opinion that the English people could not run amok. They very nearly did about a hundred years ago and neither Army nor Militia could be trusted. The soldiers don't seem to be a bit well disciplined and I think could be easily carried away. I think the Government must be afraid of this, as they are so down on any discussions of Bolshevism, Socialism or even Co-operation.

I would have liked to have tried a new experiment in the way of strikes and that would be to run the trains, that is a certain number, with food, coal and a limited number of passengers, collaring the money and paying the staff. It would be great *if* it could be done. Of course, the clerks would have to join up.

The one great thing about the strike is that they won't be able to keep up supplies to Kolchak and Co. That I think will be the one great gain and that makes me doubt if it's a plot. They do so want Russia to be reduced to slavery again. This may just save the Revolution. The blockade and starvation sound so awful: just the same policy as was adopted over here as early as the time of Henry VIII. Among the State Papers are letters from English officials in Ireland to Secretary Cromwell, telling that they were destroying the standing corn and killing the cattle.

Philip Sidney's description of the starvation in Elizabeth's time is awful. They never stopped doing this till after Oliver Cromwell's day, and after that till quite lately they starved the people whenever they could by legislating so as to produce famines.

There is a great move on at present among the English enemy to influence the Pope against Ireland, but they have not the remotest chance of succeeding. They tried hard to get a pro-English Cardinal for Australia ! The Pope wisely refrained from appointing one at all, owing to the 'strained political situation.' There was also a move on to get a Nuncio appointed from Rome to London to have authority over the Catholic Church in both England and *Ireland!* A very cute move on England's part, for of course he would have to be partial to England. But—I don't think !

Have you heard anything of this ? I got it from America.

People here tell me that a lot of this sniping of police is done by themselves, either for vengeance or money. Most poor young men would think £500 easily gained by a bullet through an arm or leg. Some of the stories are so absurd : it's certainly not any of our crowd.

I am supposed to be out quite soon now. It will be a great bore if the strike is still on. Of course I would not travel in England if they were on strike : I would always back Labour—even English ! and would not put my foot on a blackleg train. I could get to Dublin easily on a bike or walking : just give me time enough !

I wonder what you will do about food. I see you are being rationed.

You never told me about Staskow. Do try and remember. Perhaps you did not get my letter asking you. You put no address, so I write to London and hope that you will get it. Have you fixed up about the flat ?

Now good-bye and best love to you.

CORK JAIL,
October 8, 1919.

DEAREST OLD DARLING,—Such a joy to get yours, If you only knew what a joy it was to hear about Staskow. I feel as if I never know from day to day whether he is alive or not. What on earth does he want over here? He wouldn't like it if he got here. Of course if it's true that he has married a rich wife, he'd be alright, but if not I don't know what he'd do. I dare say though, that he would be safer over here.

I think you are right about the strike being engineered by those two. But I believe that the men could have won. They were very strong and Government would have had to pay the miners under D.O.R.A. A lot were already idle owing to shortage of trains. The Irish railwaymen had to be paid too. These two items were quite humorous. They were kept in, to throw Government money to finance the strike.

Do you see that the police have shot another boy? In the North this time. I hope Carson will denounce the outrage.

I can't make any plans until I get out. I will write when I do. Would your health be fit to come across? I am sure it would do you a lot of good once you got here. It's still like summer, a queer summer, with lovely autumn tints and birds singing—like fairyland.

In Tirnanog summer and spring go hand in hand in the sunny weather,
Brown autumn leaves and winter snow come tumbling down together.

It's just as mad as that here at present and quite delicious. The cloud effects in Cork are wonderful.

To go back to the strike: I don't quite believe that the middle-class crowd could have run the country for long. They could never have tackled coal: they would have been alright for a bit. But they ought to have struck during the 'season.' It would have been much more inconvenient for the idle rich and much more difficult to feed them. It seemed a very trifling thing to risk a strike for, but wages are the only thing that will move an Englishman.

The Government are counting on establishing an 'aristocracy' of Labour, well-paid and satisfied, who will go to Parliament, compromise, sell every cause, act with the police, and trample on the underdog.

Now goodbye, darling. Love to Esther and to you. Bless you.

CORK JAIL,
October 18, 1919.

DEAREST OLD DARLING,—Yours just come, and I am so glad to hear that you are better. I wish to goodness you weren't staying in London for the winter, it's so unhealthy. Why don't you go a trip to America—a warm part? It's so odd your getting a sore throat. I never remember you getting one: you used to get colds on your chest.

If I get out I will try to find out about folk-lore for you. I only know the usual things—fighting and making love, like all primeval savages. I have been reading a lot of history here, but more modern, and, like you, have been hunting for the things we have thought and done differently from other nations. The one thing that stands out is that we never produced a tyrant. There was something that prevented any man or woman ever desiring to conquer all Ireland—a sort of feeling for 'decentralisation' (modern 'soviets').

Brian Boru was High King, but he never interfered with his under-King, and so on down till now. It's very curious, for in a way it was that that prevented the conquest of Ireland, till the English enemy got rid of every family of note : at the same time it always prevented the Irish getting together under one head for long enough to do more than win a battle. This makes me have such faith in the Republic. The country is now all organised and can do without leaders, but it has learnt that it must act together. I have no fear of the North. It held out much longer than the South by some hundred years, and it's only a bit behind the times. It's begun to move at the fringes.

I don't know what this new book of MacNeill's is: it might help you. If it is any good I will send it. Have you *Ossian* ? or shall I send it to you ? You pick up yarns locally that are awfully good but I never can remember them. Also let me know : does the Book of Kells inspire you ? Do you remember about O'Daly, the blind poet of Lissadil ? He was the originator of Mrs. Clark and Co.

There were great stories about St. Brigid and other women of that date too. They were very powerful and I believe that is rather a feature of Irish History. There is something coming out in the *Bulletin* about them : I must send it to you.

I don't think I told you about a peeler in Ballingeary who was being transferred North. No one would even bid for his stock of turf, just saved and ready for the winter, so he burnt it and scattered it and then swore an information ! He got compensation levied on the district. It was headed up in the papers : 'Another S.F. Outrage !'

Best love to you both. I must try and arrange to get over and see you in London and Joe in Scotland if I get free.

MOUNTJOY PRISON, DUBLIN

October 1920—*June* 1921

[illegible]

October [illegible] 1920.

DEAREST [illegible] DARLING—I [illegible] just got [illegible] from you, forwarded from [illegible] which [illegible] more [illegible] have [illegible]

[illegible]

Insurance [illegible]

[illegible] wrote the other day [illegible] must publish [illegible] about Art and the Renaissance. [illegible] since I [illegible] here, so I could not keep it for you.

[illegible] you [illegible]. How long are you

'Remand.'

MOUNTJOY PRISON,
DUBLIN,
October 10, 1920.

DEAREST OLD DARLING,—I have just got a card from you, forwarded from Liberty Hall, which wonders most appropriately what I am doing! It must have been written somewhere about the time when I was laid by the heels again. It was very bad luck. I went for a week-end holiday with Sean, and the motor car he was driving kept breaking down all the time. We had to spend Saturday night at a place somewhere among the Dublin mountains: I at a farm house and he and a friend—a French journalist—at an inn. Coming back the same thing happened. Engines, horn and lamps all being out of order. The police pulled us up because of the tail lamp not being there: they asked for permit; he had none, so they got suspicious and finally lit a match in my face and phoned for the military. All the King's horses and all the King's men arrived with great pomp and many huge guns and after a weary night in a police station, I found myself here on remand, till—to quote their own words—they 'decide' whether to bring a charge against me or not. It sounds comic opera, but it's the truth!

Your card, talking of heat and sunshine, sounds so delightful.

It's bitter here. Storms of rain and a light frost. A hurricane two nights ago.

I saw such an appreciative note on a book Esther wrote the other day: something just published about Art and the Renaissance. It was since I was here, so I could not keep it for you.

I wonder if you will ever get this. How long are you

staying in Florence? I wonder if you love all the places I loved. I suppose it is all getting spoilt and modern. Half its charm was its old-worldness, and the absence of the English with their Baedekers. There used to be only a small and select colony, which we avoided. Do you know any Italian people? I believe they are very exclusive and don't like the English too much. I'd love to see the front of the Duomo and go up to San Miniato and look down at the sunset. I wonder where your hotel is. We stayed in a pension in the Piazza Cavour. Poor old Squidge. I wonder how she is. She was great value in Florence as she knew all about everything, and was almost as good as a guide book! How she loved Savonarola! I could never quite forgive him his bonfires of Vanities. So much beauty must have been burnt.

I've been working so hard these last few months, and quite successfully. Nothing is held up, even for an hour, by my removal. You'll be glad to hear that I am not on hunger strike at present.

MOUNTJOY PRISON,
DUBLIN,
October 16, 1920.

DEAREST OLD DARLING,—I have no facilities, alas! for sending postcards and obviously my last letter must have been stolen or you would have got it by now, as three cards took three and four days to come. Post marks (Italian) were very legible. I never thought of noticing letter. I will only say that I am well and cheerful, as usual, and that I would wish that I was with you, only that I know I am more useful where I am.

'*Remand.*'

MOUNTJOY PRISON,
DUBLIN,
October 20, 1920.

MY DEAREST M——,—Very many thanks for the delicious fruit you sent me. It is so refreshing and pleasant to get fruit and flowers in a jail.

I am spending my time trying to get ahead with Irish, but it's very difficult without a teacher. I wish you would send an odd picture card to Eva, Hotel Grande Bretagne, Florence, and tell her that I am all right. It's so bad for her to be worried, and she does so worry about me.

I saw that S—— got out all right. I was so glad. The police have finally given me back my clothes and toilet things, and all the contents of the bag are safe. I suppose someone is busy trying to concoct a charge against me. It takes a long time. I was wondering if anything would be planted in my bag!

MOUNTJOY PRISON,
DUBLIN,
October 27, 1920.

DARLING,—Just a scrawl to tell you that I'm very well and ' quite calm '—as Gaga used to say.

It is no use to put in anything about myself, as it would never reach you if I did!

Clare sent me two lovely cards from ' somewhere in Europe '—a great joy.

I hope the 'flu is better. Do take care.

Where is the lovely picture of Florence taken from? —the one with the high terrace in the foreground? So glad you like San Miniato. I loved it best of all, I don't quite know why, but all through the years I keep the memory of it, San Marco and the Campanile clearer than anything else. How I'd love to go to Italy with you and see all those wonderful places and things again ! I suppose it is very much changed, but it must always be beautiful. I hope that you are not going to come in for trouble there. Things seem to be boiling up.

'Remand.'

MOUNTJOY PRISON,
DUBLIN,
November 26, 1920.

DEAREST OLD DARLING,—Do you get your letters forwarded on from Florence, because Dulcibella was writing to you just as you were leaving.

I have now been locked up for two months. However, I believe it is all for the best. I love your post-cards. They are such a lovely little bit of colour in this dismal place.

Maud Gonne has just been to see me and was most pleasant. I do hope they'll let her alone. She looks very ill and worn.

I have just finished working three little blue birds on a black riband for you. They are very gaudy. Do you remember the picture I sent you out of Holloway Jail ? I must see if I can send you the riband when you come back, but maybe they'll think it a 'plot' if I ask to do so !

My time here is spent in working and in learning Irish. It is impossible to paint under present conditions.

Aren't you delighted with C—— ? Of course he missed a chance at his trial, but still, he's made a good start. It is curious how 30 seems to be an age for people to start on arduous and dangerous paths. I only hope he goes on. One almost pities J—— with his relations. C. was the white-headed boy of his family. I wonder if they will be decent to him or if it will be the unpardonable sin.

People are so odd and mixed in their ideas nowadays. To live up to the principles that everybody preaches and teaches seems to be the only crime for which there is no forgiveness.

Mr. Nevinson is over here again. I hope to see him. He is one of the real, nice, honourable men who are so often found among the English. What puzzles me with most of them is that they never want to hear the truth, and that the most they expect from their rulers is to conceal all disagreeable and unpleasant facts and dangerous, new ideas. It must be so dull to go on and on like that.

MOUNTJOY PRISON,
DUBLIN,
December 6, 1920.

DARLING,—I was delighted to get yours and paper *re* prison reform. Like most things, of course, the man who is able to start it and carry it out is the one indispensable factor, and such men are rare. Under the present system of making such appointments, it would be very unlikely that such a man would ever get the job.

You are quite right when you say things are lurid here! The Croke Park affair lasted twenty minutes by my watch and there were machine-guns going. It felt like being back in the middle of Easter Week. Croke Park is quite close. It's a miracle that so few were killed.

I haven't given up the Bolshies yet: I believe that they will greatly improve conditions for the world. Of course, I agree with you in disliking the autocracy of any class, but surely if they have the sense to organise education, they can abolish class. While they are menaced by the moneyed classes of the whole world their only hope lies in the success of a strong central government : a tyranny in fact, but once the pressure is relieved, Lenin survives, and he has not lost his original ideals, we may hope. Of course, they may go mad with the idea of Empire, and go out with their armies to force the world to come under their ideas and do awful things in the name of freedom, small nationalities, etc., but even so, they have done something. The French Revolution gave France new life, though all their fine ideas ended in horrors and bloodshed and wars. The world, too, gained. Nothing else would have given courage to the underdog and put fear into the heart of the oppressor in the way it did.

I believe all the reforms at the beginning of the nineteenth century have their roots in the Terror.

I don't agree about people being sheep. I don't find that here, except among a very small crowd indeed. Everyone wants to know, and reads and thinks and talks—especially the young. In Belfast you have the other thing—but the rest of the country is wonderfully self-controlled, patient and heroic. I have always used my influence towards decentralisation, and to make people think and act independently.

How are the women doing in Italy ? This is being an education to them here. Their heroism and spirit of self-sacrifice is wonderful, but outside the towns they want their initiative faculties developing. There has been less physical restraint on the actions of women in Ireland than in any other country, but mentally the restrictions seem to me to be very oppressive. It is hard to understand why they took so little interest in politics as a sex, when you consider that both Catholics and Dissenters (men) laboured under all their disabilities and yet remained politicians.

I am so glad you are staying on in the sun. Do look after yourself, and whatever happens, *don't come over here.* You are *too like me* to go about safely. I loved your long letter. Any foreign gossip is interesting. You must be lonely without Esther.

'Pending Sentence.'

MOUNTJOY PRISON,
DUBLIN,
December 8, 1920.

DEAREST OLD DARLING,—D.'s address is: Glendalough House, Annamore, Co. Wicklow. How I would love you to see it! It's tucked away amongst the hills and lakes, behind a little village. A low, straggling house of grey stone with a porch—quite unlike the usual kind of Irish house. Some of the windows open on to the lawn, which is a steep slope down. You go up a lot of steps into the Hall, and there are lovely fir trees and woods behind the house. You climb up on to the Moor in a few minutes and look across the mountain tops. In front, the ground slopes to a mountain torrent. The place is a sun-trap, in the midst of the bleakest mountain scenery.

I was awfully interested in your bit about prisons, and I am sending you a bit of the *Irish Times* in exchange. I wonder if you'll get it. They see danger in the most extraordinary things these days.

Norah Connolly has been to see me and she is full of Russian news. Glowing accounts as to organisation of railways and industries, in face of almost insuperable difficulties: but says they are terribly ruthless to anyone who is 'an enemy of the Republic.' I hope they won't treat Lenin as the French treated Danton!

Do you remember my talking to you about my 'special' work, and all my difficulties and doubts?

Well—I got it so under way that it goes on just as well without me. That wasn't too bad work for an untrained fool, was it ?

I suppose now that I can tell you that I was tried by court-martial for ' conspiracy,' and that the ' conspiracy ' was the Boy Scouts ! They have not made up their minds just what they'll do with me. I think they dislike me more than most. The whole thing is Gilbertian, for we have carried on for eleven years. Anyhow, it's a fresh ' ad.' for the boys !

I am now working hard at Irish. It's awfully interesting. There are such an extraordinary number of shades of sound in it. The people must have had wonderfully subtle musical ears. I wonder how much of the history of a race lies in the language.

' Pending Sentence.'

MOUNTJOY PRISON,
DUBLIN,
December 11, 1920.

DEAREST OLD DARLING,—Your almanack has just come. It is a joy to see all that lovely colour in the midst of this greyness. To appreciate colour, one wants to do without it for a bit.

I am so sorry that you are ill and I wish to goodness that I was with you. I learnt a lot about minding the sick when I had my two invalids in Holloway Jail, and I didn't make a bad hand at it at all, in spite of the many disadvantages I was born with.

Don't bother about me here. As you know, the English ideal of modern civilisation always galled me. Endless relays of exquisite food and the eternal changing of costume bored me always to tears and I prefer my own to so many people's company. To make ' conversation ' to a bore through a long dinner-party is the climax of dullness. I don't mind hard beds or simple food: none of what you might call the 'externals' worry me. I have my health and I can always find a way to give my dreams a living form. So I sit and dream and build up a world of birds and butterflies and flowers from the sheen in a dew-drop or the flash of a sea-gull's wing. Everyone who has anything to do with me is considerate and kind, and the only bore is being locked up, when there is so much to be done.

I have just read the lives of Tolstoi and of Danton. I rather love the latter. The former I don't pretend to understand. He was so unbalanced, and he compromised with all his principles—like an English Trades Union leader. I am now reading *Eothen.* What an oddity Lady H. Stanhope was!

Jail is the only place where one gets time to read.

I am interested in what you say about Italy. It has gone through such vicissitudes that one feels it must have learnt a good deal. Co-operation is good, but by no means a panacea. The old problem always remains: how to prevent all the money and power, etc., getting into the hands of a few, and they establishing themselves as a ruling tyrant class.

I am beginning to believe that everything must begin from the schools, and that only when all children of a nation have the same education will they have the same chances in life and learn to look after the people as a whole. Of course, education will have to be different, but now, in *England,* a few are trained to bully and rule, and the mass is brought up and educated to be fit only to be slaves. In Ireland we are not so bad, as local and family history educates the children, so our minds are more receptive and more free.

Now I've written you a long letter of rubbish and I have come to the end of my paper.

'Pending Sentence.'

MOUNTJOY PRISON,
DUBLIN,
December 15, 1920.

DEAREST OLD DARLING,—I do wonder how you are and whether you are being looked after properly in Bordighera. I wonder where Esther is lecturing and on what. I should love to hear her.

I suppose you saw all about Cork—also the explanations! It was so silly to assert that the City Hall caught fire from Patrick St. I know the city well, and a broad river and many streets lie between the two areas. An ordinary human being like myself is puzzled when the cleverest liars in the world state things that are so easily contradicted. The extraordinary policy of lying and perjury surprises me anew every day. I'd no idea people were so bad.

Italy seems to be rather lively still. I hope you won't come in for trouble. Greece makes me laugh—also Armenia. I think that they must at last have realised the capacity for lying on the part of Western politicians. I have had first-hand news of Russia. They have had a terrible lot to contend with, but they have done some wonderful reconstructive work. Of course they, the workers, were horrified with the number of executions, and thought them horribly cruel and drastic, but, comparing them to the French Terror, said that these were just, according to their own laws, and said that accusations had to be proved, and were proved, quite honestly; but that anyone proved to be acting against the interest of the new regime was remorselessly executed. Nothing approaching the orgies of appalling murders that Robespierre indulged in has occurred, although the circumstances, in many respects, are similar.

India seems to be getting pretty warm too. I see

that volunteers have been 'proclaimed,' according to the papers, and they don't do that for nothing. Ours were only proclaimed about a year and three months ago.

How one longs for peace! The old League of Nations is talking pompous rubbish (for the benefit of Democracy, I suppose) about the reduction of armaments, and each one of them is only intent to find out what his neighbour is going to do in the way of navies, etc., and tip his boss to go one better.

Tell me, do the Italians go in for polished brown leather boots and gaiters? The legs of the English Army of Occupation were one of the things that struck me at my court-martial. Such a lot of time must be wasted polishing them!

'*Pending Sentence.*' MOUNTJOY PRISON,
DUBLIN,
December 20, 1920.

DEAREST OLD DARLING,—I am enraptured with the blue bird. I think it is just perfect. It was sent into the jail for me to-day.

I wonder so what you saw in the papers. It's no use trying to write the truth to you. The papers here were not too bad at all. I can't see myself how any one with a sense of humour could seriously regard a child's organisation as a 'conspiracy,' but any stick does to beat the Irish rebel with!

I long to see you. If I ever get out, we must have a week together, somewhere warm and pretty.

You'll have to wait for a present! There are complications. My love and thoughts and good wishes and prayers are with you all the time. Take great care of yourself, and run no risks.

The world seems to be in an awful state. One

wonders so about Japan and America and England. My belief is that the English would not mind another war. They don't know what to do with their unemployed. I am sorry for the poor in places like Manchester these days.

I am now reading the *Conquest of Peru*. It's so modern. All those atrocities were done in the name of Christianity and of all the noble virtues—just like to-day. A nation of quiet, peaceful people was wiped out and their civilisation destroyed because the Spaniards wanted gold. The only hopeful thing is that the Spaniards went down, and if corruption drags a nation down and breaks up an Empire, we ought soon to see a debacle such as has never been seen before! Good-luck for the New Year.

Pending Sentence.'

MOUNTJOY PRISON,
DUBLIN,
December 24, 1920.

DEAREST OLD DARLING,—Your brooch is the greatest joy. Colour and design both perfect. The lovely card and long letter have just reached me, and both are a joy.

You have no idea of the awful things that are happening here and how wonderful the people are, so determined and so self-controlled. The enemy have found more than they expected. At other times, when they got rid of 'leaders,' the country sat down, but to-day leaders count for very little. They are mouthpieces and keep order, and there are rank after rank of men and women capable of taking their places. It is wonderful how they understand the international possibilities—isolation, etc.; everyone realises too that it is by suffering, dying and sticking out that we will win. Great attempts have been made to divide us, but nobody differs about fundamentals, and everybody has their own ideas about details of policy, which they discuss quite amiably and openly. There is no jealousy, and no one is out for self.

The whole world situation is extraordinary. The triangle—England, America and Japan—is to my mind the most exciting of all things. Against whom is the American Fleet being built? I met an Indian Prince this summer who told me of his ambitions to form a great Asiatic Empire! Imperialism gone yellow and brown. Then there are the Bolshies, who are working for yellow and brown communes. One feels that both sides would want Australia. Harding was the candidate we most favoured of the possible two, though all were sympathetic, and Dev., etc. would not take sides in a purely American political campaign. I think those who rule America must want anti-English feeling stirred up, or they would have locked us all up, as they did the Bolshie crowd.

Did you hear that Ll. George arranged with Thomas for Labour to prevent munitions being shipped for use against Bolshies? He wanted to trade with them, and keep in with the crowd by promising them war material.

I am so glad you saw the *Irish Times*. It was much the best. I can't understand how they can get so many to play their tricky game. They swear on oath again and again that they can account for every cartridge in a barrack and know when one is missing. And they swear just as often that they can get no information when half a dozen lorries full of men shoot off hundreds of cartridges. . . . But, of course, you see the papers.

It will be three months come S. Stephen's day that I was arrested.

Isn't it Gilbertian to pretend that the Fianna is a conspiracy? It was started in 1909, and has always been open and never secret. I asked them could they point to one 'cowardly attack' on the armed forces of the Crown by little boys. It was an awful performance: after being shut up alone for two months to be suddenly brought up before eight 'judges,' plus prosecutors, be-wigged barristers, enemy witnesses, etc., and surrounded by bayonets! I am glad you thought I did not do so badly.

'Two Years Hard Labour.'

MOUNTJOY PRISON,
DUBLIN,
December 30, 1920.

MY DEAREST OLD DARLING,—A happy New Year to you all! You should see how gay my cell is, with all the lovely cards stuck around. Don't forget to thank Clare for two lovely p.c.s she sent me from Germany. Tell her she should come over and help the starving Irish children, though we are not as yet so distressful as Central Europe, thank God.

I am so engrossed by my Irish studies. I know you will say 'Jack of all trades!' but anyhow, if I can only go on for two years, I *will* be master, and I began as a duty, not as a pleasure. Luckily I find it most entertaining and quite different from any other language I ever dabbled in. The letters have so many different sounds each that it is as if you had an enormous alphabet. Then the words have sort of inflexions in front as well as behind, and—above all—it is a language of idioms, and corresponds little with any other language. There is no verb 'to have.' (I think national character is shown in a language, and that shows that we are not a covetous and aggressive race.) It seems to have developed along the lines of the softest and most subtle sounds and to be capable of very definite and subtle expression of shades of thought. I wish we were together. I am sure it would appeal to your poetic instincts, and that you'd get all sorts of ideas from it. It often seems to me that Yeats got most of the charm of his writing from it.

I have just been reading 'The Celtic Twilight' again, and was surprised to find it so bad. Egoistic and frothy bubble, but a lovely poem in front. The subject is so beautiful, too, and he seems to make it so common, like Andrew Lang's fairy tales.

Things seem to be moving slowly here. Do you realise that Æ. prophesied all this and worse and that a great 'Avata' (I don't know how to spell—it might be Avatar) is to come out of the mountain country round Fermanagh and lead Ireland to victory. He should be about 20 years old now. He told me this years ago when blood and flames seemed incredible and of the Dark Ages. We'll hope the end will come true as well. I believe myself that it is only a question of holding out, and that it is by sacrifice that we shall win. The people are so wonderful in their steadfastness.

MOUNTJOY PRISON,
DUBLIN,
New Year's Day, 1921.

DEAREST OLD DARLING,—I was so delighted to get your p.c. yesterday. I have written you twice since I got the lovely bird. Mrs. Skeffington brought it over and sent it up at once. She was so afraid of its being stolen in a raid. It's a real joy. I also got an almanack and a tryptich card. Both beautiful. I can't remember how to spell 'triptych.' Where the 'y' should go is a mystery to me. I wonder so how many of my letters you get. The post seems to be awfully unreliable. One Christmas card I got took five days to come from England.

It rather amused me to see that for starting Boy Scouts in *England* Baden Powell was made a Baron. I have always heard that he did not really start them but that it was a woman. I suppose, though, that he more or less ran them and made them a success. I bet he did not work as hard as I did from 1909-1913.

It's been so warm here the last few days that some of the birds started singing, and pigeons were carrying bits of straw about in their mouths, and bowing to each other in the most absurd way.

I see that d'Annunzio's reign is over and that he says he would like to come to Ireland. I don't think he'd like it if he got here, at least, judging from the only books of his I ever read. I think he would find us too strait-laced. You could certainly write the most thrilling books of adventure, telling of hair-breadth escapes and daring deeds, but for love affairs people have little time to spare. Kathleen comes first, though people get married on the run, and go on 'running.' This last year many babies were born, whose fathers were on the run. It's awfully hard on the mothers. Curfew, too, is terrible, for you can't get a doctor. However, the women are as brave as brave, and though they suffer terribly both mentally and physically they put on a brave face and you'd never guess.

Now good luck to you and all friends, from C. de M. (cheerful though captive !).

MOUNTJOY PRISON,
DUBLIN,
January 7, 1921.

DEAREST OLD DARLING,—I hope that you have got some of my letters by now. This will be the last for some time ! Don't you worry about me, though. I am alright. I have written three times to thank you for the lovely brooch. It's a joy and came quite alright and in time for Christmas. I am working very hard at Irish. If I can learn at my time of life, I think it will be a record. I wrote you a lot about it in my last letter, which you may have got by now. One thing I like in it is the liberty. English ties you down. If you are going to be considered educated, you must speak and spell in the same way as those who are belonging to the ruling clique. They clip words and talk slang and it is all very ugly. Now in Irish, localisms are not like English accent, but add expression and beauty. Spelling, voices and words vary, and most of the changes seem to be made to soften and beautify the sound, while in English much seems to be sacrificed to speed. I think that probably the language has a good deal to say to the development of the pretty soft Irish voices one hears everywhere. I often wish that the Irish musical scale, with its quarter-tones, had not been civilised out of existence. I feel that there is some faint echo of it in the innumerable vowel sounds that glide into each other and seem almost interchangeable. I am so full of it all that I must write about it, though maybe it's dull to you. But there's not much to write about in here. I am sure we are going to have some great authors, once the younger generations get in on the language. Are you writing anything much? I wish we had you here for a laureate! I'd love to see you writing to order of the Republic! though I'm afraid you'd only get tragic themes, with now and then a dash of broad farce.

I wonder what your plans are and I do hope that you will stay in the land of the sun for the present. I think that England is getting into a very bad way and anything might happen there. After the Napoleonic Wars they met the trade depression by shipping off hundreds of jailbirds (political, labour) to convict settlements. They have not got that outlet now, and goodness knows what a more educated proletariat will do when starving. It's an awful lookout everywhere. Ll. George is still busy screwing down safety valves.

When I get out, we must have a holiday together, and Esther too, somewhere beautiful and peaceful. Perhaps in the great New Republic! Who knows?

Don't come over here just now. It would not be safe for you.

MOUNTJOY PRISON,
DUBLIN,
April 1, 1921.

DEAREST OLD DARLING,—Just had a visit from Clare, which no doubt you already know. It was delightful and we had such a pleasant talk and she is such a joy to look at, all shimmering blues and soft, pretty draperies. I did not expect her, so you can imagine the excitement.

I grub away at my plot here and have got quite a lot of things in. It was a desert when I began and I don't believe it had been honestly dug. Few people share my love for digging deep. I have a few sweet-peas quite four inches high, which is a triumph. Most people are only sowing theirs. The eating peas are just coming up and the starlings and pigeons make war on everything.

How I envy you in the land of flowers! I wonder are there starlings in Italy? I remember things they called 'ucellini'—at least it sounded like that—but I don't know what they looked like with their feathers on, as I always saw them, almost daily, in stews.

I am working hard at Irish and more and more interested every day. It is so picturesque and so utterly unlike anything else and much more difficult to learn. No other language helps you and it is all idioms and exceptions to every rule. I can write compositions and letters and I can read, of course, with a dictionary, and I think I could get what I wanted if I were stranded, but I can't really talk yet. I wish I knew why grammarians always search the world—or dictionaries—for the words you want least in a language, and give them you to learn, and leave out the words you want every day. I can talk about hawks and flails, scythes, rye and barley, magicians, kings and fairies ; but I couldn't find out how to ask for an extra blanket or a clean plate or a fork. I suppose I shall find out some day !

Have you been writing much poetry ? I forget ; did I ever send you a little book by Austin Clark ? He is the latest minor poet over here and he is quite unlike a modern. He is heroic and writes long yarns about kings and historical magnificence, which is very original, in this country, where the poets wander in dim twilight mixed with turf-smoke, peopled with peasants and mystic beings with pale hands.

Do you ever write what the writers call *vers libres* ? To me they seem the last resource of the lazy and incompetent. Send me something of yours next time you write.

Italy certainly fills one with hope, Greece too, and Poland. We are the only people left in chains. Our people are wonderful ; there is little fear of death among them, and heaven is so real to them that they look forward to meeting their friends there. The present persecutions seem to have brought the living and the dead into such close touch, it is almost uncanny. It all makes one feel that they must win. The spiritual must prevail over the material in the end. We suffer, and suffering teaches us to unite and stand by each other. It also makes for us friends everywhere, while the policy of our enemies is leaving them friendless. More ominous still, it is utterly demoralising themselves and setting all the decent of their own people against them, as soon as they find out the truth.

A volley has just gone off suddenly, quite close. It has ceased to be a novelty or to make one jump, but it is an awful bore not being able to go and see what's up. Most nights one hears them and to me it is a wonder that more people are not killed. There were aeroplanes over here yesterday, which is usually a bad omen.

I was awfully sorry about Janey. She was such a dear and there are so few of the old ones left. She somehow never grew old and only gave up bicycling a little while ago. A great many people will miss her and I was glad to hear that she was with friends and well looked after. She spent all her life looking after other people.

I was delighted with your appearance in the snaps. I hope Esther is as well as you appear to be.

I was awfully interested to hear that R—— had staged a Pearse play: I wonder which?

MOUNTJOY PRISON,
DUBLIN,
May 3, 1921.

DEAREST OLD DARLING,—It was such a joy getting the rosary and a visit from Father Sweetman the other day. Please thank all concerned. It is really beautiful and the combination of green and silver is a treat. Another great joy is the last p.c.—Our Lady, Botticelli: red dress, blue cloak and eastern headdress. I have a lot of your cards stuck up and I am always looking at them.

Such a blessing to know that you are so well. It

is a pity you have to come back just now. How I'd love to see Florence again and the country round! I did so love it long ago. I remember catching butterflies wildly across hedges and ditches at Fiesole and distressed Squidge quite unable to follow. Young ladies hadn't found their legs in those days, and mine would have been quite up to the mark—even in these days!

In times of war it is better to have at least six different banking accounts, all under different names! and all in different banks, though it is awfully hard not to mix cheque-books.

If I die in a hurry, there will be a real old treat for the heirs. I did not tell you about this before because I did not want to worry you, but it's all right now.

My garden work is beginning to repay. Peas are six inches high and new seeds are coming up every day. I have a pink carnation in bud which I am watching. We've had a spell of fearfully dry weather and a scorching sun, but to-day we had a nice soft rain, and the sun is now shining again, so the garden will be great to-morrow.

Irish is going ahead. I am beginning to get hold of more useful words. Half the difficulty comes from there being no grammars or modern literature. Everything Irish having been smashed up in each generation since Elizabeth of England's reign, the language never seems to have got consolidated into a complete whole. Some of the words exist in four or five different forms, and each little district is wildly keen to stick to its own form. I am just through the whole of O'Growney and can write composition and read a bit and talk a little. Were it any other language I could talk quite well, with the knowledge I have of words and grammar, but the idioms and exceptions to every rule are endless.

If only the Lord would give us a grammarian who would organise facts like Otto and Arne did.

I object to learning bits of Connaught, Ulster and Munster, with a smattering of fifteenth century thrown in!

Fancy if a German had to learn Cockney, Yorkshire and Somerset, with Chaucer thrown in!

It was awfully nice seeing Clare. She had such a pretty frock and a lovely Italian jewel and a shawl that was a dream. She was a treat to the eyes, surrounded by ugliness and greyness.

I delighted in your poem: 'humble-splendid' is beautiful. I wonder if you have been reading German. Do send another verse next time you write.

G—— must have been shocked at your seeing the Pope. You must be great at Italian.

Father McGuiness is a delightful person. I made a speech at a party in his honour when I was 'on the run.'

'The run' is awfully funny, and I'd love to tell you some of the adventures and hairbreadth escapes. They (the enemy) are very clever about detail, but so often don't see the wood for the trees, and they don't understand simplicity and truth.

MOUNTJOY PRISON,
DUBLIN,
June 8, 1921.

DEAREST OLD DARLING,—I had a visit from Mrs. Kent to-day and quite forgot to ask her to write to you, and tell you how well I am. It is so difficult to remember to tell everything in the rush of a monthly visit. She told me that she was raided the other night and that the Black and Tans stole a bunch of *my* letters written to her and her sister, some time before

Christmas, from here, all of which had passed their own Censor. I have been puzzling ever since as to their motive, for I can see no point in it at all, unless they mean to sell my autograph! and I never asked more than 6d. for that, and I did such hundreds for various just causes.

I long to see your book, and I know I should love it. No philosophy worth speaking of has yet come out of Ireland. Yours sounds as if it might be philosophy, and it might, therefore, be epoch-making. Mind you send me a copy if it comes out before I do. I am sure it will be educational and they let me have educational books.

Just been reading *After the Peace*. Its awfully enlightening. I am very sorry for the English working people. I don't think their leaders or their writers ever get to the bottom of the incredible wickedness of their rulers. Brailsford and others of his type seem to think them short-sighted and stupid. Over here we don't.

How delightful P.A.'s garden must be! Mine is a great pleasure. Seeing seeds grow into flowers is a great joy. My cooking peas are covered in bloom and the sweet peas are in bud, pansies are very bright, carnations in bud—and it's all come out of a desert. There are lots of little annuals coming up too but I don't a bit know what they will be like. There are baby sparrows hopping about it to-day.

The Irish is going ahead fine. I believe I could make a speech in it already and could blunder along about a great many things.

I can write much better than I can speak. I could write most of this in Irish. What I find most hard is understanding both reading and talk. There are such infinite varieties of both pronunciation and spelling for nearly every word: then again, there are so many words for some things and none for others. It's utterly unlike anything else and makes me realise for the first time how like each other French, German and English are. The idioms, too, seem to be endless and quite impossible to get at except by memorising. I am wishing for someone to work out the theories and grammar that must be at the back of it all. So far, all the grammars are based on English and are very scrappy and bad. They worry you to death explaining obvious things, and whole volumes are taken up with unnecessary phonetics and details of the tenses of verbs which are very easy and only a matter for memory. The real difficulties—(i.e. the verbal noun and prepositional and adverbial phrases) are never tackled or systematised. I have gone through three grammars and a half, and yet I don't believe I could go through an ordinary story even with a dictionary. With half the knowledge of French I could read anything in that lingo.

MOUNTJOY PRISON,
DUBLIN,
Undated (presumably after June 8th).

DEAREST OLD DARLING,—I have just finished my Irish exercises, a task I set myself each night, and it's curious how one works when it's only oneself drives one. The only thing I want at the moment is someone to compare notes with, to find out if I get on as quickly as I ought. I write about 250 words each night for an exercise of composition, as all the exercises seemed to be about things I could not conceive wanting to talk much about. Flails are things they are very keen about in grammars: cows and rye, mice and cats are favourite subjects. I do wish a scholar would write an Irish Grammar for me!

Your last poem is absolutely perfect. I like it as much as anything you ever wrote. You will be glad to hear that I have a fellow-prisoner who will appreciate it. It's quite true, too: I mean the poem. Do send me another.

The post-cards are a great joy and I often bless the inventor.

I long to see your book. Will it be big? If things work out all right here, I shall be able to help you publish it when I get out, as I have a 'job' and I will go back to it.

I am very interested in what you say about Scotus Erigina. I vaguely thought of him as a cleric and a magician but know nothing. What sort of a philosopher was he? But I still stick to it—that we have not produced a philosophy, though we may have produced a philosopher. Look at the French, Greeks, Germans. They tell me that our ancient writings were nature poems and minute family annals, with immense detail of each head of a clan and their relations: wars, marriages, the buying and selling of cattle and such like. Also histories on rather the same lines. Each family or clan had its annals told by its bards, but they don't seem to have written about abstract things much or to have indulged in speculation, thoughts or theories.

I do hope Dr. K. M. will be able to do something for Esther. I know you will do what you can.

I wish you could see my rock garden. It's beginning to be quite interesting, with little stairs up and down and paths and a sort of obelisk at the top. A most obliging warder, who was bringing me stones, offered to get a huge rock put on the top of it, so I made a flat 'plateau,' with a stairway up to it, and he got the two rocks hoisted up. Unluckily, the weather is too dry for anything to be planted. Once it begins to rain, I shall make heaps of cuttings and cover it with things. My peas are not bad, in spite of the drought. The first were ripe about ten days ago.

I can have educational books, but so far I have not got many: Irish grammars chiefly, and Brailsford's *After the Peace*, but it's quite impossible to know what to get when you are shut up. If there is anything thrilling in the line of Labour or Economics or Co-operation, you might send it to me.

I had a visit to-day from M—— and from another great friend, Moira O'Byrne. They both promised to write and tell you how well I am looking. The latter had just seen Bob Barton, who is in splendid health and spirits and can't make out why he was released. No more can I. Diplomacy is very puzzling.

There's an ambush going on outside this, and it is most tantalising not to be able to see. I never saw one, and I should love to! We heard a great explosion one day and saw dark columns of smoke. It was very exciting!

Did you ever read *My Life in Two Hemispheres*, by Gavan Duffy Sen.? He must have been a most exceptional man, and a most high principled and noble one. Fintan Lalor and he were the only real brains among the Young Ireland movement as far as I can see. He seems to have thought out and originated all the things we are doing to-day, as well as the Parnell policy. It is curious how he is not appreciated here.

Mitchel's rhetoric is like a bible to patriots and is quoted up and down the land. He put out fine-phrased things that the incoherent wanted to say and could not—and so he lived. Gavan Duffy, who went in for ideas and policies, not phrases, is practically unknown. I think that he must have been one of the noblest characters that ever came out of Ireland and one of the wisest. His weakness—if it was a weakness—was that he could not work with crooks and twisters. I wonder, was he grandfather to our friend? I am always so vague about relationships. He seems too young to be a son.

Clare got a special visit through interest; I don't know whether Gertrude could or not: it depends on whom you know. Pri. knows everybody.

Isn't the grit in this country wonderful? I do feel so proud of being Irish.

NORTH DUBLIN UNION
INTERNMENT CAMP, 1923

[illegible]

DARLING—You will [illegible]
[illegible] Those [illegible] of the [illegible]
[illegible] whole [illegible] was getting [illegible]
[illegible] necessary [illegible]
[illegible]

[illegible]

[illegible] I will not write [illegible]
[illegible] had to get things [illegible]
[illegible] getting [illegible] and [illegible] done the
[illegible]
[illegible] and [illegible] not be

North Dublin Union
Internment Camp,
Undated (*Nov. or Dec.* 1923).

Dearest Old Darling,—You will have seen how I was arrested and I hope that one of the two girls I asked to write to you wrote. I was getting on splendidly with continual meetings to ask people to sign a memorial for the release of the prisoners.

I started every morning with three girls who gave out bills and went up and down Dublin and wherever a crowd collected they said a few words. It was a great tribute to my efforts to stop them !

I went on hunger strike directly I was taken : they offered me tea in the Police Station and I just decided right off. I only did three days and I was quite happy and did not suffer at all. I slept most of the time and had lovely dreams and the time went by quite quickly. I think I would have slipped out quite soon. Tom Derrick came in, called off the strike and woke me up ! One girl is very bad : she nearly died and it only stopped just in time. She is in Hospital outside now.

Be a darling and send me your book. I meant to order it in Dublin, but could not remember the long name.

There are three very nice little girls in here with me and we are quite a cheerful little party. It is a vast and gloomy place, haunted by the ghosts of broken-hearted paupers.

Sea-gulls and rooks fly around. I saw a piebald rook to-day ; it looked so odd.

Do write a line. I could not write before, as letters are so limited and I had to get things in.

I have been sketching the girls and have done the work in water colours.

Now bye-bye and best love to you both. . . .

North Dublin Union
Internment Camp.
December 12, 1923.

Dearest Old Darling,—I was so delighted to see your dear old fist. The letter came yesterday, but the book has not materialised yet. I expect the first letter went up in a blaze! A whole row of wooden huts, in which the Censor's office was, went up in smoke and one letter and some parcels went up. It was a glorious blaze. We enjoyed it enormously—far better than the pictures! The red shirts and brass helmets of the firemen on the roof, in and out of the smoke and the orange flames, made a dramatic note, and suggested thrills and romance and heroines and the nethermost pit. But all that was burnt was beds and boots and an apple pie of mine and other rather valueless property!

As far as I am concerned, I don't know how long they mean to keep me. There can be no charge against me—that is, anything more than a police-court charge of 'impeding the traffic.' It's just spite and fear of my tongue and voice. My real democratic principles, I expect!

This place is crowded with cats, dogs and ghosts, but we are really a very cheerful little party. The hunger-strike did not involve any suffering for me, but it was very short.

Take care of yourself.

AMERICAN TOUR, 1922

[illegible] nip the bird worst [illegible] and
[illegible] small stuffy cabin and [illegible] of people
[illegible] you don't want.

[illegible] of the usual English [illegible] who
[illegible] Ireland and [illegible] the [illegible]
[illegible] those who [illegible]
[illegible]

[illegible]
[illegible] started by doing things on its own [illegible]
[illegible] away everything [illegible] and
[illegible] not only for the sake of the country [illegible]
[illegible] conducting a campaign

On Board the 'Aquitania,'
1922.

. . . I find a ship the next worst thing to jail ! and rather like it. Small, stuffy cabin and crowds of people round you that you don't want.

We had some of the usual English at our table, who started abusing Ireland and libelling Dev. the first night. We told them what we thought of them and got ourselves put on to another table for breakfast.

I've not been ill, though things were charging about the tables one day and every one was rushing from wall to wall in their progress across the room. At night, too, I couldn't sleep, because of the way I was banged about.

I'm sure I hate a big boat and would never like a voyage. It's so luxurious and yet so uncomfortable and such an inactive, lazy life, with nothing to do but eat, sleep and look at freaks. The only nice thing is the sea, and you are so far from it, it might not be there at all.

There are no birds. There were porpoises one day, also a whale which made a fountain that caught the sunlight. For the rest you have miles and miles of dirty water.

I already wish that I was home again. It's awful not to be there at such a moment. The difficulties ahead are colossal, not the least of the problems being that for a very long time (perhaps for always) we shall each and all of us be suspicious of everything and every-one. In fact, I sometimes wonder if the rank and file will ever trust a leader again.

I wouldn't be a bit surprised if the Army, or some of it, started out doing things on its own. The domestic enemy are doing a very wrong thing ; both wrong and foolish, not only for the sake of the country but for their own sakes. They are conducting a campaign against Dev.[1] and Childers, a campaign of misstatements and innuendo, utterly despicable. Dev. is the one strong, personal influence in the country. He has always used that influence for unity and toleration and sanity, for repressing personal ambitions and for turning people's minds from a desire for vengeance to higher things. I believe that his influence and his alone has made it safe for the new domestic enemies to flaunt around. I don't like to think of what might happen if they were ever able to get the people, especially the army, to distrust him and to disbelieve in his honesty, his brains and his courage. If they succeed in this I am sorry for them, for their end will be swift and sure, more sure than his.

1922.
No date, no address.

DEAREST OLD DARLING,—So far, I've had no time to write to you, it's been hustle, hustle, hustle from meeting to train, from train to meeting, interviews, and so on.

We started from New York to Philadelphia, then Detroit, Cleveland, St. Paul's, Necropolis, Butte, Montana, Anaconda, Seattle, Portland, San Francisco, Los Angeles, Springfield, Cincinnati and now we are on our way back to New York.

I often wonder, as I look out of the train window, if you passed the same way long ago and loved the same beautiful length of river, rock or group of trees. The line to-day runs in a valley following the rambles of the Susquehanna River. When we passed over it on our way West, the trees were all bare and wintry. To-day, they are all gold and green and sparkling with white flowers. In many ways it is like Ireland, only so much bigger.

[1] Mr. de Valera.

Everywhere we go we are fêted and get great receptions. Indeed, our only complaint is that we are too much entertained, for our entertainers take absolute possession of us and of our bedrooms even, in the hotel, and we are never allowed to be alone for a minute, and if they can possibly stop me, they don't allow me to walk one yard. We arrived here before the Spring had established herself in the East, but found in Detroit to Minneapolis early Spring, the first pear trees white, and pink buds on the apple orchards.

I love the way they build cities here. So few rows of gaunt bare houses all joined together in dismal uniformity as we have at home ; but each ' home ' by itself, with trees round it and on its little plot of green grass, joined on to no other house, and with no paling or wall between it and the street and between it and its neighbours. The houses too are so nice, with their big verandahs. They are so much nicer than the houses at home or in England, and so much more comfortable and much cleaner and better divided-up. The bathrooms are a joy, and even the small houses have them : walls and all of shining white tiles, and cupboards built in to the walls, so convenient.

Akron especially took my fancy. We drove out to the suburbs, and even the poor houses stood alone, among greenery.

We saw the Mississippi at Minneapolis and a lovely waterfall, by the side of which great piles of unmelted snow lay, melting slowly in the shade of the cliff crowned by flowering cherry trees and shrubs in full leaf. It was very wintry crossing the foothills and the nearer we came to Butte, Montana, the wilder and colder it grew.

Butte was one of the places that stand out for its reception, for they met us with a band and an army. All Sligo seemed to be there ! Do you remember

Paddy Carty of Kilmacannon ! His son called to greet ' Miss Constance ' as he called me and he says he'll never call me anything else. He tells me that I ' put the first pair of britches ' he ever had on him : it was a matter of ' some plovers' eggs ' he said.

Our procession marched up muddy precipices, through a desolate-looking town to the Hotel. All Hotels in America are good and clean. Snow on the fields and snow in odd corners, but you don't feel the cold, I can't imagine why, as it's all muddy and damp. The town is built on the side of a mountain, and motor cars cheerfully bustle up and down mud tracks, and the ruts so deep, up to the axle, that we would hesitate to drive an ass and cart up and down. Looking down into the plain, one held one's breath and prayed that the brakes would hold. But cars don't seem to run away and turn somersaults. Only occasionally the ruts are more than axle deep and they have to wait to be pulled out if the wheel gets in.

We started for Anaconda in a blinding snow-storm. Twenty-eight miles were before us, and the road good at both ends, but unmade for a stretch of over three miles in the middle. Our car was lucky, but the one Miss Barry was in came to grief both ways. Soon after we got on to the mud track it skidded off the track, hurled itself across the ditch and landed somewhere on the mountain among the bog and scrubby bushes. It got back in the end somehow, with a wild jump.

At Anaconda we found a white town and snow over the tops of our boots. In spite of this, the meeting was fine, and we faced for Butte at midnight in deep snow. Luckily, our motor was the second, for the one in which Mr. Kelly was got lost for hours in the snow, and Miss Barry, who preceded us, landed with hers in a ditch and there they stuck. Luckily we had a chain on board and after about an hour's work—snow falling heavily

—with much groaning and creaking, we dragged and the men pushed and the beastly thing crawled out. No damage was done.

Next day we went down a copper mine. *It was awful!* Of course the manager showed us the show parts, the great passages well ventilated and the wonderful machinery, but we saw few men working. I had been put up to things by 'wicked' friends in the I.W.W. and I started to ask awkward questions. I insisted on going into hot places and seeing men working with pick and with drill. I insisted on climbing into a stoop. I saw a man drilling the copper ore without the water appliance to keep the dust down and breathing in copper dust eight mortal hours every day. This is nothing but murder, as the dust sticks in the throat and eats into the trachea and they die *for sure* of a terrible form of consumption. The hospitals are full of men suffering from work in the mines. Two men were injured during our short stay, one internally. We saw him at the hospital and they thought him dying. They told us few men live to be old in Butte, Montana.

From Butte we went across the Rockies to Seattle, passing through the waste lands of Montana, weird, unwholesome-looking mountains, slimy rocks and hollows and slimy brown earth with patches of dead grass or sage bush, looking as if the Deluge had just drained off it, and as if each hummock might hide a scaly, prehistoric monster, and each stagnant pool a water snake. For hours and hours we passed through this, like nothing I had ever seen before, until we came to the Cascade Mountains, where innumerable brooks and green pines and great cliffs surrounded us. The railway line is a marvel. Round horse-shoe curves, up and down mountains and over ravines. I wonder that the engineers are not national heroes. They certainly ought to be.

At Seattle we visited an Indian store and went wild over the work, but things were too expensive to get there, so we hurried on into Summer at San Francisco. 'Roses, roses all the way' here. We were met by huge bouquets at the station, before the ferry and by a huge committee, and we crossed a calm summer sea and looked at the Golden Gate. When we landed we found a band and a procession headed by two American soldiers, and more roses and children in Irish dress and photographers and Press men and women. We got into gaily decorated cars, surrounded by the flags of both Republics, and processed through the city.

Roses were thrown at me from the tops of trams.

I got an hour to spare and rushed through China Town and we were driven round the resurrected city. You would never know there had been an earthquake and fire so short a time ago.

At Los Angeles we found the tropics. Great palm trees lining the streets and aloes scattered like thistles through the waste stretches of country. We passed through orange groves where the fruit hung ripe on the trees, and saw great piles of golden balls on the brown earth, ready to be packed and shipped away.

Then we passed the desert of Arizona, with nothing but sand and a scanty crop of yellow bent-like grass, and aloes everywhere. We passed day and night through this on our five days' journey to Springfield, where apple blossom, lilac and syringa met us in the full blast of Spring. I found a bird's nest there in a friend's garden.

At Cincinnati we found Summer and roses again. We stayed there with friends and had one day's peace.

I am writing this in the train and it's very jumpy at times. The great meeting is to be in Madison Square Gardens on Sunday. We find great sympathy and support here and have got a lot of money. Subscriptions and pledges given at various meetings held, tot up to over £20,000.

Nobody likes the Freak State. They are trying to block us by saying that *we* are making civil war in Ireland, and I hear that they are organising stunts every night, firing off vast quantities of ammunition at nothing and pretending that we are attacking them !

We stayed with a Mr. and Mrs. Castellini at Cincinnati—awfully nice people, who have a son, aged fifteen, who is a musical genius. I knew his father in Paris.

LETTERS AFTER IMPRISONMENT AND DURING 'TRUCE'

1917—1924 or 5

D[illegible] DARLING,—We have just [illegible] of
Thom[illegible] a heroic death in the [illegible]
last night. [illegible] K. L. went up and [illegible] admitted [illegible] was just drifting off into unconsciousness, and [illegible] ed till he died. [illegible]
and [illegible] don't know how they [illegible]

[illegible]

[illegible] and [illegible] who went for [illegible] and [illegible]
was [illegible] them [illegible]
them not [illegible] the one idea that [illegible]
their minds. We are prisoners pledged to be tried,
and we can fight in jail as well as out, and die in jail
as well as out, and it is up to us to d[illegible]
England are trying to goad us into another rising to
wipe us [illegible] General L—— is reported to have

143 Leinster Road,
Sept. 26, 1917.

Dearest Old Darling,—We have just heard of Thomas Ashes's heroic death in the Mater Hospital last night. Dr. K. L. went up and actually was admitted. He was just drifting off into unconsciousness, and she waited till he died. Isn't it all wonderful and terrible ? I don't know how they find the courage to do it. I feel afraid myself. I don't a bit feel sure that I could do it. It's different from fighting somehow, it is so awfully cold-blooded. Dr. K. L. thinks that it was the forcible feeding that did it, that they forced some into his lungs, because at the Mater they say he died of pneumonia.

Drs. D. and C. of M. jail sent for a Dublin doctor to help feed our men. Eight refused, to their everlasting credit. A Dr. Low, English, from Amiens Street, did it for them.

Isn't it wonderful to think of these boys in Mountjoy ? Some are just rough country lads, all going in smiling and confident and facing up to things like this.

I had a talk with Liddy and with Brown, during the hour they had to wait, under arrest at Limerick Station. Both said they knew what they had to do. I said : 'Think it over before you hunger-strike, for they will let you die, and it would be fatal for the Cause if you gave in to save your life.' I told them that there was no need for them to strike, and that it was terrible suffering, and in fact tried to persuade them not to, but the one idea that is in every one of their minds is, 'We are soldiers pledged to Ireland, and we can fight in jail as well as out, and die in jail as well as out, and it is up to us to do it.' I think the English are trying to goad us into another rising, to wipe us all out. General L—— is reported to have said that M—— shot sixteen, but he will not stop till he has sixteen hundred if he gets the chance. They have machine-guns and armoured cars parading the streets here and in every corner of Ireland, and masses of soldiers in every district. When I gave a lecture in Cork they mobilised a regiment, with four machine-guns in the neighbouring streets.

The charges against our men are really so absurd, too; no one speaks more strongly than I, and I am left alone. J. M. Donagh *never* spoke very strongly. No one is preaching rebellion. We are all talking of organising the country into a strong constitutional movement, with the Volunteer Force behind, whose immediate duty is to keep order. . . .

[*Last page lost.*]

Fragment. 1918.

. . . fear of air raids and no revolution looming. We are all organising for a strong constitutional movement now. I believe that by International Law, we have, by Easter Week, earned the right to be in at the Peace Conference at the end of the War, and that's what we are now aiming at.

I know that you will be glad that we do not contemplate another 'scrap' at present, and we are making our men do police duty at meetings and keep order, and they are doing it very well. We are trying to prevent all low electioneering tricks and our men are a wonderfully decent, sober, and orderly crowd. The other side is supplying drink to the separation allowance women and trying to organise riots, so far unsuccessfully.

Do you know, I sometimes almost regret jail—I loved your visits so? and now you are so far away and life is such a rush. I think the greater the gloom, the brighter the spots of sunlight. That's one of the things that make even the horror of jail bearable.

10 Richmond Av.,
After March 1919.

Darling,—I had a wonderful journey.[1] Mme. O'Rahilly and Mrs. Humphries met me at Holyhead, and they had secured sunny seats on the boat. The sun on the rippling sea was divine, and the seagulls gave the finishing touch to the reality of freedom.

I was met by deputations of everybody! M. S—— and Joe McG—— (both on the run), and C. M. B. at Kingstown with bouquet. Howling crowds everywhere. They took me to a Hotel and fed me. I was extremely hungry. It was all very official. Just deputations from all the organisations, run mostly by the women. S. McG—— was there, very pleased with himself. We motored in to Dublin to Liberty Hall. Last time was nothing to it. The crowd had no beginning or end. I made a speech, and we then formed up in a torchlight procession and went to St. Patrick's.

M—— had dropped from the sky into our midst.

We held one meeting for me and one for J. McG—— (escaped Usk). The constituency certainly appeared unanimous, and it was unparalleled in Irish History, they say. Every window had a flag or candles or both. You never saw such excitement. . . .

K. C. is better and was glad to see me. Maev also was looking much better.

I'm already very busy. We celebrated the Commune on the eighteenth, and Mrs. H—— is giving me a party to meet fellow-M.P.s on Saturday. Liberty

[1] After release from Holloway Jail 1919.

Hall is capturing Ireland and growing on every side. The Women Workers have a palace and everything is booming here.

Undated.

We are all frightfully busy here, preparing for the elections. Though personally I should not be surprised if they were put off again. The Register is a farce. Griffith is afraid that if it is revised he will be beaten. None of the Volunteers are on. We brought in a Bill to enfranchise women under 30. Griffith turned it down. Quite spontaneously the demand arose here, women everywhere throughout the country suddenly finding their position to be humiliating, and it was the fight that did it. They say they must have a say as to the Treaty, and that if they are good enough to take part in the fight, they are good enough to vote.

Things are *awful* here. There are more people being killed weekly than before the truce.

LIMERICK,
1924 (?).

DEAREST OLD DARLING,—Many happy returns of the day! As I am in Limerick, I am sending you a wee piece of lace.

Work here is *desperate* but things are going well. The tide has really turned, but it's work, work, work and no rest for the wicked. Each bye-election goes better and we have hopes of this.

People's hopes have come to life again and enthusiasm is rising and blowing on every wind.

Did I ever thank you for your 'blue Glory' of a cape? I have a horrible feeling that I did not, but it is such a joy and it was so lovely to get a birthday present, you old darling.

Up till recently, we have just been trying to block the stampede of the nation, and now it is all changed again.

I am such a fool about posts. Your Christmas present is still in my room, and I could never get it packed, but you'll get it in time.

Undated.

How I wish you had been here! but it would have killed you. You were very wise to refrain.

You will be pleased to hear that people in command are not in favour of a fight just now and do not want to shed useless blood. I haven't seen Dev. yet. O'Reilly is doing awfully well, they say. I wish I was there. I wonder if I left much behind with you? Poor you! I hope it did not fuss you too much. I was greatly impressed by Cole. I am sending you a letter for Ll. George, etc. I'm almost run off my legs already.

Dail Eireann. DEPARTMENT OF LABOUR,
MANSION HOUSE,
1921.

DEAREST OLD DARLING,—Just received the lovely brooch from Reginald. The colours are perfect. I don't know what you mean by not being able to find yellow, for the yellow is quite right.

I wish you could get over for a bit during the truce.

You'd be quite safe here now. I do hate that old channel between us, but I suppose I ought not to abuse it, as it separates us from England so crudely and so definitely and is such an unanswerable argument.

It is so heavenly to be out again and to be able to shut and open doors. It is almost worth while being locked up, for the great joy release brings.

Life is so wonderful. One just wanders round and enjoys it.

The children and the trees and cows and all common things are so heavenly after nothing but walls and uniformed people.

It is so funny, suddenly to be a Government and supposed to be respectable! One has to laugh. The English Government should publish a new decalogue.

Would you believe it, darling, I am in French Poetry these days! A man 'Camille de Mercier d'Erme' has sent me a book about Ireland 1916.

LAST LETTERS TO HER SISTER
1923—1926

[illegible]

[illegible]

D[illegible] Darling,—Please [illegible] as [illegible] all the [illegible] that lazy people make for [illegible] letters. [illegible] that it is a [illegible]. But [illegible] that [illegible] the lovely [illegible] is a [illegible] [illegible]

[illegible]

and would [illegible] by which [illegible] person in the world and of which [illegible] understand can no longer [illegible] between independent [illegible] the [illegible] [illegible] making love and neglected.

2 Frankfort Place,
Rathmines,
1923.

Dearest Old Darling,—Please take as said all the excuses that lazy people make for not answering letters. I think that it is a disease with me. Did I ever thank you for the lovely bag? It is a joy. And your book and the book of plays? I find your book very difficult for my memory is so bad and I keep muddling your symbolic words (I don't know if that conveys anything to you) but you have a language that I do not know and until I can learn to use it easily I know that I shall not benefit much by the book. But it is very thrilling trying to work it out and every sentence that I read gives me something to think about. Perhaps if we live ten years I shall be able to tell you what I think of it. The tragedy of Christ's life to me is far greater to-day than it was during the few terrible last hours of suffering. For every church and every sect is but an organisation of thoughtless and well-meaning people trained in thought and controlled by juntas of priests and clergy who are used to doing all the things that Christ would most have disliked. And yet I don't know how this can be avoided, for without organisation Christ would be quite forgotten, and all organisation seems in the end to go the same road: and if it does not go in for graft and power it just fizzles out. That is what is wrong too with all public bodies and governments, and what the world has got to think out is some scheme by which power can be evenly distributed over every person in the world and by which the foolish and uneducated can no longer be grouped in unthinking battalions dependent on the few pushers, self-seekers and crooks and made slaves of and exploited.

I suppose that all lovers of freedom are looking for this.

I do hope that you are better. I hate you to be in London in the winter. Everything here is very dull. The main thing is the appalling poverty that meets one everywhere, and the enormous increase in the numbers of huge motor-cars that threaten one at every crossing. I am still trying to get somewhere to live in my constituency but there are no houses or flats to be got anywhere. Was not my arrest funny? 'Honour bright,' as we used to say, I was engaged in no work that was not visible to the naked eye and all my activities were passivist and within the law.

I directed an election, I did lightning sketches at a bazaar each day for a couple of weeks and I went round on a lorry asking my constituents to sign the petition drawn up by the Corporation for the release of the Hunger Strikers. I always rather dreaded a hunger strike, but when I had to do it I found that, like most things, the worst part of it was looking forward to the possibility of having to do it. I did not suffer at all but just stayed in bed and dozed and tried to prepare myself to leave the world. I was perfectly happy and had no regrets. It is all very odd and I don't understand it but it was so. I had no wish to live and no regrets. I just seemed to be sliding along in a happy sort of dream. When Derrick came to me he woke me up with a jump and it was like coming to life again and I wanted to live and I wanted the others to live. I am telling you this because you have such a horror of the hunger strike and I want you to realise what it was to me, that for just one moment when I was making it imperative on me when telling the police of my decision, I had the sort of shrinking that one has before taking a header into a cold sea: just a want of faith in the unknown but that was all. Once I had begun I did not suffer either mentally nor physically, nor did I regret the step that I had taken. And by the way it has cured my rheumatism for the moment. It has done this for a great many of the strikers. Also it has cured quite a number of people who were suffering from stomach trouble. Most of those who were on for only a fortnight seem to be none the worse. One girl who was suffering from an ulcerated stomach has been absolutely cured. Of course some of those who were in for a month or longer have been very bad. One girl, Baby Bohen from Ballymote, will probably never be the same again: her kidneys are affected. She was awfully plucky and suffered a lot.

English politics are very exciting just now. I am afraid that the Labour Party are not strong enough to do anything and that they will be in a position where they can be discredited and from which they will get a big set-back and lose a great many of their supporters who expect them to do something. But one cannot tell.

I hear that it was the Orange lodges of Glasgow and the Protestant hysteria that beat Newbold. He could count on the Catholic (Irish) vote and that fact used cleverly by the Protestant Capitalist interest did the trick.

Now, old darling, I must stop. Writing on a machine always tempts one to ramble on and on.

I got you a present. I got it before I was locked up, but though it is small, it is hard to pack and laziness intervened. I must try and make an effort.

Love to you both and good wishes for the New Year. By the way, what's really happened about M.'s engagement? G. told me a long yarn. I hope that she will steer her own ship the way she wants and will not let anyone push her into doing what she does not want—'for her own good.' The more I live the more I believe in people usually knowing what is best for themselves.

Now bye-bye again, old darling. How I'd love to be with you! It was so lovely last summer and it made amends for the long months of exile.—Lovingly,

CON.

FRANKFORT HOUSE,
DARTRY,
About May or June 1926.

DEAREST OLD DARLING,—I don't suppose that you have been wondering why I hadn't written before, because I am such an awful slacker at writing and I am always so full up of work of all description.

I've been writing a play! I don't quite know what started me, but somehow a situation came into my head and I wrote a scene and then I simply could not stop. Wherever I went I had an old copybook and whenever I was not actually using my hands I wrote. I had to go and drive for an election in the middle—such hard work—and one day I got my car out at 7.0 and never stopped driving round until weary and sleepy I rang up a house at 2.30 to beg for a bed. But every minute I had to wait for someone outside a house—out with my old book, and anyhow the play is finished at last. Of course it is not literary, only just a thrilling story during the Tan war and in Sligo, but I think it is human and natural.

I loved the book you sent me. I got it in the middle of the election. It reads like truth, and one gets so fond of the hero that one longs to know what happened to him in the end. After all his adventures, it seemed so sad that he was back again into exile and slavery.

How are you? I wonder so where you are and if

you've been abroad. Poor D. has been operated on again and is so brave and patient. She misses her father very much. I saw her last night at a little gathering at a friend's house. I am sorry that she has left this, for she was great company. She has a lovely flat. Her father had just fixed it up before he died.

I wonder what you think of us all? I sometimes think that people get rather mad when they go in for politics. The latest has made me laugh since it began. Dev., I say like a wise man, has announced that he will go into the Free State Parliament if there is no oath and this has caused an unholy row. I myself have always said that the oath made it absolutely impossible for an honourable person who was a Republican, to go in, and that if it were removed, it would then be simply a question of policy with no principle involved, whether we went in or stayed out.

Dev. thinks the moment has come to start out attacking the oath and demanding its removal. Some unlogical persons are howling. They stand for principle and for the honour of the Republic and prefer to do nothing but shout continually 'The Republic lives!' It was as good as a play to hear the self-righteous fools lauding their own stand as being a stand for principle and honour and then trying to 'throw flowers' at Dev. It was Mark Antony's oration. They don't want to quarrel with him. Oh no: they know he's an honourable man. Such a queer lot of people who are taking this stand. It's quite surprising. I think the ordinary man and woman in the street will agree with us. I don't think that we'll get the oath removed, at any rate for a long time, but anyhow it is something to go for with a chance of success, and something outside Ireland might help.

Maev blew in on her way to Sligo and commandeered the car.

I love the queer little musical instrument she has and the way she has of lilting to it all sorts of silly little songs without any pretension at all but very attractive.

Is there any chance of your coming over this year at all? It is such an age since I saw you, and that beastly channel and the long, long journey costs such a lot and I never have any time or money somehow.

Is there going to be any real trouble in England with the miners? There is no work here at all. Crowds are starving all over the country. I wonder if it is as bad over there.

I would like to see you laugh at my bobbed head. I have it quite short at the back and parted at the side, covering my ears. It is quite smooth and straight as a rule, for I seldom curl it.

How is Esther? Give her my love. I often think of the time I was in London 'on the run.' I loved it. I wish they'd send me again. Perhaps they will some day.

It was rather a pity after all that I was not caught that time for I would have got a nice round sum and it would have been worth it.

They raid this place an odd time and get nothing, but I suppose they want to keep their hand in.

They have nearly gone mad, looking for the eleven prisoners who escaped so supernaturally. They looked here.

There is nothing the least interesting to tell you about. I garden and drive about.

One blessed thing about this row is that I have got out of a great deal of awful meetings.

Now goodbye, old darling, and best love.

CON.

LETTERS AFTER HER SISTER EVA'S DEATH 1926

[illegible] HER,—It was very good of you [illegible] [illegible] realise it. I know how I [illegible] how much that [illegible] it is for you [illegible] wh [illegible]

[illegible]

[illegible]

[illegible] wrong, [illegible] nothing, enough [illegible] it [illegible]

I [illegible]

face it [illegible] and [illegible] and [illegible]

[illegible]

FRANKFORT HOUSE,
DARTRY,
1926.

MY DEAR ESTHER,—It was very good of you to wire. I simply can't realise it. I know how I feel and I know how much worse it is for you who were with her the whole time.

There was no one ever like her. She was something wonderful and beautiful, and so simple and thought so little of herself. I don't think she ever knew how much she was to me.

I am so vague and stupid and can't express myself.

But her gentleness prevented me getting very brutal, and one does get very callous in a War. I once held out and stopped a man being shot because of her. And she was always there when I was down and out, she and you.

I was writing to her in answer to a letter she wrote me the other day, when she told me she was playing with 'glitterwax.'

Her letter seemed well and happy and she was full of interest in us and the Strike. Other letters had often rather frightened me, but this was quite a jolly letter and firmly written.

I was frightened too when I read her book on Saint John, for it seemed to me almost as if she had done the work she was destined to do: that her whole task in life was finished and that she had just gone on living while some strong force was working through her and in her. I can't explain.

I'm not coming over, because I simply could not face it all.[1] I want to keep my last memory of her so happy and peaceful, and nothing but love and beauty and peace.

I sent a wreath: white and her own blue.

[1] She had become ill.

Write to me when you feel you can and tell me how it happened.

I got the wire when I got home. It had been here for a day or so, while I was with a friend at the sea, and it gave me a terrible shock. Everything seemed to go from under me: sometimes I could not realise it. I had been awfully depressed and I did not know why, for days. People noticed it and I thought I was seedy.

I had always had a funny habit, since Aylesbury, of referring anything I was doing to her. Every sketch I made I wondered how she would like it, and I looked forward to showing it to her. If I saw anything beautiful, I thought of her, and wished she was there to enjoy it.

I was always dreaming and planning to take you both along to some beautiful places in the car. I was writing a play and doing a copy to send her, and so on, through everything, though I didn't write often. And then everything seemed to be cut off all at once.

But lately I've begun to feel and see her often. When I'm painting she seems to look at me and help me from the clouds. I wake suddenly and it is just as if she was there. Last Sunday at Mass, when I wasn't thinking of her at all, she suddenly seemed to smile at me from behind the priest, and I know it is real and that she, the real Eva, is somewhere very near. I know too that you will feel this in time. It is only that you were so much in touch with her human form that you miss it so, and your mind can't rest: but it will find rest, and her, only it will take time.

I'd love some personal relics of her and a photo, if a good one exists. I have no good one. My things were destroyed so often.

I want to come over and see her grave.

I always looked on you as a sort of adopted sister, Eva's twin. And you're all I have now, in that way.

FRANKFORT HOUSE,
DARTRY,
1926.

DEAREST ESTHER,—I would like to come over to you, and any time after the second week in September would suit me.

I do hope there is nothing serious wrong with you, and that you are better than when you wrote.

I love the Spanish wrap. Eva always wore it latterly when I saw her. It is so associated with her in my mind. I should love the cross: our Granny left it to her years ago and it was a thing she loved and wore so much when we were girls together.

About the Celtic Cross: they are very commercial here. I might be able to find some one: don't hurry. Let's consult first. I think something rather simple would be nicest and on the lines of some of the old ones, not too finished and correct but rather rough and bold.

Patricia Lynch called with her husband on Saturday, to show me an article he had written on her in the *Millgate Monthly*. It is really a beautiful appreciation of her, and he seems really to have understood and loved her, and to have got a far deeper knowledge of her than many who knew her better.

I had a collision in the car the other day—it just escaped being a very bad accident—and when I saw the other car rise suddenly from behind a corner wall, I just had an extraordinary feeling that Eva was there and that it was all right. I can't explain.

I am longing to sit in the room where she lived and worked again, and I know she left the feeling of peace and love that was her gift there more than anywhere else.

FRANKFORT HOUSE,
DARTRY,
1926.

MY DEAR ESTHER,—I was very glad to get your letter and to hear that you are bringing out another book of Eva's poems. The one thing we can do to honour her is to make her work known and help her to immortality here in this world through the ideals she lived for.

It seems to me that it is almost a test of a person's soul-worth, if—reading her—they understand. So many more do than I ever dreamed of.

I met a woman among the International Peace women, who had been at the Kemp's school and had acted in Eva's play. She came to me and told me how she had loved her writings, and so many others have said the same.

She has left a spiritual inheritance to those who can understand, which will never die.

I don't feel lonely as I did at first, and I know you won't, after a bit. It is only natural that you should, who was so much nearer her body than I was, for her human presence was so beautiful and wonderful; but with her the spirit dominated every bit of her and her body was just the human instrument it shone through.

It's so hard to put things like this down in a way that one can understand.

When I was in Aylesbury, we agreed to try and get in touch for a few minutes every day, and I used to sit at about 6.0 o'clock and think of her and concentrate and try to leave my mind a blank—a sort of dark, still pool—and I got to her and could tell how she sat in the window and I seemed to know what she was thinking. It was a great joy and comfort to me.

When I got out I lost this in the bustle and hurry of life, but now, just the last few days, I seem to get in touch again.

14 Frognal Gardens,
Hampstead,
1926.

My dear Mrs. Lestrange,—I feel very sad leaving this house, probably for the last time.

Every corner in it speaks of Eva, and her lovely spirit of peace and love is here just the same as ever. And Esther, too, who is her spiritual sister, I hate leaving. She is wonderful, and the more one knows her, the more one loves her, and I feel so glad Eva and she were together and so thankful that her love was with Eva to the end.